D0970465

Praise for *Promoting a Development Culture in Your Organization*

"This book provides a unique synthesis of the major challenges confronting today's organizations. The ideas and insights serve as a treasure chest for anyone involved with any aspect of moving organizations toward a development culture."

 —Marianne Matheis, Organizational and Leadership Development Center,
  The Aerospace Corporation

"An insightful description of the shift from paternalism to empowerment in career development. Offers practical perspectives for surviving—and thriving—in the emerging employer-employee relationship."

 —Lynn Trautmann, President, Congruence, Inc.

"A practical guide and step-by-step blueprint for creating and enhancing a development culture. This book makes a major contribution to the HRD field by showing how career development can be a strategic advantage to effectively compete in the global marketplace and used as a tool to successfully manage today's changing and diverse workforce."

 —Kenneth M. Nowack, Ph.D., Industrial Psychologist, Organizational
  Performance Dimensions

"The author makes an excellent case—that an organization's culture can be greatly affected by the principles, policies, and practices of a well-designed career development effort."

 —Beverly L. Kaye, Ph.D., author of *Up Is Not the Only Way*

"Organizations that thrive will take the critical steps needed to create a development culture and use it as a blueprint for the future of work. This book is an invaluable tool for those who will design these changes and for those who will live with them."

—Camille Helkowski, Assistant Director, Career Center, Loyola University

"Simonsen's new book makes a strong, well-thought-out case for why a development culture is essential to maintaining high productivity and building a flexible, resilient workforce that values employability security. This is must reading, a vital prescription for decision makers in chaotic organizations."

—Jean R. Haskell, Ed.D., Consultant, The Einstein Consulting Group, Haskell Associates

Promoting a Development Culture in Your Organization

Using Career Development as a Change Agent

Peggy Simonsen

DAVIES-BLACK PUBLISHING

Palo Alto, California

Published by Davies-Black Publishing, an imprint of Consulting Psychologists Press, Inc., 3803 East Bayshore Road, Palo Alto, CA 94303; 1-800-624-1765.

Special discounts on bulk quantities of Davies-Black books are available to corporations, professional associations, and other organizations. For details, contact the Director of Book Sales at Davies-Black Publishing, an imprint of Consulting Psychologists Press, Inc., 3803 East Bayshore Road, Palo Alto, CA 94303; 650-691-9123; Fax 650-988-0673.

Permissions credits are listed on p. 266.

01 00 99 98 97   10 9 8 7 6 5 4 3 2 1
Printed in the United States of America

Library of Congress Cataloging-in-Publication Data

Simonsen, Peggy
    Promoting a development culture in your organization : using career development as a change agent / Peggy Simonsen.
       p.   cm.
    Includes bibliographical references and index.
    ISBN 0-89106-109-6
    1. Career development.   2. Organizational change.   I. Title.
HF5549.5.C35S56   1997
658.3′124—dc21   97–26477
                                                CIP

FIRST EDITION
First printing 1997

Contents

Foreword

No organization can succeed without its people. Doesn't it make perfect sense that the managers and employees of an organization *share* the responsibility for the development of all employees so they not only are ready, willing, and able to carry out the mission and strategy of the organization, but also are continually improving in order to keep up with ever-changing business needs and to continue to grow as individuals?

Then why are so many organizations so far from this perfectly logical picture of associate development? It may be that they view such development too narrowly. As Peggy Simonsen so ably demonstrates in her book *Promoting a Development Culture in Your Organization*, to widen this view takes a fundamental belief in the value of associates, the need for associates to take responsibility for their own development, and greater manager involvement in an integrated development process. In short, it takes a development culture that permeates the organization.

In my own experience leading first the Credit Group (more than 10,000 associates) and now the Home Services Group (more than 35,000 associates) of Sears, Roebuck and Co., our biggest challenge is not developing a vision for the business or a strategy to focus our efforts or even a set of values. The biggest challenge is engaging and energizing individuals at all levels of the organization so that they connect to where the organization is going, how it's going to get there, the values that are shared within the organization, and what all this means for them personally.

I couldn't agree more with Simonsen's premise that the career development process can be an agent of change to accelerate an organization's transformation. At the heart of the relationship between an organization and its associates is the dialogue that must go on between employee and manager at all levels whereby the changing needs of the individual and those of the organization are communicated, understood, and aligned. Associates are obviously more engaged and energized as the quality of this dialogue is improved: they can see they are valued, they can see how they can grow and improve as the organization grows and improves, and they feel a greater sense of purpose as they see how they are contributing to the success of the organization.

This book not only presents a great case for the benefits an organization can derive from a development culture but also lays out an approach to creating one. If your organization, however large or small, is going through major change, if you need people at all levels to behave differently, to learn new skills, to feel more valued and valuable as individuals, read on. *Promoting a Development Culture in Your Organization* may be just what you need for breakthrough performance at all levels of your organization.

Jane J. Thompson
President, Home Services, Sears, Roebuck and Co.

Preface

Everywhere today we hear people in organizations saying that they need to change their cultures. Usually they are referring to getting employees to change their expectations and behaviors, and occasionally they also recognize that the company must change the way employees are treated and that managers need to change their behavior. But rarely do we hear what they want to change the culture *to*. There is an unspoken message that the listener must translate. I believe the same problem is found with employees in companies. They are told that the old rules no longer work and that they must change their behavior, and sometimes they are given a general description of the needed change: "Employees need to be more flexible," or "Everyone is responsible for managing his or her own career." Employees often do not know the specific behaviors that are expected to achieve this undefined future state.

I agree that many organizations must change their culture, but I propose that we must define what the new culture should look like. What are we aiming for? What will be different for managers and employees in a new desired culture? How will organizational policies and systems be different to support the new desired behavior? This book proposes that what may usually be meant by "changing the culture" is a need to build a *development culture*. The behaviors we see as desirable in employees and managers to keep organizations competitive in a rapidly changing marketplace are the behaviors that occur in a development culture: constant learning, self-responsibility, continually adding value, and flexibility and adaptability. To achieve a development culture we also must provide some support systems and rewards to ensure the kinds of changes in behaviors that are needed. Organizational leaders must recognize that to change the culture, they must change major cultural assumptions.

Part I of this book, The Need for a Development Culture, discusses the factors that are causing the need to change organizational cultures and introduces some ways to look at the concept of culture. It also provides a view of the scope of a career development intervention needed to affect the culture.

Part II looks at all the roles and responsibilities that are necessary for or support using career development as a change agent in altering the culture. And finally, Part III lays out the steps needed to implement a comprehensive career development process that can promote a development culture.

Peppered throughout this book are examples of good career development intentions that failed, or ran into significant problems in achieving their intended outcomes, because one or more of the major elements proposed in this book were ignored. In many cases, there was a need to change the culture to make the career development intervention work, but the need wasn't recognized and so an event or a good beginning was derailed. I have included these vignettes because I believe examples contribute to understanding, and because I believe many organizations are at the point in their career development efforts where they can learn from others' mistakes. Benchmarking has grown as a valuable intercompany activity because it eliminates some trial-and-error efforts.

On the other hand, I have also included as cases some examples from companies whose efforts at more comprehensive, integrated career development interventions have indeed begun to change the culture and whose attention to supportive systems has contributed to successful career development outcomes.

My career as a career development consultant, trainer, instructional designer, and career counselor since the mid-1970s has paralleled the evolution of the field. Career development has been in and out of favor over those years, and I find it amazing that in 1997 we are still having difficulty calling a process in organizations *career development.* We have experienced almost two decades of unprecedented change in structure, career paths, expectations, the nature of work, and certainly the speed (or velocity) of change. Even with all the media impact on our awareness of the changed employment contract, many leaders in organizations are still concerned that something called career development might be interpreted as entitlement to promotions. I also am amazed at how often organizational career development today is synonymous with resources for employees: a career center, a career advisor, a workshop, interest tests. That's why I think there is a need for a book like this.

Career development has so much more potential. It can be the catalyst to build a development culture because it answers "What's in it for me?"

for employees as well as addressing the critical need of the organization to remain competitive. A career development culture can contribute to the recognition of the importance of the organization's and management's role in developing employees. Perhaps organizations have to apply the concepts of career development to themselves first as an endangered species before they can fully appreciate the changing roles of managers in organizations as they evolve development cultures.

The intended audience for this book is broader than career specialists: human resource and organization development professionals, senior and line managers, internal and external consultants, and, of course, career specialists charged with holding their finger in the dike of a flood of career and development issues that individuals and organizations are facing in our whitewater world of work today.

Acknowledgments

This book is a tribute to the learning and synergy that result from many years and innumerable experiences consulting in organizations, counseling individuals, and collaborating with supportive colleagues. I acknowledge the contribution of my clients, some of whom are highlighted in the vignettes in this book, for taking on the challenge of creating a development culture in their organizations. They have contributed to my learning and appreciation for the complexity of changing organizational culture.

I especially want to thank my staff who contribute to and challenge my conceptual framework and the practical application to our work. Jan Hann brings her organizational development perspective and consulting skills and a wealth of resources. She pushes the scope of my narrower career development focus. My husband Bill, who as business manager for Career Directions, Inc., frees me from the bookkeeping and administrative management tasks to do what I do best—build consulting relationships with my clients. Bill will be pleased, with the publication of this book, to get his weekend sailing partner back. Debi Rajczyk, who as project secretary took this book on as another project and was undaunted in managing the edits of various versions of a 380-page manuscript with tables and figures that were written on various laptops and desktops and stored on numerous disks and hard drives. And all the others on my staff, who work so well as a team on client projects and on building our own development culture and have helped us to grow and mature as an organization.

Introduction

What really binds people together is their culture,
the ideas and the standards they have in common.
—Ruth Benedict

Historical Perspective

The significant changes in work and workplaces we are experiencing today have created a need to think differently about our "human capital" in organizations. The organizations that will emerge successfully from the turmoil of the 1990s will reinvent themselves—the paternalism and dependency that evolved with the industrial age are no longer viable. Everywhere we hear that the old employment contract has changed. Most employees have heard that *they* need to change, but most organizations do not yet recognize that the organizational culture needs to change as well. And of those organizations that are aware that the changes to be made must be so pervasive as to require a change of culture in the organization, some may not yet have defined the new culture that must emerge. This book provides a perspective of using career development as a change agent to create a development culture and describes the elements of a development culture, the roles and responsibilities needed to take on the task, and the process and components of a successful outcome.

Organizational career development has evolved significantly over the last twenty years. It first began to emerge in the late 1970s as a "nice to have" program in companies with progressive human resources or training functions. Many of my first organizational contacts had backgrounds in education—where the career planning field was beginning to blossom—and then moved to organizational training and development, where they saw the same need in employees that they had addressed in college students. To a large extent, career development in the early 1980s involved programs, primarily self-assessment, that were targeted to individuals.

Then the corporate deregulation of the 1980s occurred, and merger-and-acquisition fever began. In addition, technological changes, long predicted, hit staffs and company systems in a major way. The resulting organizational changes were unprecedented in most employees' lifetimes and caused upheaval unanticipated by any previous career planning process. Career development planning had to "get real." Through the 1980s there was confusion between outplacement and internal, proactive career development planning and career management. Many career centers that had been established to assist employees whose jobs were being eliminated began trying (with little success) to help the survivors deal with the changed expectations and new roles.

In my consulting practice in the late 1980s and into the 1990s, I saw, and worked with, a growing number of organizations that recognized the need to disconnect the old culture and old messages for development from the evolving needs of the business. Some solid programs were designed and implemented in the 1980s, but it has been the impact of the 1990s that has elevated the need for a comprehensive change in the emphasis on development. Instead of a program for targeted groups within organizations, career development has become an agent for creating a development culture. In order to do so, career development processes must be aligned with business needs and integrated with other change efforts. Career development must expand beyond resources for employees and ensure alignment of selection, development, and reward systems.

Quick Fix or Significant Intervention?

Organizations are recognizing that a "quick fix" cannot change the culture and is not the answer to development needs. Employees and managers must change their expectations; behavior must change to support new organizational realities; and human resources systems need to be updated, or reinvented, to support the new behaviors. And, increasingly, there is a recognition in organizations that to build a development culture, the old culture needs to change or be changed.

I have heard many senior executives espouse the need for employees to change their expectations, but I don't believe that many of them truly understand at the outset the scope of the intervention they are undertaking to accomplish the type of changes they envision. I have also worked with many human resources professionals who see the need for, and believe in the vision of, a development culture but are restricted in power, budget, or other resources to accomplish the changes needed.

Career development can be a tool (or, better defined, an *intervention*) to affect organizational culture significantly enough to initiate a development culture. In this book, I attempt to provide a perspective for, as well as some guidelines and suggestions on, using a career development process to build a development culture in your organization.

Career Development and Organizational Culture

The goal today of comprehensive career development programs (or, more accurately, *processes* or *systems*) is to change the current culture and create a development culture. This book will focus on building a development culture through a comprehensive, integrated career development process. We seem to know intrinsically that a development culture is good. But what exactly is a development culture, and how do we attain it? The following vision statement made by one organization describes it well:

In our desired future state, our company has a competitive advantage over our competition. We are the employer of choice, and every employee is adding value. Individuals are constantly developing in ways consistent with the direction and needs of the organization as well as their own goals. We have very few employees whose goals don't align with the company's goals because our selection process has the same criteria as the development process. We have an agile workforce, ready to change and apply new skills as business needs change. Managers encourage and support the development of employees, who are substantially self-directed. Organizational systems reinforce the selection, development, and rewards of employees who contribute to the success of the company. We live in a development culture.

In a development culture, employees are not held back from development options, as long as their goals are aligned with the direction and needs of the department or organization. The problem occurs, of course, when the broader needs of the company and the goals of the individual conflict with the specific, present needs of the manager to achieve results today. This is when development and mobility policies are important. If the company values development, some questions need to be addressed: Will managers encourage skills development even though those skills are not needed now? How can the environment be developmental without affecting the volume and quality of work to be done? Under which circumstances is it appropriate for a manager to object to an employee's move?

How can managers be rewarded and not punished for letting a good person go from their area, thus contributing to the good of the company?

A development culture can be compared to Peter Senge's (1990a) *learning organization*. "Learning is about enhancing capacity. Learning is about building the capacity to create that which you previously couldn't create. . . . It is intimately connected to action." Senge (1990b) defines a learning organization as "an organization that is continually expanding its capacity to create its future." Similarly, a development culture is one in which individuals grow in ways needed by the organization, even as the organization expands its capacity to create its future. Employees are expected to grow, supported in their efforts to do so, and are rewarded for success as measured by their contributions.

Recognizing the Power of Culture

In considering the concept of organizational culture, we can think of culture at two levels. Kotter and Heskett (1992) wrote, "At the deeper and less visible level, culture refers to values that are shared by the people in a group and that tend to persist over time even when group membership changes." These values—that individuals are valued and have intrinsic worth, that it is critical to meet changing customer needs, and so forth— constitute the driving force for a development culture. Other values that are part of the culture—the emphasis on innovativeness or risk taking, for example—might be quite different in different companies. Sometimes it takes a crisis or major changes to force an organization to look at its values. Organizations must ask themselves if the values of the past support their direction today.

Kotter and Heskett wrote further that "at the more visible level, culture represents the behavior patterns or style of an organization." It is these behaviors and attitudes that may need to be changed in building a development culture. When new behaviors and attitudes are encouraged, modeled, and rewarded, changes will gradually occur. As a change agent, you need to be patient, but not passive. Cultures exert a powerful influence and change slowly, if at all, so you might not see effects of a successful intervention on deeper culture for some time. But behavior changes, in a critical mass of employees and managers, begin to signal changes on the surface level of culture. Celebrate successes! Kotter and Heskett added, "But even when successfully implemented, the behavior patterns that represent a given strategy are not cultural unless *most group members tend actively to encourage new members to follow those practices.*" We have our work cut out for us.

Table 1

Corporate Culture and Performance

Conclusions from Kotter and Heskett (1992) research:

1. Corporate culture can have a significant impact on a firm's long-term economic performance.
2. Corporate culture will probably be an even more important factor in determining the success or failure of firms in the next decade.
3. Some corporate cultures inhibit strong long-term financial performance by encouraging inappropriate behavior and inhibiting change to more appropriate strategies.
4. Although tough to change, corporate cultures can be made more performance enhancing.

Adapted with the permission of The Free Press, a Division of Simon & Schuster, from *Corporate Culture and Performance*, by John P. Kotter and James L. Heskett. Copyright © 1992 by Kotter Associates, Inc., and James L. Heskett.

There is growing evidence that organizations with development cultures see an improved bottom line. Sears Merchandise Group (1996), for example, engaged the University of Michigan to determine whether there was a correlation between employee satisfaction, customer satisfaction, and investor satisfaction. They found that an increase of 5 percent in employee attitudes about the job and company as measured on employee attitude surveys resulted in a 1.3 percent more favorable customer response. When favorable customer feedback increased even 1.3 percent, it generated a .5 percent increase in revenues. In a multibillion-dollar company, the outcome is significant. Similarly, a 1.3 percent increase in customer impression plus a 1.0 percent increase in customer retention drove a .9 percent increase in revenue. The group called their new model the Sears Transformation Model and adopted the following values statement: *Making Sears a compelling place to work, to shop, and to invest.* These beliefs and the major change effort in the company are driving efforts to build a development culture. Managers are less likely to question why they need to be developing their direct reports—they see the relationship between productive employees and their bottom line. They are also rewarded for achievement of company goals, and thus are more likely to ensure that their department's goals, as well as the goals of their direct reports, are linked to the business objectives.

Kotter and Heskett conducted research that showed the importance of corporate culture on organizational performance. Their conclusions are summarized in Table 1.

Patricia McLagan (1996) has written:

A growing and impressive body of research is establishing a very
strong relationship between participative human resource practices and bottom line performance. It strongly supports the need
for congruent, integrated sets of people practices. It also confirms
that staffing, development, performance management, assessment,
and reward practices that both involve people and align them with
the business' goals are the best. These practices will not emerge
naturally from the operating assumptions of the past "superior/
subordinate" culture. The New World of Work requires something
new. And people must become aware enough of this New World to
want to put the new practices to use.

Linking career development efforts with needed changes in culture will
provide the opportunity to make major changes in your organization. By
harnessing employee behavior in ways beneficial to themselves and the
organization, new attitudes and behavior patterns become established, and
both are rewarded. A development culture celebrates successes of people
who have found the right career or who are comfortable with the journey.

Clarifying Terminology

In most of the literature in the field today, *career development* is used as a
generic term. Most organizations use the label *career development programs* or *systems,* and professionals refer to the *career development field.*
Schools even call their career planning assistance *career development.* In
its specific definition, *career development* is the result for an individual of
successful *career management.* Historically, career planning was considered the individual's responsibility, and career management was the
organization's. These distinctions have blurred recently, with the emphasis on individuals taking responsibility for their own careers. The message is pretty clear today—employees must not expect their employer to
be responsible for their careers.

In 1994, the Career Development Professional Practice Area of the
American Society for Training and Development (Simonsen, 1994)
updated its definition of career development:

Career development is an ongoing process of planning and
directed action toward personal work and life goals. Development
means growth, continuous acquisition and application of one's
skills. Career development is the outcome of the individual's career

planning and the organization's provision of support and opportunities, ideally a collaborative process. . . . The purpose of career development systems is to ensure the best fit possible between the individual's interests, skills, values, needs, and work preferences and the requirements of the position, work unit, and organization. . . . Increasingly, organizations are viewing career development as a means of linking individual goals to business needs.

A commonly misused term is *career pathing*. It is sometimes used interchangeably with *career development,* contributing to the out-of-date expectation that there is such a thing as a predictable career path in organizations any more. Employees still stuck in the old paradigm (see Table 2 in Chapter 1) hold on to the belief that there is a road map to moving up in the organization, if someone would only tell them what it is.

We use the term *strategic career management* to change the mind-set of entitlement and to communicate instead the process of managing one's career in ways consistent with the direction and needs of the organization. Just as organizations need to do strategic planning to anticipate and prepare for market changes and competition, so do individuals need to plan their careers strategically. Career development planning is the first step in managing one's career strategically.

In the past, career development in hierarchical organizations equaled promotions, so many organizations were cautious of using the term *career development* for their programs. Managers expressed the concern of raising unrealistic expectations on the part of employees. Education was needed to change the mind-set, but many chose to use the terms *employee development* or *professional development,* or even just *development*—omitting the word *career.* Others kept *career* and paired it with *renewal* or *action,* tiptoeing around the issue of needing to help managers and employees alike to reframe their thinking.

A related process is *performance management.* Typically representing development and evaluation of performance on the present job, performance management in a development culture must move from strictly *performance evaluation* to a more proactive process involving managers and employees. Career development systems are best linked or merged with performance management systems, since opportunities on the job or in the company are based on strong present performance. In some organizations, career development planning is a subunit of a comprehensive performance management process, and these two together form a strong element in a development culture.

A phrase that has not changed meaning is *succession planning.* While the approach to succession planning is different in organizations with a development culture, the intent is still a selection and development process to ensure "bench strength" or "heirs" to senior positions in an organization. Traditionally, succession plans have been established for the top 6 percent or so of an organization's hierarchy, and perhaps the top two positions in a division or department. Succession planning was also traditionally a secret process, with even those on the "list" unaware of their selection.

In a development culture, succession planning must evolve to a more open process. Candidates become partners in assessment, developmental assignments, and perhaps mentoring. If active career management is addressed at all levels of the organization, people will not resent those elite few who are targeted for top positions. An interesting dynamic is driving a renewed need for succession planning in many organizations today. After the downsizing of recent years, companies are finding they have eliminated layers of management that used to serve as the feeder positions for key leadership roles; so now new high-potential identification and development processes are needed.

We may be using the same terms today as in the past—*career development, employee development,* and *career management*—but they represent a new reality. One of the purposes of implementing a career development system is to ensure that employees' goals, managers' support, and organizational systems align with business needs. Today's world of work requires that people be constantly growing, increasing their value to the organization. A development culture is both cause and outcome. A development culture, approached appropriately for the realities of the times, will meet the needs of organizations *and* individuals.

Focusing on Your Vision

An individual, no matter how enthusiastic, cannot successfully take on the task of creating a development culture alone. To champion efforts to create a development culture, you will need to identify your allies at all levels in the organization and enlist their support, expertise, and leadership. Clarify, communicate, and put your efforts into achieving your vision—even though you may need to start on a small scale. If you can envision a desired future state, you can then assess where you are today and define a plan to get there. A successful leader of the process will be one who can enlist others to contribute and together with them envision the outcomes, lay out a plan, and gather the support and resources necessary to move forward. The organization and its employees at all levels will be the beneficiaries of your successful interventions and designs.

Part I of this book seeks to define organizational culture, the factors causing the need for a change of culture, and a philosophy of development that, when implemented, can create or at least contribute significantly to a development culture. Part II focuses on the roles of all the stakeholders and contributors to the process. Part III details the approach of using career development as a catalyst to create a development culture.

The Need for a Development Culture

A Radically Changing World of Work

I'm successful because I don't go where the puck is,
I go where it's going to be.
—Wayne Gretsky

The Changing Nature of the Workplace

We are experiencing a revolution in the world of work no less dramatic than the industrial revolution of the nineteenth century that caused major changes in the way people made their living. We are, of course, in the information age, and the long-predicted changes in work are happening now.

Many factors are influencing this revolution. Competitive global markets require companies to compete or die. Quality and customer service require that front-line people have the power and authority to respond quickly and to solve problems. Global competition requires that productivity be at its peak and that people power (especially at U.S. wages) not be wasted. Organizations have to be lean, and everyone in the company must add value. Bureaucracy is slow and deadly. Autocracy does not value or reward the intelligence and skills of even the high-level professional, let alone the entry-level worker who brings needed current skills. As organizations create "just-in-time" production and maintain only core staffs, outsourcing and virtual offices become a reality for many workers.

In response to this revolution, there must be many changes: Skills must change and grow; attitudes and expectations about work and jobs must be updated; management practices must evolve; work processes and practices need to be reengineered; communication about business needs and realities must keep pace; attitudes about people development must be updated. Opportunities are different from those in the past, and employees need to be ready for new challenges. In any aspect of organizational life, the status quo is immediately passé. In this environment of change, certainly careers and career expectations must change as well.

The concept of the organization as a pyramid allowing successful employees to move up the ladder (be promoted) is no longer functional. Even though many organizational charts are still shaped like a pyramid, the organizations they illustrate are flatter than in the past. And the pyramid does not account for the many ways work is being done and evolving. Contract workers, hired on a project basis, don't fit into the pyramid; nor do experts or services to whom work is outsourced. Vertical ladders may be representative of some functions within a department, but they don't depict the team structure. How is a self-directed team represented in a hierarchy?

Work is changing so fast that job descriptions are obsolete almost as quickly as they are written. Not only job descriptions, but the nature of jobs themselves! As William Bridges (1994) has written, work is not going away, but jobs are. The possibility that an individual can be hired to do a specific job and nothing else is long gone. People doing whatever needs to be done to make the business a success represent the new entrepreneurial model. Many companies are asking employees to "act like an owner."

Specialist skills can quickly become too narrow or out of date, yet generalists can lack enough depth or current skills to be valuable. People whose only career development planning involves the expectation of promotions to management or to higher levels of management may find themselves on an indefinite plateau or even downsized.

With the speed of changing business needs, employees must balance the current demand for growth with long-range strategic career planning. And they must do both with the realities of the workplace in mind. Career development planning certainly cannot mean just "next job" thinking. The very job being targeted may be gone next year, or the work and skills required may change. In the old culture a common dilemma was expressed: "If I learn new skills now that I can't use in my present job, they will quickly become outdated; yet, how can I be qualified for other assignments if I don't have the new skills?" In a development culture, this dilemma does not occur.

So the old systems of hierarchy, titles, putting oneself in line for the next higher position, career paths, and so on are contradictory to realities in today's—and will be even more so in tomorrow's—organizations. Is it any wonder that employees need help reframing their thinking about careers in this chaotic environment? With the old paradigms no longer viable, new ones must be developed and communicated. As careers change, so must career planning and development resources.

Building a Development Culture

The culture of organizations is changing as they redesign themselves to survive. Those who will succeed in the next century are the individuals and organizations that can read the trends, quickly adapt to new demands, and contribute to a positive though changing culture. Today we see many organizations in flux. The massive downsizings of the last decade have taken their toll, not only on those who lost their jobs, but on the "survivors" as well. There is chaos in many organizations as the old culture is dying and a new one is emerging. In some cases, the organization's culture has evolved to represent a new reality, but many employees and managers have not kept up; in others, employees are embracing the changes, but organizational systems have not changed to support the new message. An example of this confusion occurs in many companies that are now encouraging employees to grow in place or make lateral moves to broaden their contribution, rather than seeking limited promotions in a flattened hierarchy; yet the compensation systems in these organizations often still reward only upward moves. Employees in this situation can rightfully ask, "What's in it for me?"

A comprehensive, integrated career development system can be the catalyst for bringing individual expectations in line with organizational realities. It can be the framework for updating or creating systems that support new behavior to achieve the results needed to survive and thrive. The approach to career development must align with, or support, the organization's new or desired culture to make the greatest impact. Without understanding the forces driving the culture or a goal to create a development culture, many companies have tried to implement career development or other programs that came to be referred to as "the flavor of the month." While well meaning, they weren't sustained because the components didn't fit the new culture or cause enough change to contribute to the development of a desired new culture.

Assessing Your Organization's Development Culture

As you begin to consider characteristics of a development culture, use the assessments and case studies in this book to help you determine (1) where your organization is in its evolutionary journey, and (2) the course you should take to achieve your desired outcomes.

Survey 1, "How Developmental Is Your Culture?," can be used to determine characteristics of your organization's present development practices. On a scale of 1 to 5, assess your organization, your management practices, and your employees' involvement in development. Note the areas of strength and those that need attention. Then continue through this book for perspectives and approaches that will help promote a more developmental culture in your organization.

continued

DEVELOPMENT CULTURE SURVEY

How Developmental Is Your Culture?

Does your organization provide an environment to grow and improve performance? Do you have an energized, motivated, and committed workforce? Answer the following questions for a quick assessment of organizational needs, using this scale:

1	2	3	4	5

Not true of my organization   *Somewhat true of my organization*   *Very true of my organization*

____ 1. Our organization values managers who develop their employees.

____ 2. Our managers are skilled and comfortable coaching employees.

____ 3. Our employees seek feedback about their performance from their supervisors.

____ 4. We have systems (job posting, position descriptions, and so on) and open communication so employees can gain information about opportunities in the organization.

____ 5. Our managers/supervisors know how to help marginal employees.

____ 6. Employees here initiate new work procedures, activities, and responsibilities.

____ 7. Managers' and employees' responsibilities for performance and development are clearly identified and stated.

____ 8. Our managers work with employees to enrich their current jobs.

____ 9. Employees have written development plans.

____ 10. Our organization provides access to career assessment and planning tools/materials for employees.

____ 11. Our managers use performance appraisals as a developmental activity.

____ 12. Our new supervisors are trained in managing the performance of subordinates.

____ 13. We prefer to grow people internally rather than to hire from outside.

____ 14. Our managers help employees explore career goals other than promotions.

____ 15. Employees like to work here, as demonstrated by high morale.

____ 16. Our organization provides training and development for managers and employees.

____ 17. Managers know how to reward and keep top performers motivated even when promotions aren't possible.

____ 18. Our professional/technical employees can grow without moving to managerial positions.

____ 19. We have "bench strength"—that is, employees prepared to move into key positions in the organization.

____ 20. Our managers give employees frequent, candid feedback on performance.

____ 21. Our productivity is high.

Record the score for each question below:

1._____	2._____	3._____
4._____	5._____	6._____
7._____	8._____	9._____
10._____	11._____	12._____
13._____	14._____	15._____
16._____	17._____	18._____
19._____	20._____	21._____

Now total each column:

I._____   II._____   III._____

Grand total of all 3 columns: _____

Column I: Refers to *organizational systems* that support growth and development for improved performance.

Column II: Refers to managers' contributions to the *development of employees.*

Column III: Refers to *employee needs and awareness* of responsibility for their own development.

continued

If your grand total is:

82–105 Super rating! Yours must be a great place to work! Perhaps one action you can take is to ask your employees and managers if they agree with you. Maintain your developmental environment by offering new career development services, assisting managers in even better approaches, or expanding opportunities for all employees.

43–81 Take a serious look at the areas where problems exist. Intervention now can emphasize development and improve performance before it deteriorates. Create a long-term plan while initiating short-term actions.

0–42 Take action immediately! You probably need to put efforts into all areas to improve performance and the environment in your company: systems, managers' skills, and employee responsibility. Ignoring problems will make things worse, not better! Start by building organizational support systems, and then consider training interventions. Recognize that you need more than a "quick-fix" approach. People are your most valuable resource!

Acknowledgment is given to Caela Farren, Beverly Kaye, and Zandy B. Leibowitz, Career Systems, Inc., for the influence of *Managers and Career Development: A Critical Commitment,* and to Career Directions, Inc., *Performance and Development Index.*

A *Look* at *Organizational* Culture

Edgar Schein (1986) defines organizational culture as "the pattern of assumptions that the group has invented and evolved in learning to cope with both its problems of survival in the external environment and its problems with how to manage itself as a group." Culture is a shared way to perceive in an organization. One of Terrence Deal's (1986) definitions of culture is the following: "Culture is a closed circle of assumptions, beliefs, and understandings." If culture, as Deal further defines, is "the way we do things around here," and market forces cause those things to change radically, the culture too will change.

Culture is a composite of an organization's values, and as such is not easy to change. Just as with one's personal values, someone can't just decide to change the organization's values. For example, if you personally value autonomy in your work, you would likely experience conflict with a new manager who micromanages you. In a similar vein, an organization that has never valued or rewarded risk taking will need more than a verbal commitment to change its behavior. It must undertake a process to change the group's pattern of assumptions. In the meantime, there will be value conflicts between the old culture and newly espoused values. When there are a number of values that must change in an organization, an uneasy time of conflict between the old, established culture and the culture that must evolve with the changing organization can be expected.

There is much attention today to dealing with and managing change. While it is essential to recognize the ubiquity of change in our world today, just telling people in an organization that they need to change won't usually cause a change of behavior. A change in "the way we do things around here" requires a change in the culture. The stronger the culture, the more difficult it will be to change. And change efforts must then require a process that will have a big enough impact on enough people in the organization to change its old assumptions, beliefs, and understandings. Employees must know that change is needed, understand why they personally must embrace changes, learn new behaviors to be able to operate in new ways, and be rewarded for doing so.

Changing the Culture

In order to create a new synergy between employees and the organization, cultures that evolved in the past need to change. Cultures are represented not only in people's attitudes and expectations, but also in formal systems that represent official policy and in reward systems. They are strong or weak to the extent that words match deeds. Organizations may post their values and mission in their lobby but contradict them with executive decisions and managerial behavior. To move an organization forward and establish a new culture, deeds must match words, as the following example illustrates:

A financial service organization that had been paternalistic in its expectations and practice experienced major reorganization. With much more sophisticated technology and tough external competition, it needed employees' technical and customer service skills to grow fast. In a consolidated environment, there were fewer opportunities to move, but many jobs had greater responsibility than before. The culture needed to change, and employees needed to buy in to a new environment and new expectations. The message that was stated was this: There is a lot of room for growth and there are many new challenges, and even reward systems other than promotions. But then a new vice president implemented policies to hire from outside instead of developing and promoting from within, putting the brakes on an evolving developmental culture. Just at the point when the company's actions were gradually changing employees' assumptions, beliefs, and understandings, its change in course belied the message.

Career Development as Change Agent

Career development, or "the way people get ahead around here," can be positioned as a change agent to bridge old and new realities, reinforce the messages of change needed, and educate employees about "what's in it for them." Pritchett and Pound (1996a), in *High Velocity Culture Change,* claim, "You must hit with enough shock effect to immobilize the old culture at least temporarily."

An integrated career development system can affect the culture in positive ways. Table 2 contrasts old elements of a typical culture with a new paradigm for individuals brought about by a successful career development system.

Job security—the promise of lifetime employment with one company—is a thing of the past. *Employability,* where the organization and individual join to ensure the skills necessary to get and keep a job—whether in this organization or in others—has taken its place. Instead of guarantees, employees need to take responsibility for keeping themselves current and adding value.

Continuous learning is a significant factor in the new paradigm. *Credentials or a degree* no longer guarantee a professional level of employment, or even a job. Today, even those with advanced degrees in their field must continually upgrade their knowledge and skills. Continuous learning may be supported by company-sponsored training or education, but even when it is not, individuals must take responsibility for their own growth and development.

Entitlement to a job, raise, or promotion can no longer be sustained by organizations in a competitive market. Everyone must continue to *add value,* and often even determine the value that is needed. In a development culture, employees who passively repeat the same work and set the same standards year after year set themselves up for failure, downsizing, or at least no additional compensation. The status quo is rarely acceptable, and it certainly no longer carries entitlement.

Table 2

The Changing Individual Paradigm

Old Paradigm	New Paradigm
Job security	Employability
Credentials/degree	Continuous learning
Entitlement	Adding value
Job description and title	Portfolio of skills and roles
Success equals promotions	Success driven by individual values and needs
Next job focus	Broad career, nonjob focus
Dependence on the organization	Commitment to work in one's field and to making a contribution

Since work is changing so fast, *job descriptions* and *titles* are used less to define who one is and what one does, and there is an increased recognition of the need to build and record a *portfolio of capabilities* to be offered in a variety of roles. Above all, organizations today require flexibility. Having an arsenal of capabilities to offer in a variety of roles that evolve to meet needs allows individuals to be ready to respond and ensures their employability.

In flattened and reengineered organizations, *success* no longer *equals promotions* for most people most of the time. Success today needs to be defined differently and must be *driven by each individual's values and needs.* In a development culture, a growing recognition that success means different things for different people has replaced the consistent expectation that everyone will move up.

Similarly, equating development with moves—that is, having career goals that are targeted only to the *next job*—is not a functional way for most individuals to plan for career development. In a changing world of work, *career plans must be broader,* more flexible, and perhaps *not tied to positions* at all. Focus is on the contribution the individual wants to make and the direction appropriate for his or her total career. Emphasis can be on building a reputation in one's field, profession, or industry.

All of this, of course, leads to a need to reduce the *dependence on the organization* and replace it with a *commitment to work in one's field and to making a contribution.* This can be a mutually beneficial relationship, perhaps long term, for both the individual and organization; but it is based on interdependence, not dependence. The individual has competencies to offer and shares values and goals with the organization, which in turn offers an opportunity to contribute, grow, and be compensated for the contribution.

Given the changing paradigm, managers and employees need a new mind-set about careers in organizations. Especially for those with a long tenure in an organization in which careers developed in the old paradigm, the new realities are hard to accept. Even senior managers who believe in developing people still feel that development means moving up and being ready to move up. After all, that was their successful experience. The example below illustrates a new paradigm expectation in the context of the old culture:

A manufacturing organization has a well-established succession planning program that spots high-potential employees early in their careers and moves them up as fast as they can handle, sometimes faster. There is a list of these fast trackers that represents about 5 percent of the division; employees, however, are not told they are on "the list." Others in the organization are not happy with the process—after all, many senior professionals find themselves reporting to a youngster the same age as their own children. Long-term employees, having bought into the old mind-set of loyalty, resent having their only shot at management filled by someone they perceive as less qualified than themselves. After downsizing and flattening, with fewer opportunities for promotion overall, employees are disgruntled. Hearing management say everyone must be responsible for his or her own career development without any help or tools to do so (a new paradigm expectation in the context of the old culture) has left people cynical.

Organizational Realities

Old career paths are gone in most organizations. The steps a senior manager took to become a senior manager are probably no longer possible. Assistant manager positions or general manager of a field office are likely to be the jobs that were eliminated in a downsizing. Reorganization and reengineering have changed reporting relationships, eliminated entire departments, and reduced the number of jobs. Functional "silos" with upward career paths are being replaced by cross-functional product or project teams.

Another reality is the speed at which employees must learn new skills. Settling into a job without continuous learning quickly leads to obsolescence, especially in a high-tech field. Being rigidly tied to a job description or comfortable tasks brands a person as unadaptable. Working linearly, one task at a time, makes an employee seem slow, unable to juggle in a fast-paced environment. Expecting a manager to look out for one's development and opportunities in the company is naive in today's competitive, multifaceted environments.

Organizational realities require that employees be flexible, fast learners, actively updating or changing their skills and managing their own development and careers. Realities also require that individuals link their goals and career plans to organizational needs and direction. When head counts are reduced or departments reengineered, it is those who don't fit or add value that lose out.

More than just saying that "people are our most important resource," progressive organizations recognize that it becomes a strategic advantage to develop people. New technological advances are quickly replicated by the competition, at home or abroad. But in the information age, a well-developed, adaptable workforce with skills that contribute to strategic business needs becomes a critically important resource.

Just as individuals must change their mind-set about careers and development, so too must organizations and the people who lead them develop new paradigms (see Table 3).

In a development culture, *paternalistic* messages that the company knows what's best for employees and will take care of them have to give way to *empowering* messages in which employees take responsibility for their own work and growth. Individuals cannot be empowered if the organization and managers continue to command and control. Empowerment is not a one-way street—employees cannot operate in the new paradigm unless organizations do so as well.

Development must occur too fast and continually to be *owned by managers*. Yet individuals do need direction and support from their managers to ensure appropriate, efficient, and targeted goals and development options. The new paradigm must be a *partnership for employee development*.

As discussed in the introduction to this book, *defined career paths* are an artifact of stable, hierarchical organizations. Today people need to be

| Table 3 |

The Changing Organizational Paradigm

Old Paradigm	New Paradigm
Paternalistic	Empowering
Development owned by managers	A partnership for employee development
Defined career paths	Multiple ways to move, or grow in place
Secretive plans for top employees	All employees involved in own development
Organization information not shared	Open information about company goals, needs, and HR systems
Compensation rewards upward moves	Compensation rewards contribution

considering *multiple,* perhaps constantly changing, *ways to move or grow in place.* When employees or managers expect that the organization should or even can define career paths, they show that they have not yet accepted the new paradigm of thinking about careers. An organization that, for example, expects employees to identify the positions they want for the next five years, through a career plan or on a performance appraisal, is reinforcing the old paradigm.

There is no room for *secret development plans* in a development culture. *All employees need to be involved in their own development,* proactively managing it. This doesn't mean that companies shouldn't have succession plans or replacement plans for key positions, but if people are being developed for leadership positions, they must be active participants in the process.

In the old culture, *information about the organization was not shared—* it was hoarded for the sake of power or control. *Open information about company goals, needs, and human resources systems* is essential for individuals to plan their development and careers strategically. How can individuals develop in ways the organization needs if information is guarded?

When *compensation rewards only upward moves,* it reinforces the old paradigm. No matter what is said, people experience a contradiction. The organization cannot claim that it is operating by the new contract until reward systems support the new behaviors expected of individuals. If the message is that individuals must add value, then *compensation must reward contributions,* not just upward moves.

Many organizations are in limbo between the old, paternalistic culture that worked in a hierarchy and the new culture with the evolving needs of today's world. They expect employees to change, yet their management practices and organizational systems are based on the old paradigm. The most common cause of this kind of conflict is lack of open communication: It occurs when business plans or predicted changes in product lines or department direction are not communicated. It occurs when the competencies expected for success are not communicated—even though selection is based on them. It occurs when job descriptions and position requirements are not shared until an open position is posted. And it occurs when certain people are targeted for opportunities that others did not even know were available.

Any time there is important information that is not shared with those who need to know, that is a symptom of a paternalistic culture. Senior managers who expect new behavior from employees must take the time to evaluate their own behavior and take whatever action is needed to change it.

Career Development as Organization Development

The fields of career development and organization development have a lot in common. As the field of career development has grown over the last two decades, it has taken what might be called a *systems approach*—that is, an approach that integrates career development with other organizational systems and takes into consideration strategic business needs and direction. This approach addresses the effects of changing business needs on employees, managers, and the organization itself. Career development is less likely to be targeted to a special population within the organization and more likely to be broad-based.

If career development is to be a means of creating a development culture, it needs to be institutionalized and pervasive—owned by line management as well as the human resources department. Any interventions must be based on real and perceived needs and have buy-in from stakeholders. That is not to say that a successful career development effort cannot start small, but it must be planned and designed for long-term commitment rather than for a quick fix.

Company opinion surveys today are likely to indicate problems with employee morale and to express a need for improved performance management and career development systems. This feedback from employees is driving much of the initial interest in "doing something about career development." However, management's need to respond and show some action can cause premature interventions that will not sustain the kind of change the organization needs or the kind of help employees are seeking, as the example below illustrates:

A rapidly growing high-tech company is experiencing turnover in its educated, highly skilled workforce. In exit interviews, employees say they don't see any opportunity within the company. In addition, senior management sees the need for skills to be increased constantly, putting pressure on employees to keep pace. With morale down in general, management made some unilateral decisions about what was needed. They decided to create a skills assessment process, requiring employees to be tested and enroll in certification courses where needed. They also decided a rotation system would be good to provide opportunities for learning and applying new skills and preparing a more broadly based pool of readiness. But without employee or management involvement in identifying the need, planning, or even communication about the decisions that were made, employees haven't bought in. They are living in the old paradigm and perceive rotation as a punishment rather than a development experience. The new paradigm has not been accepted and, therefore, will not change the culture and behavior in the ways needed by the company.

A process for designing and implementing a career development intervention that will contribute to a development culture will have many of the same components of an organizational development approach. Mink, Schultz, and Mink (1986), in their book *Developing & Managing Open Organizations*, say the following:

The idea behind sociotechnical systems is that any production or service system calls for both a technology and a work relationship structure relating human to technological resources. That is, an organization's total system has a complete set of human activities plus interrelationships to the technical, physical, and financial resources and the processes for turning out products and delivery services.

Career development will also be based on action research and planned for big systems change, and will involve stakeholders in the process, attend to the effects of interventions on related groups and processes, and contribute to organizational learning. Career development systems, approached appropriately for the realities of the times and the changing needs of the organization, should meet the needs of both individuals and organizations. The following chapters in Part I will address the new employment contract, help you envision a development culture, and explore ways that you can link career development with organizational needs.

A New Employment Contract

Do not rely on convention: career paths that were winners for
most of this century are often no longer providing much success.
—John Kotter, *The New Rules*

Changes in the Employee–Employer Relationship

The relationship between employee and employer is changing. No longer
can employees expect employment for life with one company. Security
no longer comes from working for a "good" company, but rather from
knowing who you are and how marketable you are. This is a hard lesson
to learn for those employees who bought in to the old contract and
played by those rules. They were obedient to the company's wishes, even
when it wasn't in their own best interest. They typically worked hard,
kept out of trouble, and expected a raise every year. Now, at midcareer or
later, all that has changed and these employees feel betrayed, as the example below illustrates:

Steve had worked all his career for a heavy equipment manufacturer
in sales, sales management, and administrative management. He had
moved his family fourteen times during his career because the company
had asked him to, and he was rewarded with promotions and salary
increases. With increasing competition from foreign manufacturers,

however, the company had to streamline and become more efficient; so in the early 1990s, the company reorganized into product lines, with each facility a profit center. In the process, the workforce was reduced by more than 25 percent, and Steve lost his job. Now in his fifties, Steve was angry and bitter and felt betrayed. He had given his entire career and a good piece of his life to the company, and this was the thanks he got. He felt that he had upheld his end of the "contract" but that the company had let him down.

Steve's story has been repeated millions of times in the last decade with the massive downsizings of white-collar workers, managers, and professionals. Although the blue-collar labor force had experienced widespread layoffs in response to economic downturns, the extensive layoffs of white-collar workers had been, until recently, unprecedented.

Jack Donahue (1993), Assistant Secretary in the Department of Labor for the first Clinton administration, presented an even more ominous picture. He described the difference between the aftermath of the effects of the recession of the early 1990s and those of previous recessions. Following most recessions, he noted, a substantial number of workers get their jobs back—but not this time. Most of the current layoffs would be permanent. Yet even after the economic factors indicated an end to the recession, people kept blaming the economy for the layoffs. They blamed the North American Free Trade Agreement (NAFTA) or the General Agreement on Tariffs and Trade (GATT) and any other scapegoat they could find for the loss of their jobs. Donahue emphasized a need to identify jobs that were likely to be permanently eliminated and to help workers in these jobs move in new directions *before* the job ended. He also emphasized that unemployment compensation should be thought of as support during retraining rather than as temporary income while waiting to return to work. People may have a sense that "things aren't right" in the world of work, but most of them do not understand the scope of the problem. Most know the old contract is no longer valid. They may be survivors of a downsizing (and wondering if they will be next) or close to someone whose job has been eliminated. But most people, employees and former employees alike, do not know what the new contract is.

The fact is that organizational changes are systemic and, to a large degree, caused by rapidly changing technology. For example, General Motors produces as many cars today with 300,000 employees as it did in 1976 with 500,000 (Rifkin, 1995). The jobs have gone away, not because of NAFTA or the GATT treaty, but because of automation. There are fewer bank tellers because of ATMs and fewer drafting technicians because of computer-aided design. One field in which jobs are increasing is the human services field—not only because of the aging of the population, but also because those jobs are harder to automate.

The organizational changes have been massive, and along with the loss of jobs, have included the loss of the old employment contract. Even employees whose jobs continue will face different expectations. Longevity of employment is no longer valued for its own sake, and employees must continue to add value to the organization. And in order to add value in a rapidly changing environment, employees must be flexible and resilient. In an often quoted article published by the *Harvard Business Review,* Waterman, Waterman, and Collard (1994) define a career resilient workforce as

> a group of employees who not only are dedicated to the idea of continuous learning, but also stand ready to reinvent themselves to keep pace with change; who take responsibility for their own career management; and last but not least, who are committed to the company's success.

To establish and reinforce the new contract, compensation and benefits need to change. Traditional compensation rewarded longevity, which became one of the issues in cost-cutting moves. Long-time employees who had received raises every year were often compensated above market value for the position they held or the level of work they were doing. When it came to deciding which positions to cut, they often became the first to go. Compensation systems that reward upward moves are still reinforcing the old contract, even when it is no longer viable. Compensation systems are slowly evolving to reward contribution rather than tenure. This often means variable pay based on company profitability, department or team contribution, and individual value added. Changes in compensation are another frustration for employees stuck in the old paradigm and another erosion of the old entitlements and security.

Benefits, such as pensions, are becoming more portable. The growth of 401k plans, often replacing traditional defined benefit pension plans, reflects a more independent approach to retirement. Health care is slower to become independent of employers' programs, but the passage of the Health Care Portability Act in 1996 is a move in the right direction. It is less likely with today's employment contract that an employee will stay in a job solely because of the need for continued health insurance or because of a vested retirement fund.

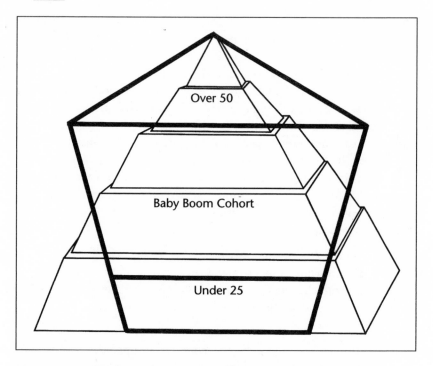

Figure 1   Population and Organizational Hierarchy—The MisMatch
From *Managing Your Career Within Your Organization,* by P. Simonsen, 1993.
Rolling Meadows, IL: Career Directions, Inc.

Redefining Success

With all this revolution in the world of work, individuals must redefine success. The concept of "working for a good company that will take care of me, increasing my pay every year, and moving up the ladder" was once the common definition of success. But there is no longer a ladder to climb, and no longer the top of a pyramid to aim for. Organizations are flattening and reducing layers of management. This is occurring at a time when the baby boomers are at midcareer. Overlay the population bulge on a pyramid-shaped organization (see Figure 1), and it is readily apparent that there is a mismatch. So even without a change in the structure of the organization, the old mind-set of success meaning moving up could not be realistic for most people most of the time.

In addition, as organizations evolve from hierarchies that are too slow to respond to rapidly changing market demands, the concept of moving up becomes even more problematic. Product or project teams may be established for long-term working relationships or brief assignments. Problem-solving teams may be ad hoc. An individual may be linked to more than one team at a time and report to more than one team leader. With the depth of knowledge and specialized skills necessary in many environments, a matrix structure can be practical. An employee may report to a technical manager or project manager as well as an administrative manager or development representative. "Manager" may be a temporary title.

In 1996, a growing percentage of the workforce consisted of contract workers or temporary employees. This phenomenon affects all sorts of occupations, from engineers to day laborers, from word processing clerks to executives. A major change following all the downsizing is the unwillingness of employers to add new employees to their payroll unless the positions are essential to the core business.

Work that does not involve the core competencies or business strength of the corporation is likely to be outsourced to a firm that specializes in that product or service. Employees still holding on to the old contract resent the elimination of their jobs through outsourcing. They feel that they are being devalued and sometimes resist the change, even though retaining the jobs in the company may mean losing business to a competitor who can produce the product or service at a lower cost. The following example shows the devastating costs to one company that faced this dilemma:

> An automobile manufacturer recognized that by outsourcing some jobs it could cut costs of production substantially, making its prices more competitive. Doing so would mean the loss of a number of union jobs that paid an hourly starting wage twice that of what employees at some outsourcing companies earn. Reassignment of jobs within the company for the affected individuals was not an option. So before contract talks began, the union struck two of the plants that would be most affected by outsourcing, shutting down production at most of the company and costing $900 million for the lost time and production.

The old mind-set of entitlement drives this kind of action. A strike is an industrial age tactic that can't work long-term to solve problems in a competitive, global economy. Automotive analyst Professor David Gregory was quoted by *USA Today*, September 20, 1996, as saying: "The new

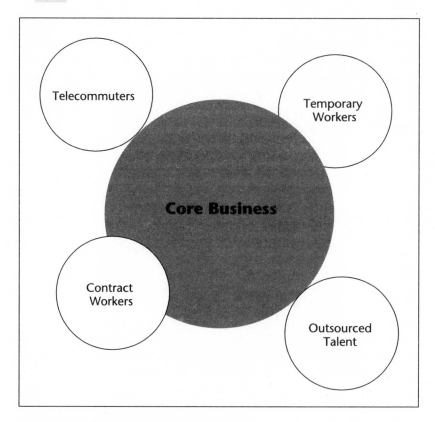

Figure 2   The Changing Shape of Organizations

union leadership (UAW President Steve Yokich) is saying a strike is the residue of an era that doesn't apply anymore."

Perhaps a *molecule* is a better model than a *pyramid* for organizations today, with employees contributing to the core competencies in the center, and peripheral bodies representing contract workers, temporary help, and outsourced talent attached but not part of the nucleus (see Figure 2).

Workers in this model may be full-time employees if they have skills that contribute to the core competencies of the organization. If not, they may find their niche with the supplier to whom work has been outsourced.

There is no shortage of leadership needs in today's organizations—no shortage of challenges, and therefore of opportunities. But the successful new career path will look different from the old linear ones. The new career path (recognizable as a path only in retrospect) will have horizontal moves, will perhaps include moves out and back into the organization, may stay for long periods of time at one level and even in one position, and will respond to changing and expanding demands. Superior employees may choose to remain individual contributors because of their depth of technical expertise and be valued and rewarded for doing so. Employees may move to outsourcing, especially if the work they do is no longer a core competency of the organization. For example, before Continental Bank of Illinois was acquired by Bank of America, it had outsourced its entire accounting operation. The employees did not lose their jobs, but became employees of Arthur Andersen instead of the bank, while doing the same work.

Another manifestation of the new employment contract is the phenomenon of the *portfolio career*—reconceptualizing a career in terms of using skills and knowledge in diverse settings and roles rather than with a single employer. People with portfolio careers balance projects, assignments, or part-time jobs, not expecting to work for just one employer for any length of time. The following example illustrates how one woman moved into a portfolio career:

Sandy had been a human resources director for the real estate division of a large corporation. When the company reorganized to focus on its core businesses, it decided to sell off the division that handled the company's properties. In the process, Sandy's job was eliminated. She received a severance package and immediately was hired as a full-time consultant for six months to design a human resources system for a division of a Fortune 500 company. While working in this temporary position, she considered other corporate employment offers and decided to combine consulting for an established consulting firm with counseling (using her master's degree) for a community agency.

Today success needs to be defined by the individual. For some, success means a balanced lifestyle with enough income for basic comfort. For others, it may mean acclaim, or at least peer recognition for one's expertise. For still others, success is in achieving and maintaining a high level of accomplishments. For many, it is a sense of control of their destiny. Money can become a stronger measure of success when other measures are missing. For example, if an employee hates his work, resents what the company is doing to the workforce, feels unappreciated, and generally feels like a victim, money may be the only reason left to work, and therefore pay looms larger than reality. The people who will thrive today and tomorrow are those who "know how to thrive on ambiguity in an environment of perpetual change—the very talents that moving up the ladder discouraged" (Gottlieb and Conkling, 1995).

Success, and certainly security, are being defined today as *employability*. When organizations can no longer guarantee employment—especially for life—employees need to know where their knowledge and skills are valued in today's market. Employers keep people as long as they add value and as long as they can afford to keep them; employees should stay as long as the organization adds value to their career and as long as they can afford to stay. Work is seen as a privilege rather than a right. Whether the relationship is respectful and built on trust or is mercenary depends on whether the organization builds the necessary foundation for the new culture or allows the old one to die a slow death, leaving surviving employees resentful, angry, and looking out only for themselves.

A Shared Vision

If people are competing to be "the one"—the one not downsized, the one promoted, and so forth, there becomes a competitive win-lose environment, not a developmental win-win atmosphere. Competition needs to be directed externally, not internally against the team, co-workers, or another department.

If employees feel like they are "on the corporate battleground, [they are there] for one reason only—personal profit. [They] are no longer working for the corporation, [they] are working for themselves" (Gottlieb and Conkling, 1995). If the new expectations are superimposed on the old culture,

> sometimes it works for a while. Stripped of the camouflage, it goes something like this. There will never be job security. You will be employed by us as long as you add value to the organization, and you are continually responsible for finding ways to add value. In return, you have the right to demand interesting and important work, the freedom and resources to perform it well, pay that reflects your contribution, and the experience and training needed to be employable here and elsewhere. (O'Reilly, 1994)

What is missing in this message is a shared vision for a new development culture.

If employees understand and accept the new contract, and the organization is building a development culture, both win. "The new workforce will help the company achieve objectives if it can achieve its own personal goals as part of the bargain" (Gottlieb and Conkling, 1995).

The new contract can be a positive force or it can be resented, depending on the support, the communication, and whether the company "walks the talk." The questions organizations need to ask is this: Is management operating by the old rules while expecting employees to behave according to new rules?

Changing Values About Work

Employees' values about work are changing, exacerbated by the massive changes occurring in organizations, but evolving because of other influences as well. Values are so much a part of our being that we're often not even conscious of them. Values are influenced significantly by our upbringing, with parents the primary factor for most people. However, factors external to the family also play a critical role in forming our value system as children. Television has been found to have a significant impact on youth due to its pervasiveness as well as the nature of the medium itself. Societal events also play a major role in forming our value system. Depressions, wars, boom times, and recessions all influence our collective value system. We can be sure that the scope of the downsizing in organizations is having a major impact on the values of young people preparing for or starting careers today, as well as on the lives of everyone personally affected by the massive layoffs.

Sometimes we assume that others' values are the same, or should be the same, as ours. In the case of societal values, such as honesty and integrity, that is true. But work values—those motivators that are important to us about work—are very personal. Why does one person value and thrive on competition, for example, while another shuns it and is stressed by it? When our values are not met at work, we will experience dissatisfaction at best, or even stronger conflict with the nature or tasks of the work. Value conflicts can occur when a value that is important to an individual is missing in the work environment or when a value that is present in the environment is undesirable to the individual. For example, if an individual values collaboration and teamwork and is in an environment where people are out for themselves, there will be a felt value conflict. On the other hand, an atmosphere that encourages micromanagement will be frustrating to a person who values autonomy. Often people do not recognize the dissatisfaction as an issue of differing values. They think there is something wrong with the other person or with the organization for not recognizing their needs, or for doing things differently. Employees and managers often do not see that there are no inherent rights or wrongs with work values, but merely differences.

Many workers who matured with expectations of the exchange of loyalty to the company for security are feeling value conflicts because of the changes occurring today. It is typically less of a problem for younger employees, for whom security was not a priority in the first place. If they grew up in the "me generation" of the 1970s, personal satisfaction or self-actualization may be their driving force. Many who came into careers in the rapidly changing growth years of the early 1980s were driven by accomplishment and financial gain. These are stereotypes, to be sure, but society's influence *does* affect generations. No one likes to lose his or her job, of course, but the impact is more difficult to bear if the main reason for having the job was security. Someone who is in the job because of the challenge may find an imposed job search just another challenge.

Career Anchors

With the old contract null and void, security as a value driving employees is in conflict with today's prevalent culture. This brings us to the question: What other values are supported in today's organizations? In research conducted with various employee groups by Edgar H. Schein (1978) of the Sloan School of Management at MIT on *career anchors*—motivating forces or composites of values that tend to constrain and influence an individual's career development throughout the career—security dropped from a primary anchor in the 1960s to fourth (out of eight) in the late 1980s. Perhaps it would be even lower today.

Eight basic career anchors have been identified by Schein (see Table 4). Career anchors are defined as the dominant elements that govern career choices. They determine how you select your experiences, identify the contributions you wish to make, and generate criteria to make career decisions, pursue your ambitions, and measure your success. Anchors influence the choices we make and how we respond to the events that are not of our choosing. Career anchors are not likely to change substantially in the short run, and we generally can't consciously decide to change them. Even if career circumstances change, our career anchors hold us. They are an element of the self-concept that is so much a part of us that we feel conflict when they are not being met. People can become uncomfortable, ineffective, and even miserable if their work conflicts with their personal career anchors. Development cultures value differing motivators for different

Table 4

Eight Basic Career Anchors

Managerial Competence

The career development focus is on progress toward greater and greater responsibility. People with this anchor enjoy and thrive on the emotional and interpersonal crises of being in charge of something complex. They welcome the opportunity to make decisions that have a far-reaching effect. They like directing, coordinating, and influencing others more than perfecting a particular skill or way of doing things. They feel most successful when carrying a large amount of responsibility.

Technical/Functional Competence

The career development focus is on building expertise and proper fit between the individual and the job. The primary concern of people with this anchor is doing a specific kind of work. It is extremely important to increase and demonstrate skills for their particular work. They are reluctant to take on work that is not within their specialty. They feel most successful when recognized as an expert and given challenging work rather than being given promotions and raises, although these may be important as recognition of expertise.

Security and Stability

The career development focus is on maintaining satisfiers, such as pay, benefits, and recognition. People with this anchor enjoy the prospect of continued employment with an organization they can rely on. Long-running career stability, good job benefits, basic job security, and involvement in one community are very important to them. They look to the organization to recognize their needs and competence and to define how they can contribute to its goals.

Pure Challenge

The career development focus is on new, challenging assignments and problems to solve. People with this anchor are motivated by the chance to solve difficult problems, win out over tough opponents, and build (and be recognized for creating) something new. Novelty, variety, and challenge become ends in themselves; people with this anchor dislike routine.

Autonomy and Independence

The career development focus is on greater freedom to make decisions and carry out responsibilities. People with this anchor enjoy being on their own and setting their own pace, schedule, lifestyle, and work habits. They are primarily interested in maintaining the workstyle of their choosing. They prefer to determine the nature of their work without significant direction from others.

Table 4

Eight Basic Career Anchors *continued*

Lifestyle Integration

The career development focus is on achieving and maintaining balance between work and other aspects of one's life. People with this anchor are concerned with making all the major sectors of their life work together as an integrated whole. Career decisions are strongly influenced by the need to maintain a balance with family, personal concerns, and other activities. Their identity is more tied with their total lifestyle than with a particular job, field, or organization.

Service/Dedication

The career development focus is on making a difference to society, to the organization, or to the people it serves. The primary concern of people with this anchor is to contribute to a cause or achieve some life value through their work. They pursue opportunities that permit them to make a difference in their area of concern. They feel conflict in an organization that holds values that are different from theirs, and refuse opportunities unless they are compatible with their cause.

Entrepreneurship

The career development focus is on gaining more "ownership" and total responsibility for a unit of work. The primary concern of people with this anchor is to create something new, involving overcoming obstacles, taking risks, and attaining personal prominence in whatever is accomplished. This anchor does not necessarily mean starting one's own business, but rather creating and developing a concept or project inside or outside an existing organization.

Edgar H. Schein, *Career Dynamics* (adapted from chapters 10–12). © 1978 Addison-Wesley Publishing Company, Inc. Reprinted by permission of Addison-Wesley Longman, Inc..

individuals, as long as individual values do not conflict with the organization's values.

Often the anchor with the highest identification in research groups (highly educated professional employees) is technical/functional competence, which can be defined as *expertise*. In other words, more people today are motivated by their fit with a job that uses and contributes to the development of their skills (Schein, 1978). In addition, a growing number of employees and managers identify lifestyle integration as their primary anchor. Not identified in the initial anchor research, lifestyle integration was added because of the increasing number of individuals who said something along the lines of the following: "My career is important to me, but it is only one of many factors that will drive my decisions about my life. My family, my community activities, my wellness, all matter as much."

This orientation is influencing the number and timing of moves an individual is willing to make for the company, the commitment of hours per week, and the whole issue of loyalty. Therefore, some individuals are choosing not to seek the managerial route for their careers because of the higher commitment and broader responsibility demands. This comes, perhaps valuably, at a time when management ranks in most organizations are shrinking and layers are being eliminated. However, it also coincides with the downsizing, which in most instances has increased the workload of the survivors.

In a 1995 survey by Merck Family Fund (see Davis, 1996), 28 percent of Americans polled had "made voluntary changes in their lives that had decreased their earnings, such as reducing working hours or switching to less stressful or time-demanding jobs." "Voluntary simplicity" is one of the top ten trends of Trends Research Institute (Davis, 1996). Perhaps this change from *loyalty in exchange for security* to *contribution in exchange for lifestyle integration* contributes to a win-win culture.

Shared Values

The ideal in a development culture is a set of shared values as the basis for the new work contract. Companies are saying they want employees to be loyal, but not dependent. Employees expect respect and open information, not paternalistic care taking. If values are to be shared, organizations and employees must know their values and act on them. Ken Blanchard (1996) has written

> This means that management must clarify and communicate what values the organization stands for, and then use those values as guiding principles in all organizational practices—especially in determining who is hired. For example, Disney holds a strong value in customer service that serves as a basis for hiring decisions. In almost all of its positions, Disney looks for service-oriented people who truly enjoy helping others. By hiring individuals who already believe what the organization stands for, they are better able to tap into a deeper sense of commitment to the organizational purpose and practices that follow as a result. Training becomes easier and organizational pride and morale are strong. Employee friendliness and dedication to service serve as competitive advantages to Disney.

A career development philosophy can be linked overtly to the company's stated values, contributing to a clearly defined development culture.

case **1** DEVELOPMENT CULTURE IN ACTION

Sales Division of a Manufacturing Firm

Values Statement

By contributing to a development culture, the career development process supports the organization's values. Research has shown that satisfied, productive employees lead to satisfied customers, which, of course, results in business success.

Trust, teamwork, and innovation are essential elements of a development culture. Trust is built between every employee and his/her supervisor/manager and co-workers as well as customers.

A building block for *trust* is open communication: about business needs and processes and also about individual goals, aspirations, and development needs.

In today's organization, individual goals are best met by contributing to the group's goals. This requires being receptive to changing and developing new skills. Teamwork creates a win-win situation for everyone.

Career development planning requires proactive thinking, to be ready for the challenges and opportunities ahead. It means anticipating needs and being *innovative* in our approach to work and meeting challenges.

Customer focus, sense of urgency, and passion for business drive the organization's goals, which then cascade to individual development goals. An expected outcome from the career development process is strategic career management—individual goals aligned with the organization's goals and direction.

Active career management results in accomplishing our goals and adding value to the organization. When we feel we are truly making a difference and are being valued for doing so, we take pride in our work, enjoy the ongoing challenge, and *have fun.*

Development Culture in Action: Case 1 describes the company values presented in the career development brochure used by a division of a manufacturing company.

Company values become beacons for goal setting and development actions by individuals as well as a set of operating principles to guide the development process organization-wide. For example, one company has a stated value of "becoming the preferred employer," which is defined as having competitive compensation, good benefits, quality products, and a stimulating, motivating, and encouraging environment. This value drives the expectation that managers will attend training sessions on managing employee development and will apply what they have learned with every direct report.

With existing employees, especially survivors of downsizing and reorganizing, it is critical that new organizational values be clear. Otherwise individuals sometimes expect things to go back to the way they were. "If only the changes would slow down," they think, "we could get back to business as usual." What these people don't recognize is that business will never be as usual in the past. Gottlieb and Conkling (1995) noted that "survivors need direction. . . . They long for some objective evidence of their worth. . . . They want to know what the future is and more importantly, their part in that future." Survivors must be clear about what the company expects from them now and in the future, and they must be clear about their own values. If there is a conflict between what the company stands for and an individual's values, it is difficult to reconcile. The employee must recognize that the company is not going to change its values to accommodate him or her, as the following example illustrates:

Susan was a hard-working employee who worked for a small high-tech company. She didn't avoid work, but she did resent the number of hours everyone was expected to work. She was slightly older than her co-workers and had outside interests not shared by them. Her co-workers typically worked long days and then socialized with the boss on Friday after work. When she didn't join in, she was criticized for not being one of the gang. Susan found herself in a "work-hard, play-hard" culture, with values different from hers. She initially blamed others in the company for their behavior but gradually came to recognize that she didn't share their values, couldn't change them, and wouldn't change hers. She needed to seek an environment that matched her value system better.

Key to building a development culture is to first clarify mutual values, and then build new relationships accordingly. This means that employees must have an opportunity to clarify their own values, and managers must talk to employees about their values. "A final shift in the new work contract is the need for managers to be responsive to what employees need (to do their jobs well). This is a reversal from past practices in which employees were expected to primarily be responsive to what their managers needed" (Gottlieb and Conkling, 1995). When differences between the individual's values and what the company needs are not reconcilable, perhaps the employee must make the tough decision to leave the organization, as did the employee in the following example:

Sam, a twenty-eight–year employee of a major manufacturing company, had always made his life decisions based on security in his factory job. He took the job because of the expectation of lifetime employment, stayed in the same town because of the job, joined the union for the salary and benefits it negotiated for members like him, and is building up substantial retirement benefits. Always in the classification "unskilled," Sam never much thought about learning new skills. He did what the forklift operator job required. Now with global competition and higher-level skills needed to operate automated equipment, the company and union have agreed on a technical training program that workers will need to attend in order to continue to hold their jobs. Sam's security and entitlement values conflict with the company's need for lifelong learning and "upskilling." He says, "I'm too old and uneducated to go back to school at this point in my life." So instead of continuing to work past his thirty-year milestone as he had planned, he now expects to retire instead of changing to meet the new needs of the company.

Where values are clarified and shared, productivity and job satisfaction increase. For example, one manager recognized that her employee valued independence and service. Since the company needed employees to be self-directed and responsible to customers, the manager decided to make sure that her employee had what it took to handle the job, and then basically left him alone—except for feedback and communication about the department needs and changes that affected the work being done. They discussed development needs identified by the employee or the manager, as well as ways to accomplish new learning. This employee is both productive and satisfied. He feels valued and is adding value to the company.

Operating with shared values requires new behaviors of managers and other leaders in organizations today. Gottlieb and Conkling (1995) describe the new leader:

The new leader derives power and influence from being trusted and by being able to develop collaborative behaviors in diverse groups. . . . The new leader for dynamic, turbulent organizations must possess the flexibility and tenacity to guide and manage an anxiety-ridden workforce through the choppy waves of change. He or she must have the ability to provide employees with a focus, a direction which will revitalize the department; directly contribute to the success of the organization; and most important, empower individuals to take charge, initiate change, and create a new organization that will have ownership from top to bottom on the organization chart.

Gottlieb and Conkling (1995) define a *transformational leader* as one who is able to:

- Formulate and articulate a vision of the future organization
- Share that vision with his or her employees and facilitate their ability to translate that vision into achievable tasks, goals, and objectives
- Value individual differences and understand the need to sensitively guide employees through the change process, to rebuild trust, and to encourage teamwork
- Provide continuous feedback and communication as cornerstones for future success
- Become a catalyst for facilitating individual self-esteem and internal motivation, though not offering unlimited job security

Employees who have the good fortune of working for a transformational leader can put their effort and energy into contributing in ways the company or department needs, rather than waiting for the paternalistic organization to take care of them. Instead of blaming their manager or the company, employees begin to become self-reliant, recognizing that their career security is in knowing their skills and adding value. In a development culture, all managers are in the process of becoming transformational leaders.

What About Employee Loyalty?

Companies are no longer able to promise long-term security, promotions, or even predictable raises. Where does this leave employee loyalty? We may need to accept a different definition of loyalty. Today *mutual commitment* may be a better term than loyalty in the old sense of "I'll hang in there through thick and thin, no matter what they do to me or my job." Loyalty today must be earned—by both employees and the organization. If the organization acts in ways that communicate that it can't be trusted, any residual loyalty (usually from long-term employees) is continually eroded, and new loyalty will not grow. Gottlieb and Conkling (1995) express the following concern:

> By replacing the idea of working together for a common goal, product, or service with the resolve of working for one's own security, career, and life meaning, we are toying dangerously with basic motivational values and theories. . . . We are cutting the heart out of the organization and replacing it with a superbrain.

A more hopeful perspective is found in a 1992 study of 3,400 employees of fifteen Fortune 500 companies by the Families and Work Institute, cited by Gottlieb and Conkling (1995). These findings indicate that loyalty and commitment have taken a different shape from what they were in the past. Today's worker commitment comes from an inner drive for development and fulfillment, for building self-reliance and independence. This drive will take the form of commitment to the organization as long as employees' needs for achievement, self-actualization, and recognition for contribution are met. Of course, employees are still looking for external satisfiers, such as making a good income and having control of their work. The study found that an amazing 93 percent of survey respondents felt loyal to their employer ("extremely loyal," 27 percent; "very loyal," 37 percent; and "somewhat loyal," 29 percent). These employees communicated a desire to help their employer succeed.

The Families and Work Institute study also attempted to determine which factors influenced selection of the current employer. The results are listed in Table 5. Notice that quality of work life factors and relationships on the job were rated significantly higher than salary.

The Families and Work Institute study also found that employees will be committed to their work if they

- Are in a highly participative work environment
- Have meaningful and interesting work
- Are significantly contributing to a higher goal
- Can achieve a healthy balance between their work and their personal and family life
- Are in an environment in which career development and growth are valued and encouraged

The new set of work values driving many employees' attitudes and behaviors today encompasses issues dealing with workload, job autonomy, work schedule, control, work-family balance, social relationships at work, perception of equal opportunity in the workplace, and supportiveness of their culture (Gottlieb and Conkling, 1995). So, while blind loyalty

Table 5

Reasons Considered "Very Important"
in Deciding to Take Job with Current Employer

Reasons	Percentage of Respondents Indicating Reason
Open communications	65%
Effect on personal and family life	60%
Nature of work	59%
Management quality	59%
Supervisor	58%
Gain new skills	55%
Control over work content	55%
Job security	54%
Co-workers' quality	53%
Stimulating work	50%
Job location	50%
Family-supportive policies	46%
Fringe benefits	43%
Control of work schedule	38%
Advancement opportunity	37%
Salary or wage	35%
Access to decision makers	33%
No other offers	32%
Management opportunity	26%
Size of employer	18%

From *Managing the Workplace Survivors,* Marvin R. Gottlieb and Lori Conkling. Copyright © 1995 by Quorum Books. Reproduced with permission of Greenwood Publishing Group, Inc., Westport, CT.

may be an artifact of the past, the quality of the work experience is driving commitment and loyalty today. Employees are typically willing to put in extra hours and effort for the short term or to deal with a crisis, but they may not be willing to work that way indefinitely.

Workforce productivity is promoted by building a development culture in which employees are prepared, know what to expect, and feel supported in their efforts. To change the old paradigm, perhaps organization leaders should be seeking and supporting *commitment* from employees rather than loyalty.

A Philosophy of Career Development

Organizations that are trying to create a shared vision for a new culture need to define and communicate a philosophy of career development that will drive the change to a development culture. As with any change process, a clear vision of the future can help people steer a course through the chaos and ambiguity of the present.

Creating a philosophy of career development often means educating executives as well as employees and managers. After all, most executives got to where they are under the old contract, and they may be giving mixed messages at best.

Many senior managers recognize the demise of the old contract and the speed of skill development needed by employees today. They see the changes in human assets essential to being competitive in the future, but they may not understand the importance of changing systems (selection, development, rewards) to achieve that end. Other executives are themselves firmly enmeshed in the old culture, equating career development with promotions. The influence of these managers may doom a career development process if they are not educated about the changed definition. In order to build a development culture, a philosophy of career development must be formulated and used to update the thinking of and to gain support from the organization's executives.

The CEO of a small, fast-growing software firm was asked what outcomes he expected from a career development process being initiated. He responded that he wanted every employee to have an entrepreneurial approach to working there. He wanted employees to be innovative and thought of as leaders in their field, to take ultimate responsibility for solving problems, and to act like owners in all ways. He was willing to change the work structure and the selection, development, and reward systems to achieve this vision. This is the beginning of a career development philosophy and the foundation of an emerging development culture.

Linking Career Development to the Organization's Mission

To build a successful development culture in organizations today, efforts must be directly related to the organization's mission and vision. Often a general "people policy" is stated as part of the mission, but it may not be interpreted at the level of detail that individuals need in order to act on it. A development philosophy, with actions defined for managers and

case 2   DEVELOPMENT CULTURE IN ACTION
Sears Merchandise Group

Linking Career Development to the Organization's Mission

Make Sears a compelling place to shop, to work, to invest.

In response to the newly articulated direction of the company, the Information Systems (IS) department of the Sears Merchandise Group targeted the goal of creating a compelling place to work in its effort to develop and implement an integrated performance management/career development process. In order to link people development with the direction and needs of the organization, they instituted a "goal cascading" process to ensure that individuals knew the goals of the company, division, and department before writing their performance, skills development, and career goals. Performance and skills development goals are required of each associate and are written and discussed between the associate and his or her manager. Career goals (longer range than present job needs) are voluntary and are discussed in a midyear development dialogue.

Once goals have been written, the next-level manager reviews those of his or her direct reports to ensure consistency and to make sure department goals will be achieved by employees' efforts.

Used by permission of Sears Information Systems department

employees, can be the base upon which the rest of the design of a development process is built. The Sears Merchandise Group underwent major reorganization in the early 1990s. With Arthur Martinez as the new president and CEO, a new vision, a new mission, and new values were defined and communicated throughout the organization. Development Culture in Action: Case 2 describes the process they used to ensure that employees were aware of the new goals.

The new employment contract not only is a result of the changing culture—it requires it. Employees—especially those affected by downsizing and reengineering—blame management and the company for their problems. At the same time, organizations witness the old behavior in employees and blame them (or even fire them) for their unwillingness to change, for lack of current skills, or even for longevity that has raised salaries above market value. Both management and employees may be aware of the new contract, and have certainly heard or read about the turmoil in organizations today, but are so firmly rooted in the old paradigm that only a change of culture will get their attention.

While reducing the number of employees and reorganizing departments and reporting structure, most companies have not substantially changed the infrastructure or implemented a major change in policies and behaviors. All of these elements are needed to plant the seeds of a development culture. A contract by nature involves two or more parties, and all parties need to buy in to the new employment contract for it to become operational.

Envisioning a Development Culture

You'll have trouble creating a new culture if you insist on doing it in ways consistent with the old one. . . . It doesn't make sense to try to change culture according to the old rules. The rules themselves are part of the problem.
—Price Pritchett, *High Velocity Culture Change*

Undertaking a Change of Culture

One of the characteristics of culture is that it is self-perpetuating—it defines "the way we do things around here." In order to build a development culture, particularly if your culture has been the opposite (closed, paternalistic, autocratic, hierarchical, and so forth), a major change process will be needed. For example, career planning in the old culture was often done secretly—by both the individual and the company; but in a development culture, career goal-setting must be collaborative. To make the change, there will be significant cultural norms to break through—lack of trust, lack of rapport between employee and manager, and perhaps even a history of recrimination by managers against "disloyal" employees. Simply telling people to discuss their career plans with their managers will not break through the old norms and change behavior. You will need to create a shared vision of the new culture with a "critical mass" of employees and be ready to use strategies for change that will break through the old expectations and cultural norms.

Changing the culture is not for the faint of heart. An expert in organizational change, Price Pritchett (Pritchett and Pound, 1996a), offers the following advice:

> Corporate culture has a very strong immune system . . . [and] it will launch a fierce counteroffensive. Usually it wins. . . . You must hit with enough shock effect to immobilize the old culture—at least temporarily. . . . Attempts at incremental change—tweaking the culture—ordinarily die for lack of energy. If you try to go slow, bureaucracy and resistance to change will cancel out your efforts. Let your opening moves leave no doubt that the old culture is incompatible with what's to come.

I personally have seen this play out many times in my consulting practice. If a company says, "We need to get employees to take more responsibility for their own development. Can you conduct a workshop to teach them how?" I know they will not achieve the outcomes they expect. Even when employees enthusiastically accept their new charge, they go back into a system that reinforces the old ways of doing things, and their enthusiasm fades. Even when both employees and managers are involved, with most buying in to the new roles and relationships, the changed behavior will not be sustained without an underlying culture change to support it.

A pilot program was generated by a self-directed team in an organization that had undergone a major reorganization to using a team structure. An employee group planned, researched, and proposed a career development planning process for its members, which was accepted and funded by the management team. Employees went through assessment, career planning, and improvement of "soft skills," such as communication, problem solving, and conflict resolution, and they wrote goals and development plans. They monitored each other's progress, but they didn't feel supported by their managers. So they went back to the management team and requested that their managers attend training with the same concepts and expectations that the employee group had learned, preparing them to conduct career discussions with employees. The pilot group's managers were trained to have career discussions with their employees. The program was deemed successful by all who participated, and did have successful outcomes for many employees, who felt more in control of their own careers within the company. But two years later, when the trained managers were asked their opinion of the process, they responded that they had believed in the process and went back enthusiastically after training to implement it with all their employees, not just the members of the sponsoring team. But they were not supported by *their* managers in the process—there was no accountability for them to put in the extra effort, and, in fact, they were measured only on achieving their numbers. There was no indication that employee development was valued by the division management team, so the changed management behavior was not sustained.

Pritchett and Pound (1996a) noted in their book *High Velocity Culture Change* that "culture change is hard to come by unless people can see a big payoff for behaving in different ways. Buying in to a new culture must bring pleasure." If it cannot bring pleasure, it must at least provide a view of the positive outcomes that occur as a result.

As you consider using career development to change the culture, recognize that a coordinated effort is essential. Some organizations face the reality of needing to do something quickly to address a problem that is driving the need for career development, such as high turnover of skilled professionals or lack of technical skills to meet changing demands. While responding to the immediate crisis is necessary, recognize that you must design a coordinated approach, with the message that the immediate intervention is part of a more comprehensive process to come. Some organizations, such as the one presented in the pilot program example, learn quickly from their mistakes and salvage a good effort that did not go far enough or did not have the proper support structure. Whether you are initiating a new intervention or salvaging a previous career development effort, attending to the change process itself will position career development for success in promoting a development culture.

The Change Process

Experts and practitioners alike agree that it is essential to have a clear vision of the future state that will result from the change. Richard Beckhard and Reuben T. Harris (1987), in their book *Organizational Transitions: Managing Complex Change*, identify the first condition for effective management of change to be "a vision of what the institution should look like, and direction toward that vision." Pritchett and Pound (1996a) agree: "Energy gravitates toward clear goals, so start by giving your people a clear aiming point. Tell them precisely what you're shooting for in terms of culture change. . . . Show commitment to the new culture [so you'll] disarm the old one." They further state that when culture is changing, for the people affected,

> the tendency is to drift, confused and aimless, unless there is an aiming point that captures their imagination. There must be a vision that holds their attention and hooks their hearts. . . . The vision must be like a beacon that defines where the culture is headed. . . . Promote it, sell the dream. . . . The vision must be articulated.

Joan Farrell, a human resources manager for Lawson Marden Label Co., was quoted in the *Personnel Journal,* July 1996, in regard to management's role as change agents in her organization: "We were prepared to lose our jobs before we [would sacrifice] our vision and the people's effort in working toward it."

A clear, articulated vision of the desired future state is absolutely essential in the change process. If people can't look to the past because it's gone, and the present is in flux, they must have a vision of the destination. So a starting point in managing the change process to achieve a development culture is a definition of the future state. What will the organization look like in the desired future state? What is driving the need for change? When these issues or problems are solved, what will be happening? How will behavior be different in a development culture? Be careful to define not only the activities needed to achieve the future state, but also what the organization will look like when the desired state is achieved—that is, why these activities are important. An example of an activity would be "employees and managers having career discussions" or "employees with active development plans." Ask yourself why it is important to have these activities.

In addition to vision to guide the culture change process, pay attention also to the speed of change. People often think change will be more successful if it occurs slowly. Not so, says Price Pritchett: "Unless you move quickly, people will spend their new energy in ways that interfere. They'll waste it on self-protective behavior. Or even worse, it will fuel resistance to changes, . . . and perpetuate the old culture" (Pritchett and Pound, 1996a).

While it is likely that a career development process cannot be rolled out to the whole organization simultaneously, several efforts can be in progress so that a development culture is seen as evolving on a number of fronts. For example, if competency analysis is an element of your approach and it will take several months, you can be building your communication strategy during this time as well. Design and conduct an orientation program so people aren't hearing rumors or thinking that nothing is happening.

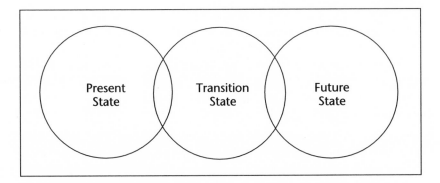

Figure 3   The Change Process
R. Beckhard and R. Harris, *Organizational Transitions.* © 1987 Addison-Wesley Publishing Company, Inc. Reprinted by permission of Addison-Wesley Longman, Inc.

Work on analyzing and modifying the other human resources programs that could conflict with the new culture or reinforce the old undesirable behaviors you are trying to change.

That doesn't mean everything must change—that you will throw away the proverbial baby with the bathwater. *Personnel Journal* (July 1996) quoted Coleman Peterson, senior vice president of the People Division of Wal-Mart Stores, as saying, "In a strong culture, change can sometimes look like the enemy of what already has been accomplished. It's important to understand that the change process is holding on to the successful elements of the present culture and adding new elements that are important to propelling that culture into the future."

While the change process needs to evolve from the present state through transition to the future state (see Figure 3), Beckhard and Harris (1987) recommend a different order. They suggest first identifying the need for change, then defining the desired future state, followed by an assessment of the present circumstances in order to manage the transition (see Figure 3). The transition then involves planning and implementing the activities and commitments required to achieve the future state.

Defining the Desired Future State

Beckhard and Harris (1987) define the future state as a midpoint goal between the present state and achievement of the vision. The clearer this goal, the more support and buy-in you will get from the stakeholders. So instead of starting with the present, and perhaps getting bogged down in all the problems to be overcome, start by defining the desired future state. To achieve a clear understanding of this desired future state, it is necessary to leave the present circumstances behind for a while and get people focused on the future. An advisory group, a career development team, or focus groups of key stakeholders can be tapped early in the planning process to contribute to the future vision (see Chapter 10). First these questions will need to be asked: What will be the characteristics of the organization in this future state? What will people be doing? How will behaviors be different? Does everyone agree on the desired outcomes?

Once there is some consensus by the steering group, the characteristics and outcomes of a desired future state can then be written and validated by other stakeholders. If these outcomes are achieved, the following questions can be asked: Will you be where you want to be? What will still be missing? What time frame is realistic? Members of the organization can then visualize themselves in this future state, and enthusiasm and support for the process will build. A defined vision for a development culture will lead to less misperception about the results of change and how it will affect individuals, thereby reducing resistance to change.

Characteristics of a Development Culture

Trust

People consistently identify trust as the most critical element in building development cultures. Jennifer Laabs (1996a), in an article titled "Expert Advice on How to Move Forward with Change," quoted the following statements on the matter of trust: "Trust is the most important ingredient in any corporate change process. Without it, management may find itself constantly fighting rear guard skirmishes with employees instead of leading everyone toward the future" (Robert Levering). "The ingredients you need most in a corporate culture for change to stick are trust and an unwavering view of the future" (Jennifer J. Laabs). Stephen Covey, as quoted in Laabs's article, used the term "360-degree trust," which comes from individual integrity, but also from "philosophically aligned structures and systems."

Trust comes from trustworthiness. If the organization is not perceived as trustworthy, even the best initiatives will be suspect, because employees will look for a hidden agenda. Of course, you can't build a trusting

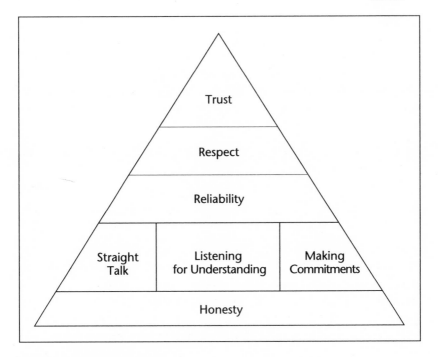

Figure 4   The Trust Pyramid

environment just by recognizing that it is needed. You must establish an atmosphere of credibility and fairness that will be worthy of respect. Trust and respect must be earned. The pyramid in Figure 4 shows the building blocks needed to build trust. If any are missing, the basis for trust will falter and perhaps collapse.

Straight Talk   Straight talk is essential to building trust. An important step in building a development culture is to intervene in the communication processes. Even if senior managers are seen as "walking the talk," communication typically breaks down when there is a lack of feedback between middle managers and employees. In a development culture, there is open and direct communication and information at all levels about the direction and needs of the organization and department, and about competencies needed by individuals to meet those needs. Employees communicate their goals, and managers give clear and objective feedback as a basis for appropriate development actions.

Listening for Understanding   Listening is also basic to building trust. In a development culture, people work to understand the meaning behind what is said. Listeners clarify communication one-on-one and in small groups. People attend to the feelings as well as the message of the speaker. If employees feel they are listened to and heard, they are much more willing to turn ideas into positive contributions and to be open about their own development needs in career discussions.

Making Commitments   To build trust, those involved must first be clear about expectations and commitments, and must then be willing to support the stated commitment. People know they can count on others because those others have proven themselves. This applies to the organization and its leadership as well as to each manager and employee.

Reliability   Reliability means that people do what they are committed to or what is expected of them on an ongoing basis. Reliability means that they follow through on explicit and implicit commitments. A perception of reliability is built up over time—daily actions can either enhance that perception or hinder it. In a development culture, promises are kept; organizational systems don't contradict the straight-talk messages.

Respect   Individual dignity must be respected, and integrity must be the basis of the way employees are treated as well as the basis for business decisions. Robert Levering, co-author of *The 100 Best Companies to Work For in America*, was quoted in *Personnel Journal* (Laabs, 1996d) as saying: "The very best policies in the world make no difference if they aren't well integrated with all the other aspects of the company's relationship with employees." Achieving a development culture may require change in the way people treat each other.

Honesty   Underlying all of the above elements of trust is honesty. Even though employees sometimes don't like what they hear, and may not accept it well, they consistently say they want honest feedback. Nothing destroys trust faster than failure to tell the truth. Studies consistently show that employees want to be in on things; they want to know what is happening—even if it is bad news.

Openness

Organizational Structures   "As organizations experience dynamism, flux, and change, the management and organizational structures should remain as open as possible, encouraging participation and role exchange among their employees" (Gottlieb and Conkling, 1995). Organizations need to speed up the process of changing from highly structured, autocratic environments to more flexible, egalitarian environments. "Internal control systems are often based on a zero trust premise" (Gottlieb and Conkling).

Bureaucracies are deadly to a development culture. "An open systems model [of organization(s)] offers the needed alternative to bureaucracies. . . . It presents a way of understanding and developing organizations so that management processes and individual human potential work together instead of against each other" (Mink, Shultz, and Mink, 1986). A rigid structure with systems that are increasingly dysfunctional will not be able to respond to a rapidly changing environment, support changing work ethics and motivation in the new contract, or tap the expertise of a diverse workforce that brings the very skills needed today.

Just as careers today need to be based on a principle of adaptability rather than predictability, so do organizations. "Open organizations consider process more important than structure . . . and free human interaction more effective than a chain-of-command hierarchy" (Mink et al.). In a development culture, feedback is critical. There is a continual interchange of information, breaking down traditional restricted information and interaction by cross-functional systems, teams, moves, and assignments. The unifying forces are (a) shared purpose and goals, and (b) leaders with a system-wide perspective to solve problems through collaboration rather than authority. "The process assumes that people have the capacity for creativity, responsibility, and growth" (Mink et al.). A proactive rather than reactive environment anticipates and plans for changes so there are fewer crises and a greater ability to deal with ambiguity.

Strategic Direction and Communication   In order for employees to develop in ways needed by the organization, both formal and informal communications systems must be open. Organizational leaders must define strategic direction, and managers at all levels need to translate organizational purpose and goals into specific objectives for work in their units, as discussed in Chapter 4. A development culture requires clear and focused direction, and with the elimination or blurring of functional units, strategic coordination of projects and initiatives is also essential. How can employees manage their careers strategically if they don't even know what the company or department needs? Employees must be in on the organization's goals in order to contribute in ways the organization needs. Managers need to work hard to keep their people informed of and involved in the direction the corporation is taking. Open communication and acceptance of both suggestions and complaints must be encouraged.

Collaboration Versus Competition

Development cultures focus on external competitors and build collaboration internally. Career development today is not about beating out the competition for a promotion, but about successful teamwork so that everyone is adding value and contributing to a team goal and the organization's success. It is about ensuring one's own *career security,* not job security, and that becomes a win-win situation for everyone. Leadership in a development culture is less about position and more about skills and knowledge. The people who do move to senior positions are collaborators who lead an informed group of knowledge workers and even form alliances with competitors when it is in the best interest of both parties.

Managed Conflict

When ideas are open and individuals are empowered to take action, conflict will arise. Conflict is a result of ambiguity, which is a byproduct of change. So conflict-resolution skills are essential in our changing organizations. Conflict is also a result of complexity, so as organizational structure changes—with less clearly defined reporting lines and job descriptions—individuals are challenged to improve communication strategies and understand differences in order to be able to identify and work toward shared goals. In a development culture, conflict is managed rather than avoided and everyone has and uses skills to move from *argument* to *planning for solutions.* The outcome of conflict situations becomes problem solving rather than ongoing disagreement or win-lose challenges. Rather than wasting energy on personal conflicts, energy is directed at the problem and solutions. Thomas J. Bergmann and Roger J. Volkema (as quoted in Meyer, 1989) offer the following advice on managing conflict:

> Conflict that is not identified, understood, and managed effectively can lead to inefficient use of organization resources, stress on the conflicting parties, and misdirection of the energies of those affected by the conflict situation. On the other hand, conflict that is effectively managed can result in increased creativity and innovation, a rethinking of goals and practices, and a better informed work group.

Risk Taking

A development culture encourages smart risk taking. Change requires exploring the unknown, which ultimately means taking risks. Changing the individual paradigm from security and entitlement requires that individuals take risks. Instead of playing it safe, people need to move out-side of their comfort zone. They need to be open to new ideas, challenge their own perceptions, and be willing to climb a steep learning curve. If organizations expect individuals to change, they must reward the desired behavior. If they want employees to be less dependent and to act like owners, allowances need to be made for mistakes and failure along the way.

In a development culture, risk taking is rewarded, not punished, and innovation as a result of risk taking is celebrated. Employees and managers understand the difference between foolhardy risks and calculated risks, and they understand how to monitor risk factors. This understanding reduces the likelihood of failure and increases the probability of success.

Systems Aligned with Messages

Development cultures reward appropriate behaviors, such as open com-munication and taking risks. Compensation systems reward contribu-tion rather than tenure or position; intrinsic rewards, such as showing respect and acknowledgment, show individuals that they and their work are valued. If employees are expected to be self-directed, then decision-making systems allow and support that behavior. If employees are pushed to keep their skills current, then employee skills are tapped before hiring from the outside. If risk taking is needed, then individuals are not punished (demoted, fired, given less power) when calculated risks fail. The organization and its leaders "walk the talk."

Learning Versus Training

A development culture thrives in a learning organization—not a training organization, but a learning organization. Companies can provide a full training calendar and be neither a learning organization nor a development culture (witness an employee who left a full-day session at noon because he had achieved his forty required hours of training for the year). Indi-viduals in a development culture are always in process, never "there yet," just as the organization is continually improving. Everyone is expected to learn from experience and apply what they learned to improve their own work and contribute to the goals of the company. Career development planning includes needs assessment, to determine appropriate training and development activities, and measurement, to determine whether any learning took place.

A development culture involves and affects individuals, work groups, and the entire organization. Individuals need to expand their self-awareness. They need to know who they are and what they have to offer so they can then reach out, listen, and be open and sharing. The work group is concerned with team goals as well as with all who are contributing and committed to goals. They can then be sensitive to others' needs and can generate cooperative interaction with other teams. At the organization level, units can interact to move everyone forward, with shared information and resources, to achieve the purpose and goals of the organization.

Assessing the Present State

Once the desired future state is defined, and before moving on to the details of planning how to achieve it, an analysis of the present is required. What are the conditions or characteristics of the present state? Who are the champions of and who are the resisters to changing the culture? Which organizational systems support the new vision, and which need to be changed?

Surveys, interviews, focus groups, and other methods are useful data-gathering steps that can provide a broad view of the current state. Focused on all aspects of a development culture, input from a variety of levels and departments can emphasize what is currently being done well, where the problems lie, and the severity of issues perceived by members of the organization.

A division of a Fortune 500 manufacturing company that was initiating a major change effort around career development administered to its employees an opinion survey. Results showed that questions about career development and performance management received the lowest ratings of any items on the survey—an average rating of 40 percent compared to ratings above 60 percent on all other items. Focus groups with employees indicated that the reason for this low rating centered around the perception that selection processes were unfair, especially in a flattened organization where there were so few opportunities anyway. People were cynical about the job posting system. They also felt they did not get any feedback on why they weren't selected for openings or feedback from their managers on development needs.

Interviews with managers indicated that they felt employees were unrealistic in their expectations of promotions—after all, not everyone can become a manager. The reward systems were also a point of difference. Managers felt that employees' expectation for raises was unrealistic, as the division was very competitive in its compensation levels. This perspective was clearly different from that of employees, who were concerned not about the amount of pay but rather about the seeming unfairness of the way the incentive pay was determined. Needless to say, trust was low, and both groups clearly knew that.

In this example, a constellation of problems emerged around lack of open communication between managers and employees, particularly individual feedback. Another constellation was identified in regard to employee expectations and understanding of the new paradigm. An underlying issue was the lack of trust.

Beckhard and Harris (1987) delineate three steps to diagnosing the needed changes in a present system:

∎ Identify and set priorities within the constellation of change problems
∎ Identify relevant subsystems
∎ Assess readiness and capability for the contemplated change

Relevant subsystems in the above example include the selection process itself, development opportunities besides promotions, and policies of the compensation system. Manager and employee groups could also be considered subsystems, since they are operating with different perspectives on problems.

Employees at first glance may seem to be very ready for change; after all, they are unhappy with the current situation. But the underlying cynicism and lack of trust can cause suspicion and resistance to any change efforts rolled out by managers. Readiness for change is indicated in willingness, motives, and aims. Capability is another matter and includes power, influence, authority, information, and skills. Employees may need educating before they can change their expectations about this thing called career development if they are still operating in the old paradigm.

Managers, on the other hand, may be *capable* of change: They have evolved the present systems and have the power and authority to change them as well. The issue is whether they are *ready* for change: They may think the problem is unrealistic expectations on the part of employees, and thus may not yet have recognized that there is a problem other than getting employees to change their attitudes.

Beckhard and Harris identify some elements of potential change, to include attitudes and values, organizational policies, managerial practices, control and reward systems, and technical skills.

In defining the present state, it is also appropriate to identify a "critical mass"—the minimum number of supporters needed to accomplish the changes. Do all managers need to be on board to achieve the desired future state? What percentage of employees must participate? Can implementation be voluntary, and if so, what about the individuals who need to change but who don't participate? Should the first interventions be with those who are most supportive of the change efforts, or with those who are most resistant? How will you get a critical mass of the latter group? How will you overcome the old attitudes and behaviors to prepare people to move to new ones?

Walter Oliver, senior vice president of human resources at Ameritech, was quoted in *Personnel Journal,* July 1996, as saying, "It's absolutely critical that everyone move toward a certain level of involvement and engagement in the change process. Otherwise a wide divergence of focus concerning the reasons for the change can slow or derail the entire process."

Planning the Transition

Once you know the characteristics of the desired state and sense the pulse of the present situation, you can start designing the process and components of the transition process. This involves determining the objectives of each element of the change process and then the activities required to move forward. Chapters 11, 12, and 13 identify essential elements and components of an integrated career development system and the design questions that must be answered in the planning.

One decision to be considered in the initial planning is where to start. Will you intervene first with top management—perhaps through a series of executive briefings—to communicate the findings of data gathering and get buy-in for the initial change efforts? Or will you work first with the group that has been requesting help, either because of readiness or because of significant problems that are driving the need for changes? Will you initiate your communication strategy with everyone so that people know there is an intervention coming, or will you wait until the details are in place?

Overcoming Old-Culture Objections to a Development Culture

As you prepare to initiate a change process, you will most certainly run into interference and objections. Some of the questioners may be devil's advocates, helping you anticipate the kind of resistance you will face, but others will be expressing or suppressing real concerns or biases. Pritchett and Pound (1996a) note that "a good 20 percent of the people will buy in to the culture change immediately. They'll embrace the idea, enjoy the challenge, and help drive the effort. Another 50 percent of the group will

Table 6

Common Objections to Career Development

- We can't promote everyone, so why raise unrealistic expectations?
- We have a space on our performance appraisal forms to indicate what career plans our employees have, and our managers are supposed to discuss these career plans with their people. What else is there to do?
- Our company can't even *think* about career development. We're downsizing!
- What if employees "develop" in ways that won't be useful to the organization?
- We don't have the staff needed to implement career development.
- I'm sure it would be nice, but we can't afford it.
- If we develop our employees, they will just jump ship to our competition.
- We already have a career development program. We have a lot of internal courses and a generous tuition reimbursement program, and employees don't even take advantage of these now.
- We don't have time for career development; we're busy with TQM or quality initiatives right now.
- Our managers are technical people—they won't be good at career development.
- We do things differently in (Europe/the field/plants)—the (U.S./corporate/home office) style won't work here.

be undecided . . . on the fence . . . slow to commit themselves one way or the other. The remaining 30 percent will be anti-change, and that attitude isn't likely to go away." It is wise to anticipate the resistance and be prepared to overcome it. Table 6 identifies some common objections to implementing a career development process.

Most objections arise out of the old paradigm. People expressing these concerns aren't ready to embrace change; they first need to be educated, to look at development from a new paradigm perspective. Rick Maurer, in his 1996 book *Beyond the Wall of Resistance,* says,

> People resist not out of spite but out of fear. They may fear that this change will result in a loss of status, money, power, even their jobs. Some people will fight back when they believe that the change threatens their own best interests.

Maurer suggests that rather than confronting resistance, we engage the resistors by responding to their concerns, so that people believe that the change agent hears them. Pritchett (Pritchett and Pound, 1996a) says,

> You need a tremendous amount of high-quality communication to sustain a culture change. [People] typically underestimate the effort

Table 7

Benefits of a Career Development System

- Reduced turnover of highly skilled or experienced employees
- Revision of outdated expectations for career opportunities after flattening or reorganizing
- Motivated employees who take responsibility for their own development and continue to add value
- Understanding by employees of the urgency to keep skills current
- Employee and manager buy-in to the need for continuous learning
- Increased "bench strength" (based on increased retention of experienced employees) for succession planning
- Ensured equal opportunity for minorities and women
- Managers who are convinced of the importance of developing employees
- A competitive organization through productive and motivated employees
- Flexible employees who can move out of functional "silos" or narrowly defined roles
- Matching of realities in the organization to recruiting promises
- International flexibility
- Employees with meaningful development plans

that is required. First, people need to hear the logic, the rationale behind the decision to change the culture. You must give them a clear understanding of what's expected regarding new ways of work.

"Good communication can't guarantee success in your efforts to change the corporate culture, but poor communication guarantees you'll fail" (Pritchett and Pound). To overcome objections to a comprehensive career development process, you need to be ready to communicate the benefits. Analyzing the present state uncovered problems or needs that your desired future state will solve. Now is the time in your planning to translate those problems and needs into business terms, if they are not already described that way, and to communicate in every way possible the vision, benefits, purpose, and goals of the intended changes. The need for change must be clearly communicated to each stakeholder group.

Selling the Career Development System

Table 7 identifies typical benefits derived from an integrated career development system. To sell the benefits of such a system, you will need to show how it can address the needs recognized by the decision makers.

The following example illustrates how one organization was able to sell the career development system to senior management:

The senior management in a finance organization had been promoted on the fast track to their current positions. They believed that if they weren't promoted every two years, something was wrong, and their experience, by and large, supported this expectation. When the organization flattened considerably and closed satellite offices, opportunities for moves—particularly promotions—became very limited. The jobs that remained now required a greater variety of skills for successful performance. Senior management was concerned that many of their managers wouldn't be able to handle the greater scope of their jobs now. However, they resisted implementing a career development process because they knew there were limited opportunities to move up: "Why have career development discussions when you can't offer good employees any opportunities? And besides, most managers aren't handling their present jobs well, so expectations for promotions are unrealistic."

An executive briefing communicated a redefinition of career development and emphasized the need for quickly improving skills. Focusing on the outcomes of a development process—the right people in the right jobs with the right skills—the plan got the managers' attention. In their own minds, their own career development may still mean promotions, but they agreed that a reeducating process was needed for everyone else, and hence they supported the implementation of a career development program.

Celebrating the Successes

Once your change efforts begin to take shape and you begin to see some new behaviors, it is essential to reward these new behaviors and celebrate successes. In order to change behavior, people must first recognize that change is needed; second, they need to know what the new behavior looks like and what skills will be needed to perform in the new ways; and, finally, they should receive reinforcement when they display the new behaviors. When you see acceptance of the new culture displayed, either by a group or by an individual, you must be ready to reinforce and reward the desired new behavior.

For example, managers of a department in one organization asked for training in how to conduct development discussions with their employees. They recognized that they needed to encourage skills development in their technical professionals and to counteract the turnover they were experiencing in their best performers. First of all, it is essential that these managers be supported in their initiative. This recognition may take the form of an announcement to employees that their managers are trained and ready to discuss individuals' career goals and help create development plans. A celebration, such as a group awards ceremony for those individuals who have achieved a valued certification, may be appropriate. For most people, recognition of achievement is a tangible outcome that rewards their effort and demonstration of new behaviors. The following example illustrates how valuable recognition can be:

A high-tech company that had experienced rapid growth instituted job descriptions and pay levels for the first time. This meant that in some cases individuals were reclassified, not always in the categories they expected. There had been some departmental announcements about the changes, and a job descriptions booklet was made available to all managers. But these actions caused morale problems, because some individuals felt they were treated unfairly or even demoted. There had been no individual discussions about the impact of these changes on employees' careers, and managers feared opening a Pandora's box if they tried to rationalize the decisions. Managers realized that they needed to face employees and deal with the issues head on, so they asked for training in conducting career discussions. After most of the discussions had been conducted, managers saw less hostility and anger on the part of employees—an intrinsic reward for them. A more tangible acknowledgment occurred when multirater survey scores showed employees valuing the relationship with their manager and believing that their manager supported their development.

As you design a career development system to contribute to a change in your culture, consider some systematic ways to reward new behaviors:

■ If the new message is that achievement of diverse goals is valued by the organization, then acknowledge these achievements, not just promotions, in your company newsletter or announcements.

■ If employees are encouraged to grow in place because of limited options for moves as well as increasing job demands, then ensure that that kind of growth is rewarded financially—either through a broader base of discretionary pay or through incentive compensation.

■ If undue emphasis has been placed on titles, then devise other ways for worth to be publicly acknowledged, such as "distinguished" status or selection as a mentor.

■ If employees have been passive about their development, waiting for the company to make decisions and take action for them, then celebrate accomplishment of individual goals such as completing a degree or gaining expertise in the latest technology.

■ If employees push the limits in bringing a new product to market, throw a celebration to acknowledge and reward the behaviors and commitment necessary to make it happen.

■ If you are encouraging open communication, then make it okay for individuals to talk to managers other than their immediate supervisor.

Be careful not to reward the old behavior or punish the desired new behavior:

■ If a manager encourages his or her best performer to make a move that is good for the company, make sure that systems or budget constraints don't make it difficult for the manager to replace that person.

■ If managers put in the necessary effort to develop their direct reports, make sure their reward system is based on having more productive employees and not just on technical production.

■ If you know that some employees' jobs are going to be eliminated, facilitate their cross-training for other positions within the company before the door is closed.

■ If managers are beginning to give corrective, and sometimes tough, feedback, train employees to accept and build on it rather than to argue and resist change.

■ If employees are exploring other areas of the company for long-range options, make sure that systems are in place to prevent punishment by a resentful boss.

■ If employees are encouraged to develop teamwork skills, don't reward only individual performance.

■ If you value diversity, don't allow managers to purposely overlook nontraditional applicants or prevent employees from using flextime (for child- or eldercare, religious observances, educational pursuits, and so on) or other benefits.

If you like the behavior change you see, don't take it for granted. It is far too easy to revert to the old behavior if the new is not reinforced. And then it is a much greater uphill battle to elicit the desired behavior again. Run interference in advance to ensure that company procedures do not contradict the cultural change message. Creating a development culture is fragile at the beginning. Make sure the messages are consistent, that everyone is buying in to the change, and that your champions are visible and making a difference to achieve the desired new state.

> You need to change what you celebrate, what you honor, and who you hold up as heroes. . . . If [people's] behavior hasn't changed enough—if you're still stuck in the same old culture—you need to make bigger changes in your rewards and sanctions. (Pritchett and Pound, 1996a)

If the old employment contract is no longer viable and the culture is changing—perhaps drastically—then the message is that individuals must take responsibility for their own development. Employees have a right to ask what they should be developing and what they should be developing for. Just as the future state of the new culture must be clear to all, so must the direction and actions of each individual. In the next chapter, we will take an in-depth look at linking career development efforts to organizational needs.

Linking Career Development to Organizational Realities

Before you can determine the route, you need to
know the destination.
—Branch Rickey

Aligning Individual and Organizational Goals

If career development is going to influence a change of culture, the single
most important element is a clear and strong link to the strategic direction of the organization. If we want employees to act like owners, make a
commitment to the success of the endeavor, and align their career goals
with the direction and needs of the organization, they need to know the
strategic direction and what is required of them to add value.

If we want leaders to value the efforts and expense of a career development process and recognize that it is essential to build the workforce
required for competitive advantage, they need to understand how the
alignment happens and what outcomes to expect. Attention to employee
development (at all levels, including executive development) is not just a
nice thing to do for employees—it is essential for the survival of the business. John Naisbett and Patricia Aburdeen (1990) put it succinctly in
Megatrends 2000: "In the global economic boom of the 1990s, human
resources are the competitive edge for both companies and countries. In
the global economic competition of the information economy, the quality and innovativeness of human resources will spell the difference."

Directly linking development to strategic business needs is a change in the purpose and message of career development efforts since the late 1970s and early 1980s. Most companies today recognize the need for a well-developed, flexible workforce that will respond to rapid changes in the market and environment. In fact, Gutteridge, Liebowitz, and Shore (1993) define organizational career development today as "a planned effort to link the individual's career needs with the organization's workforce requirements." They describe it as "a process for helping individuals plan their careers in concert with an organization's business requirements and strategic direction." While people responsible for career development programs often agree that it should be linked to organizational strategy, few do so systematically. In Gutteridge, Leibowitz, and Shore's international research on career development systems, they found the U.S. sample (compared with samples from Europe, Singapore, and Australia) to be the only one in which linking to the organization's strategic plan was not among the top three factors influencing career development. Perhaps a corollary finding is that career development systems were rated effective or very effective by only 29 percent of the U.S. respondents, compared to 52 percent in Australia, 62 percent in Singapore, and 58 percent in Europe.

There are two issues here: First, there must be a link between the strategic direction and employee actions; second, employees must know what the needs of the business are. This requires open and honest communication about mutual objectives, explicitly about the link. Cynicism results when you tell people they're partners in the business but then don't treat them that way. Individuals need to know the vision of a development culture and share it with the organization; the organization needs to act on its vision, not just have it as a slogan on the wall.

If the employment contract has changed so that employees no longer believe they are rewarded for loyalty and employers do not want blind loyalty, mutual goals need to be defined to establish and cement a commitment. Employees need a reason to be fully engaged and committed to the organization. In a recent study of employee attitudes by Towers Perrin, an organizational research consulting firm (cited in Laabs, 1996b), results indicated that employees felt undermined by all the changes going on in organizations today, yet they believed they have opportunities to make a bigger difference to the success of the business. Employees look toward an increasing importance in their present roles rather than toward moving up the ladder.

The Towers Perrin study covered the four areas listed below, and percentages indicated represent the percentage of employees who thought their company was successful in this area.

- Career (not job) security—whether employees had a sense of shared destiny at their firms (63 percent)
- Business alignment—the extent to which employees share the company's vision (70 percent)
- Management effectiveness—employees' view of how well a company is managed (59 percent)
- Customer focus—employees' opinions of their company's responsiveness to customers (69 percent)

Employees appeared to be in tune with company needs and issues. Steve Bookbinder, who conducted the research at Towers Perrin, concluded that "companies have a vast reserve of excellent raw material in the form of a willing and able workforce. . . . Companies that fully tap into this are likely to see significant increases in productivity, quality, and profitability."

Employees want to contribute to the success of the business, but they often believe they don't have all the information or resources to do so. As one employee put it, "They want me to run the mile faster than ever, but they are holding my ankles!" Employees who feel they are in on things and can be trusted with strategic organizational information are more likely to be realistic about their own goals and intent on aligning these goals to the organization's needs. The following example illustrates the struggle one organization had with this issue:

A Fortune 500 electronics firm implemented career development training for employees and managers to try to change the mind-set from entitlement to more individual responsibility for growth and development. They instituted career discussions between employees and managers and had employees submit quarterly reports on whether they thought their careers were on track. As an outcome of the workshop, employees are expected to complete written development plans. There is top-down commitment to employee development, and the company has a well-established training program. But in the design of employee career development workshops, the career development team was reluctant to provide information on the strategic direction of the company and was particularly concerned about putting proprietary information in writing. As a consequence, individuals who attended the workshops and tried to write career development goals had no company information to link them to. They clarified their self-insight and determined what they wanted to achieve, but they didn't have a basis to determine whether their goals were viable. In a fast-changing environment, with technical skills evolving rapidly and applications changing at breakneck speed, employees needed some organizational information on trends and needs to drive their own development planning. Managers felt somewhat on the spot to provide the crystal ball for employees. Depending on their level, most managers had the same information needs that their employees had. So, while employees had the willingness and intent to link their goals to the needs of the organization, they were mostly left on their own to sleuth out what that meant. In evaluation surveys, employees reported they knew they were responsible for managing their career (a change from the past), but a majority still report that their career is not on track.

Open Communication

In many organizations, the company's mission and vision are articulated. In a growing number of companies, the annual goals are presented at the beginning of the year. However, most organizations do not have a *process* for helping managers and employees translate this information into action. Even when goal setting is part of the performance management process, department goals are often focused on short-term projects rather than on longer-term developmental planning.

What Needs to Be Communicated?

In order for employees to plan their own career development and contribute to a development culture in general, they need to have information about the strategic direction of the company and of their department. For example, if new products are being introduced, people need to know the company's goals for increasing market share, expected volume of production, and staffing requirements. Most individuals then need to be alerted to the changes and taught how to translate that information into their own development planning.

In some organizations, demographic information is critical for informed development planning. Development Culture in Action: Case 3 describes how important the business unit of a manufacturing firm felt this type of information was for career development planning.

case 3	DEVELOPMENT CULTURE IN ACTION
	Old-Line Manufacturer

Communicating Demographic Information

Forty percent of the workforce is over fifty years old, and 60 percent is over forty-five. While the workforce is stable now and young people don't see much opportunity, within five to ten years there will be tremendous opportunity for those who are ready. The division is preparing for the loss of huge amounts of organizational knowledge and critical skills. They are communicating this information to employees and managers for career development planning so individual goals can be aligned with the company's future needs. The company is even involving those over forty-five in planning, although some of these employees feel their careers are past developing. For some, their experience will be valued in new assignments if they are prepared. For others, their knowledge and skills can be tapped in a mentoring or instructing capacity before they retire. The intended development culture especially needs the contributions of those with organizational knowledge to pass on.

Because of all the downsizing and reorganization, many organizations are not doing any long-range workforce planning or human resources planning. Although exact numbers cannot be predicted, broad demographic needs and areas of emphasis can be; these should be a part of strategic planning. This information is useful, and in some cases essential, for individuals and managers in the development planning role. If you want employees to be proactively managing their careers, and not waiting as victims for their jobs to be eliminated, information about changing demographics is important to share. In a development culture, eveyone's focus is on needs for the future.

One organization calls the demographic information they share *internal* labor market information. This information includes age distribution data as well as the percentage of positions in each broad functional area and the growth trends of these areas. This information is presented graphically in career planning workshops, with the macro perspective of realistic possibilities in the company. For example, a management representative pointed out that 44 percent of professional (exempt) positions in the company today are in product and process design, with only 4 percent of those jobs in management positions—and those positions are decreasing. So for an engineer trying to decide whether to get a technical master's degree or an MBA, the statistics are compelling. An additional 21 percent of the jobs are in operations. By contrast, only 6 percent of jobs in the company are in human resources, with 1.5 percent in management, and this area is not anticipated to grow. The message here is this: If you expect to stay long term with this company, prepare yourself in the fields that the company needs. If you choose to go in a support direction, your chances for management are slim, and that may mean leaving the company for you to achieve your goals.

When major changes are about to occur, it is only fair that employees hear about them from within rather than in the news. The information they receive needs to extend beyond the announcement of an event, such as a merger or acquisition; individuals need to understand what the event means to their job and career. If employees are resilient, which is one of the goals of a development culture, they can respond and alter their goals. But they need information about the predicted changes to be able to assess the situation and respond appropriately. Without accurate information, rumors run rampant and people become resistant rather than adaptive.

The reason executives often give for not communicating to employees is that they don't have all the answers yet or the changes are in progress and no one knows yet what impact they will have on individuals. While this is true, and it is usually difficult to predict with any accuracy what outcomes will definitely occur, any information is better than none for individuals to be able to be proactive. Partial information, with the disclaimer to "stay tuned" for future updates, makes employees feel that they are being treated with respect and can plan their actions accordingly. In today's rapidly changing organizations, the change is ongoing and no one ever has all the answers. This is the nature of a development culture.

On the other hand, employees need to learn how to work with information in progress and not to translate it as gospel. With the speed of change occurring today, nothing in the future is absolutely predictable. Yet decisions are made on educated guesses, strategic plans are based on forecasts and models, and market research influences production planning. Usually missing from these future perspectives is the impact on staffing or human resources planning. If new skills are going to be needed, employees must know which skills are needed and how they will need to be used. If functions are going to be reduced or expanded, employees need to plan

Figure 5   Cascading Goals

their direction accordingly. If new ways of working will make the organization more competitive in the future, the more that individuals are preparing for the changes the better prepared the company will be.

Goal Cascading

As organizations identify and communicate business goals, career development processes can be the catalyst to "cascade" the goals through the business units to individuals for their development planning, as shown in Figure 5. There are several steps to the cascading process, depending on the size and complexity of the organization.

The Information Systems department of Sears Roebuck and Co. recognized the need for constant development of its associates, both to maintain current technical skills and to be ready for emerging technologies. Evolving from a traditional hierarchical organization to one requiring self-directed associates, it was imperative that individuals take proactive responsibility for their own development. Development Culture in Action: Case 4 describes how they designed a goal-cascading process to ensure that associates' development would align with business needs and would be an ongoing process that would drive development and contribute to individuals' career goals.

case
4

DEVELOPMENT CULTURE IN ACTION

Sears Information Systems (IS) Department

Business Strategy Cascading Process

The business strategy cascading process in the Sears Information Systems (IS) department links the business goals of the company with the strategic goals and key projects of IS. Figure 6 graphically summarizes the cascading process described here.

Senior management meets with the business partners to determine the business requirements for setting IS goals that align with corporate goals and to prioritize projects for the coming year. The senior managers' strategy, goals, and key projects are shared with their direct reports, the department heads who now set their own goals and take ownership of key projects for their department. When the goals are aligned for these two groups, the department heads then meet with their managers to continue the cascading process. Strategy, goals, and projects form the content of the conversations at each level, and alignment is reached before moving to the next level in the organization.

This process requires a series of meetings in January and February, beginning with each IS senior manager holding a full department meeting. This ensures that all associates have the big picture and understand the strategy and key projects of their own area. System managers then hold group meetings to define their own goals and start associates on the individual goal-setting process.

All managers and associates were trained to write performance and skill goals for their current job, as well as career goals for longer-range planning. Performance and skill goals are reviewed as projects end or at performance appraisal time. Skill goals must support performance goals, and ten days of training (based on an individual development plan) is a minimum annual requirement for every IT (Information Technology) person. Each associate maintains a skill profile in an online career development system to identify his or her job competencies and opportunities for development.

Development is a comprehensive, ongoing process of identifying the competencies for development and setting skill goals to reach the desired proficiency. There are a variety of ways that someone may increase his or her proficiency in a skill. Achieving skill goals may involve formal training, self study, on-the-job training, or coaching. Longer-range career goals are not evaluated but are written based on a self-assessment and exploration process. An associate may choose not

continued

to write career goals or may carry long-range goals from one year to the next and update the action plan. Career discussions focus on the experiences needed to increase and apply proficiency in skills needed for future goals.

As with any culture change, there was mixed acceptance at the beginning. The first year was a major learning curve as people learned the goal-setting process. The strategy cascading process is critical for individuals to see the big picture and develop appropriate goals. Managers are pleased to have a more formal process for the strategy cascading and a consistent process for the whole division. There is still discussion about the difficulty of setting and achieving goals in a rapidly changing environment and the need for more exact measurements of goals completed.

In the third year of the project, with managers and associates becoming more skilled in the goal-setting process, renewed emphasis is being placed on longer-range, individually driven career goals.

Used by permission of Sears Information Systems department

Concerns that managers typically express when a career development process is first being discussed include the following: "What if people develop in ways that don't benefit the company?" or "Won't we just be raising unrealistic expectations?" Neither happens if career development is strongly linked to the business needs and goals, as shown in the Sears IT case. Employees clearly know the organization's short- and long-term plans, and managers help translate big-picture perspectives into goals to which each individual can contribute. Because this is an annual process, the other concern about sustainability of a development effort is also answered.

Employees also need to do their own longer-range goal setting based on their values, interests, and career aspirations. But having these plans (typically resulting from a career planning process) without knowing the company perspective is, in effect, asking employees to plan for development in a vacuum. It would be unreasonable to expect employees, on their own, to translate company vision and mission into strategies, read the career implications of those strategies, determine personal goals, and then identify action steps based on these goals. Leadership and management must assist in the process. Patricia McLagan (1983) uses the term *futuring,* which she defines as the ability to "project trends and visualize possible and probable futures and their implications" to describe a competency that many need to learn.

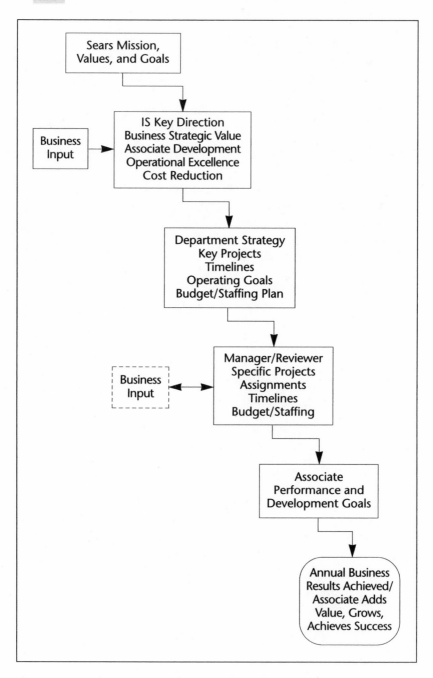

**Figure 6   Linking Business Goals with Associate Performance and Development
            Goals Requires Effective Strategy Cascading**
Used by permission of Sears Information Systems department

Individuals usually want to link their goals to the needs of the organization. They recognize that as they contribute to a development culture and take responsibility for proactively managing their own careers, they need current organizational and personal information on which to base realistic planning.

Occasionally an individual goes through this process only to confirm that he or she does not want to support the direction of the organization. If individual values clash with the organization's values, remaining with the firm will not be a positive relationship for long. Or the individual may be committed to a profession that deals with a function soon to be outsourced by the company. So instead of trying to find a fit elsewhere in the organization, he or she may decide to leave. Sometimes this person has been unhappy and perhaps unproductive for some time, and this process clarifies the need to take action. Development cultures support no-fault exits.

Undertaking a comprehensive change to a development initiative requires management to recognize that not everyone should stay. But the numbers of people who leave after participating in a career development program are always fewer than expected. In fact, often companies will institute a career development process specifically to reduce turnover, which is most often caused by individuals' sense that the company doesn't care about their development. Communicating the direction and needs of the organization, being clear with employees about their development needs and opportunities, and providing resources for assessment and development change that perception. Employees stay longer, even if they truly have outgrown their job, if they feel that the organization and their manager care about them as individuals and are contributing to their development.

Focusing on Core Competencies

Another way to communicate the pervasive need for development and to ensure a linkage between organizational needs and direction and individual goals is by focusing on core competencies. *Core competencies* are defined both as business strengths and as knowledge, skills, and attitudes needed by the organization to meet present and future business needs. Core competencies help individuals change their focus from next-job thinking to total development in ways needed by the company. If competencies are defined by behaviors that demonstrate the needed knowledge, skills, and attitudes, and if assessment is incorporated into the process, individuals can identify areas of development needed and build development plans accordingly. Development may thus affect individuals' performance on their present job, but it may also be targeted for longer-range opportunities in the organization. Since targeting a specific position for the future is fraught with uncertainty as change continues at a rapid pace, individuals need a different focus for their longer-range planning. Developing competencies that are broader than any one job or even functional area creates the flexibility and potential to respond to opportunities as they occur.

It is essential in a development culture that future competencies be identified along with those needed in the present. In many situations, the star performers are already demonstrating competencies that will be needed in the future by everyone. However, in rapidly changing environments there may be technical skills that no one has yet, but that will be required in the future for some job families. For example, in the last few years there has been a major shift in information technology from mainframe computers to client–server technology. In some MIS departments, this has meant a need for many computer professionals to develop new competencies for the future, even though they were still functioning in a mainframe environment. For longer-range development planning, there must be a future focus and an awareness of how changes will cause some skills to become obsolete and will require that some new ones be developed.

As with goal cascading, employees often may need help translating the identification of competencies into actions for a development plan. Naming competencies is not enough in itself. Behaviors need to be defined and an assessment process needs to be created so individuals can objectively assess their level of competency and identify appropriate development options. The following example illustrates how one organization translated core competency identification into their executive development process.

An accounting firm spent considerable time identifying competencies needed for creating a career path to the partner level. This resulted in a list of fifteen competencies that, on the surface, seemed viable. But after the work was done, several questions remained. First, the competencies had not been validated in any way. Were these truly the core competencies for partners? Second, was there any assurance that all present partners had these competencies? If not (and there were clearly some gaps in the partner ranks) would the list be considered valid? Third, how could individuals be objective about their own ability in each of these areas? And finally, if managers developed and demonstrated these competencies, would that ensure promotion to partner?

It became apparent that what was needed was an *executive development process,* as opposed to a *partner career path.* The goal was to ensure that leaders in the firm were changing and developing in ways needed to remain competitive. Competencies had to be validated by studying the behavior of master performers and identifying the critical behaviors. An assessment instrument needed to be developed out of the validated list, and then candidates and their managers needed to conduct an assessment and gap analysis as a basis for creating meaningful development plans. So, rather than targeting a position, or in this case a *level,* in the firm, the focus of development was changed to preparation and growth needed for success. With this new emphasis, even existing partners could not rest on their laurels, as they recognized that the core competencies applied to everyone. Partners, as well as those aspiring to the partner ranks, needed to be brought in to the development process.

In addition to core competencies, many organizations are defining competencies by job families or functions as a means of guiding individual development. Scott Parry (1996) defines a competency as "a cluster of related knowledge, skills, and attitudes (K, S, A) that affects a major part of one's job (a role or responsibility), that correlates with performance on the job, that can be measured against well accepted standards, and that can be [learned]." Not defined by specific jobs, competencies need to be seen as broader and more transferable from one role to another to have value for development in a changing environment. For example, the competency of customer responsiveness may be essential in a customer service position, but it is also needed in technical support, sales, pricing, and administrative roles.

Some organizations are using 360-degree feedback as a process of assessing competencies or more narrowly defined skills, but more commonly, a manager/employee assessment process serves as a tangible basis for development planning. Managers and employees are given separate computerized or paper assessments and differences in ratings are analyzed. This is followed by a career discussion between manager and employee to come to agreement on priority of needs and appropriate development actions. These actions can be targeted to present performance or future opportunities. In an integrated system, individuals can have access to competencies needed for other roles and assess the viability of

case 5
DEVELOPMENT CULTURE IN ACTION
Hewitt Associates

Competency Assessment Process

Hewitt Associates' Compensation Practice has a nonhierarchical structure in which development for associates means growing in the skills and scope of the work they do rather than moving up a ladder (see Figure 7). By linking the business results and strategy to the specific needs of the Compensation Practice, project managers were able to determine the capabilities essential to ensure achievement of business results. Recognizing associates' needs as well resulted in the people programs and actions to "Improve Business Results Through People." They identified two types of competencies needed by associates: *core knowledge areas* and *process and consulting skills.* They created a rating scale that defined the level of each competency needed in different roles, as well as the level currently demonstrated by the individual. Using a software assessment process, CompAssess™, managers rate associates and individuals rate themselves on each of eighteen core knowledge areas and fifteen process and consulting skills. The software identifies gaps between their ratings and provides specifics for a development discussion between the manager and each associate. After agreeing on competencies to work on, managers and associates look to the software to suggest a variety of developmental options.

Associates also participate in a career-planning process to determine their own future goals with the firm and to make sure they are contributing to the needs of the firm and their own development by developing their competencies. The process results in development plans that have ongoing implementation and are updated annually.

Used by permission of Hewitt Associates LLC

movement goals accordingly, or they can build a development plan to prepare for other assignments.

Development Culture in Action: Case 5 describes how Hewitt Associates LLC, a compensation and benefits consulting firm committed to the development of its associates, instituted a competency assessment process in its Compensation Practice.

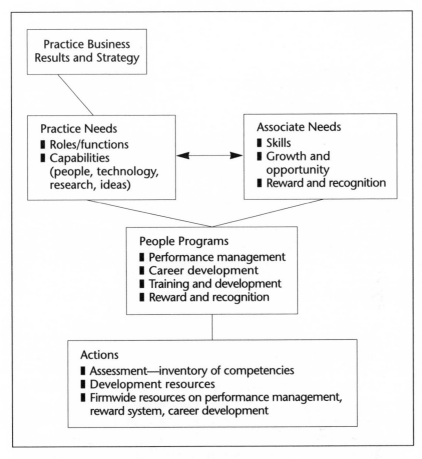

Figure 7   Improving Business Results Through People
Used by permission of Hewitt Associates LLC

Performance Management in a Development Culture

Linking individual goals with needs of the organization, particularly if performance and development planning is required of everyone, brings up some questions: What is the difference between performance management and career development? What is the difference between performance appraisals and career discussions? The answer is that both performance management and career development, and performance appraisals and career discussions must be related because opportunities for the future are based on present performance. In a development culture, an

Table 8

Performance Appraisals Versus Development Discussions

Performance Appraisals	Development Discussions
Review of past performance	Relate present performance to future opportunities
Job-specific strengths and weaknesses	Broader skills, strengths, and potential
Manager as evaluator	Manager as coach
Focus on present job	Focus on long-range planning
Linked to immediate department/ assignment needs	Linked to future needs of the company
Manager-initiated and directed	Employee-initiated and directed
Evaluative	Developmental
Often antagonistic relationship	Collaborative relationship
Annual	As frequent as needed

From *Managing Career Development,* by P. Simonsen, 1994. Rolling Meadows, IL: Career Directions, Inc.

ideal system is an integrated process that may come under the umbrella term of *performance management.* In reality, however, most organizations today still do performance appraisals that are primarily evaluative. The purpose of a career development process is primarily developmental. Table 8 lists some differences between performance appraisals and developmental discussions.

In a development culture, strategies are communicated for longer-range planning, and business goals are cascaded for annual goal setting. Individuals must attend to developing on the present job and commit to strong performance and achievement of short-term goals, but they are also encouraged to plan and prepare for future opportunities.

As more performance management systems replace performance evaluation systems represented by forms, the distinction between career development and performance management will blur. But some differences will continue to exist. Many organizations do not want to require participation in a career development program. After all, if the new paradigm message is for individual responsibility for one's own career management, perhaps it is contradictory to require participation. But it is essential that performance management—contributing and growing on the present job—be expected of everyone and be the basis of discussions between employees and their managers.

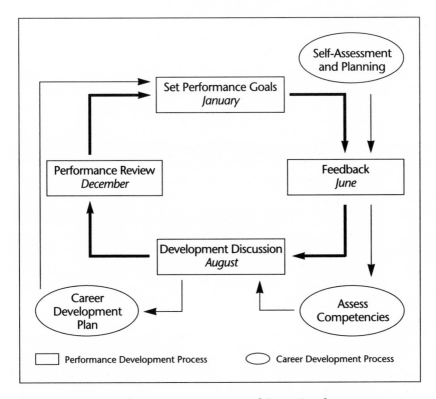

Figure 8   Linking Performance Management and Career Development

Career development planning tends to be longer range and based more on the individual's interests and motivation, albeit linked to the strategic direction and needs of the organization. If it is determined that there is a divergence between the individual's goals and organizational goals, a person's long-range plans may be to move out of the organization. If employment for life is no longer a valid expectation by employees, it shouldn't be an issue for the organization, either. The goal of an aligned performance management/career development process, as with a development culture, is a win-win outcome—that is, to maximize individual potential while contributing to organizational success.

In today's overworked environments, a practical way to link performance management and career development is to design a continuous system with elements of each merged into one system and cycle (see Figure 8). If the two systems share a common goal—individual development—they are compatible processes. The organizational goals and direction that are communicated at the beginning of the cycle serve both purposes. Competency assessment may take place early in the cycle if it is a basis of performance planning, or later if it is strictly for development. The development planning discussion between manager and employee shortly thereafter can target both performance goals and assignments for the present job as well as longer-range career goals. Feedback during the cycle can be about present performance as well as how present performance and experiences contribute to the employee's longer-range goals. If 360-degree feedback is used, it fits naturally here. Along the way, individuals can participate, at their own pace, in self-insight and career-planning activities.

A development discussion takes place midyear, not to evaluate present performance, but to discuss career goals and identify appropriate development actions on the present job or to target other opportunities. It is important for this discussion to be separate from the evaluation or appraisal. For some individuals and in some cultures, there has not been a lot of trust between employees and managers, so to honestly discuss career plans that may mean a move out of that manager's area is seen as risky. If that discussion occurs at the same time as evaluation, with compensation pending, there will be even less openness. Development and evaluation are separate roles a manager must play in the performance management process, and the development message tends to be lost if tacked on to the evaluation discussion.

Of course, the ideal in a development culture is regular discussions and feedback about development, not semiannual, prescribed sessions. But in the transition from a closed, autocratic environment to an open environment of trust and shared responsibility, many managers and employees need the structure to support new behaviors.

In the performance management cycle, the final event is the appraisal or evaluation process. As organizations evolve their whole people-management philosophy, this too is taking on a more developmental angle, but the majority of companies still use a rating system of some sort. And since compensation decisions still need to be made, most companies link them to performance ratings in one way or another. As compensation systems change (see Chapter 5), the appraisal process changes, but it is still typically evaluative. The critical factor, however, is that evaluation be made of mutually agreed-upon goals and contributions, with objective measurement criteria—not an after-the-fact "you should have done this" retribution. If performance management is not about forms but about positively changing and molding behavior, then career development and performance management can be integrated or linked. Both will contribute strongly to the successful implementation of a development culture.

Accountability

These two questions are frequently asked by organizations considering a career development system: "How can we ensure that managers do this, that they don't abdicate their responsibility for supporting employee development?" and "After the kickoff and initial excitement, how can we ensure that our career development process continues—that it is not just seen as the program of the month?" Neither question will be an issue if there is a process for linking career development to the organization's needs and strategies. The current status and plans are communicated annually, triggering a cycle of planning and goal setting.

If competencies are current and an assessment process is available, managers and employees can revisit the status annually and use both the individual's goals and the levels of competency expected for development planning purposes.

If career development is a component in the performance management process, and there is structure for that to occur on a cyclical basis, the development component will build a better rapport and enrich the outcome for both manager and employee.

In both competencies and performance measures in a development culture, developing employees is a managerial *requirement*. Managers are measured and held accountable for ensuring that their employees have the skills needed in their changing environments, developing high-potential employees so they don't leave the organization, ensuring that employees are ready for new challenges, and getting increasingly challenging work done through their people. These managers become known as good managers to work for.

If the compensation and reward systems are also aligned with accomplishment of goals and contribution to the business strategy, both for managers and employees, the expectations are cemented. People say the leaders are "walking their talk." If "the way we say we want to be" conflicts with "the way we do things around here," the old culture will win. If building a development culture is truly important to the organization, then efforts to encourage, support, and reinforce new behaviors are essential.

Development for employees is not just an option for those who feel like it—it is an expectation. In development cultures, in addition to performing satisfactorily on the present job, employees are expected to keep their skills state-of-the-art. When everyone buys in to the new development mind-set, they recognize that the status quo is not acceptable. Even employees who say, "I like what I'm doing; I don't need career development" recognize that they must be moving forward or they will be falling behind. They have the discretion of being very goal oriented for their own sake or of responding to the goals needed for their area, but everyone knows they must make a continuing contribution. In a development culture, accountability is not a matter of punishment, it is a matter of fulfilling expectations—the carrot, not the stick.

Aligning Organizational Systems for a Development Culture

Make no little plans: they have no magic
to stir men's blood.
—Daniel H. Burnham

Supporting a Successful Change of Culture

In many evolving cultures, people have begun to internalize the new paradigm of behaviors and beliefs about their career in the organization, but the systems continue to reinforce the old paradigm. In other environments, the systems are changing but people haven't caught up. The change process never will be totally synchronized, of course, but it is essential to plan and initiate changes in the total system as well as to implement programs for people. Most career development initiatives take the form of programs—a series of events in which employees and maybe managers can participate. Some organizations are able to define this process, create a model for the flow of the process, and provide good services—but if an organizational model for career development doesn't exist, the process will be seen as another human resources program. Peter Senge, in *The Fifth Discipline*, says it is essential to have systems thinking. Without it, you can't have a learning organization. Just as great training programs do not make a learning organization, great career development workshops do not make a development culture.

Jennifer Laabs (1996b), in an article on employee commitment, remarks:

> Workers find it's no longer enough to come to work faithfully every day and to do their jobs independently. They now have to think like entrepreneurs while working in teams, and have to prove their worth. But at the same time, the structure within which they're expected to follow these rules remains unchanged. The ensuing gap between old systems and new realities has left employees not only confused, but struggling to be committed to a company that, they feel, has jilted them. The good news is that they want to strengthen their relationship with the company as much as the company wants to strengthen it with them. Build the bond by sharing both risks and rewards, and by bringing old systems in line with new realities.

Nonalignment inevitably slows the process and creates frustration with employees. Instead of a focus on development that supports key business objectives, the focus is on HR systems. And instead of a focus on the future, energy is spent on contradictory messages. For example, instead of recognizing new ways to develop, people focus on the fact that compensation only rewards moving up. HR won't be seen as a change agent if it can't change its own systems.

A development culture must align its selection systems, development systems, and reward systems with strategic business objectives and work-force planning, as shown in Figure 9. Focusing on development without changes in the other systems will lead to cynicism and will not result in a development culture, as illustrated in the following example:

The sales division of an old-line manufacturing company initiated a career development program because there was widespread frustration at the lack of career opportunities and the perceived unfairness of its promotion practices. The goal of most employees was to get promoted, even if they didn't particularly want to do the work of supervisors or managers. Many people in support roles didn't have the field experience required to be on the fast track, but promotions had always been the mark of success in the unit. After reorganization and downsizing, the company's message was that development was the individual's responsibility; however, individuals were firmly entrenched in the old paradigm expectations, and systems still supported it.

As consultants designed a career development process, they made recommendations to address the selection and reward systems as

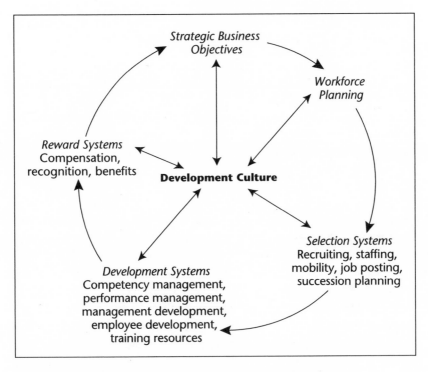

Figure 9   Elements of a Comprehensive Career Management System

well as development planning for employees. Since compensation is a companywide system, it is not at the discretion of individual business units to change, but compensation clearly reinforced upward moves. And since selection for openings had always been at the discretion of the hiring manager, there was reluctance to change that process. The job posting system was the cause of more frustration than help. Not all jobs were posted, of course, and individuals who used the system got no feedback on their status or why they were not selected. Human resources saw communication about selection as a Pandora's box they were not willing to open.

As the career development program was kicked off, employees were skeptical. People with positive outlooks could see the value of taking more responsibility for their own development; they valued the self-assessment and education about how to use the existing systems more proactively. But the cynics in the group—and there were many—said, "Been there, done that; this is just another program of the month. What will make this any different from all those other programs that have been launched and forgotten if HR isn't willing to make any changes in the way they do things around here?"

It is harder to get people to change their behaviors if they don't see the support systems changing. "If you don't make significant changes in the reward system, you'll actually reward resistance. Don't expect employees to change their behavior significantly unless you make it worth their while. Reinforce the behavior you want" (Pritchett and Pound, 1996a). You cannot create a development culture by focusing only on individual development.

Workforce Planning

The very forces driving the need for continual development in organizations will continue to change the workforce of the twenty-first century. As products and services become commodities and technology allows easy duplication, the factors that differentiate one company from another are the speed and customization of response to customer needs. Organizations are recognizing that a skilled and committed staff is the variable that makes or keeps them competitive and effective. Finding, keeping, and developing people to meet these demands cannot be a reactive process. Workforce planning is essential.

If restructuring means defining and creating a core of essential competencies the organization needs, with other functions provided by a contingent workforce, managers and employees need to know this as they establish and implement development plans. Planning needs to include identification of roles and competencies that will be in demand in the future. The process also needs to recognize those areas that will be outsourced, diminished because of changing technology, or changed so substantially that incumbents cannot keep their jobs without substantial reskilling. Planning is a matter of reconciling anticipated future needs of the company with expected staffing requirements.

Workforce planning is important to ensuring a link between career development and the strategic direction of the organization. The human resources function is increasingly involved in strategic planning and is moving toward changing from a functional unit to decentralized services that support line managers and employees in their teams or work units.

Training is evolving toward performance improvement driven by developmental needs rather than a catalog of training courses.

While most organizations put some effort into strategic planning, often driven by financial and operational goals, many skip the essential step of translating the vision into people terms. Others who know their general people needs for the future are reluctant to communicate to managers and employees because the projections are not definitive. Once again, if companies expect employees to create and carry out development plans that will contribute to the needs of the organization, they must know those needs. If employees need to reskill, the sooner they get started, the more likely they will be ready when technology changes occur. If, after retraining, those skills are not needed or if market forces take the company in new directions, the individual is still more employable than before. A company may have to take a job away, but it cannot take an individual's skills away.

An increasingly viable way to translate business needs into people terms is by identification and assessment of competencies, either by levels in the organization or by job families. To contribute to readiness for the future, competencies need to be future focused. The knowledge, skills, and attitudes needed today may not be those that will be needed in a changing environment.

Workforce planning can also contribute to internal "redeployment" or "inplacement" when staffing needs change. If individuals have advance notice and information about the competencies needed in other, growing areas, many will actively prepare themselves for new opportunities within the company. Mobility systems make internal moves possible for qualified candidates. The company benefits from internal placement by retaining organizational knowledge, building trust, and shoring up morale that would be lost without such effort. Individuals benefit by adding skills and attitudes that make them flexible and more employable, and of course by staying employed.

Selection Policies

For most employees in an organization, selection policies that affect them most directly are those that govern internal moves and promotions. External hiring should also be aligned with the development philosophy, or problems will occur. If individuals are expected to develop to be ready for new challenges in their present job or to be flexible as changing business needs require moves, there needs to be a system that supports these expectations. If "hot skills" are always recruited from outside, why should employees bother learning them? If individuals are kept in maintenance positions while new employees are brought in for the challenging assignments, what motivation will people have for taking on the development challenge?

It becomes a chicken-and-egg dilemma. If a manager doesn't have the skills or leadership internally, and has business demands requiring fast response, she finds it necessary to hire from outside. But why doesn't she have the skills internally? Are the employees incapable of or unwilling to change? Has she not given them the opportunity to develop the new skills? Are they too busy putting out fires in the present situation to be able to think about future needs? Is there no system for identifying the skills individuals do have? Or is there no way to identify individuals elsewhere in the company who might be qualified? If these questions are not addressed, the problem will be perpetuated.

Another area for contradiction between selection processes and the development message is in internal mobility systems. Are employees working on development plans, but then held back when an opportunity presents itself because they are too valuable where they are? Are employees told to manage their own careers, while management continues to use the old paternalistic methods for selecting and promoting people? Are individuals unaware that there is an opening until a new person is hired? Do individuals who want to progress lack feedback on what areas they need to work on in order to be seen as qualified?

Equal employment opportunity and affirmative action policies are linked to both internal and external hiring. Organizations traditionally focused on external hires, ensuring compliance with regulations and company policies. But with today's focus on career development programs, it is essential that these policies be linked to both the message and the practice of selection. In some organizations, it is the diversity initiative that is driving the career development process to change the old practices that held some people back and to ensure equal opportunity internally to all.

Table 9 summarizes the alignment issues of selection, development, and reward systems. Misalignment of many of these elements jeopardizes efforts to promote a development culture by undermining the development message.

Table 9

Aligning Selection, Development, and Reward Systems

Selection Systems	
Policy/Procedure	**Alignment Needed**
External recruiting	• Recruiters/managers must convey *positive reality* about development and advancement when hiring.
Internal staffing	• Internal candidates must have access to information about position openings and requirements. • There is a means to consider internal candidates when hiring. • The job posting system has integrity.
Mobility systems	• A policy about cross-functional or intradepartmental moves must balance business needs and the needs of the individual. • Reality (what really happens) must align with policy.
Succession planning	• Career development policies for top employees must align with the philosophy and practices for all employees. • There is a process for identifying people capable of filling leadership positions. • Secret lists and procedures are not aligned with a development focus.

Development Systems	
Policy/Procedure	**Alignment Needed**
Competency management	• People need to target competencies for development instead of focusing solely on promotions.
Performance management	• A developmental performance management process needs to be integrated with the philosophy of development. • The performance review meeting should be separate from a career discussion.
Management development	• Managers' role in developing employees needs to be assured. • There should be accountability for employee development as well as for financial goals.
Employee development	• Training—in house or external—needs to be available and attendance encouraged. • There must not be conflict between development plans and action (such as enrollment in training) to achieve development goals.
Development resources	• Development needs should be the catalyst to determine training needed. • A variety of on-the-job development and self-directed resources must be available. • Coaching should supplement formal training classes.

Table 9

Aligning Selection, Development, and Reward Systems *continued*

Reward Systems	
Policy/Procedure	**Alignment Needed**
Compensation	• Compensation must be structured to reinforce the development message. If there's a need for a broader base of experience, lateral moves should be rewarded. If the need is to grow in place, compensate accordingly.
	• Reward (for managers as well as employees) must be aligned with the desired actions.
Recognition	• Recognition, celebrations, and nonmonetary rewards—and not just promotions—should support appropriate goal achievement.
Benefits	• Alignment works best when individuals can choose the benefits that contribute to their development and needs.

Recruiting

There needs to be alignment between the recruiting message and the realities of development. Bright recruits who are promised the world to accept a position don't stay long if those promises fail to materialize. If they have a lot to offer, they can offer it elsewhere, as the company in the following example found out:

A public utility company recruited high-potential individuals—typically with bachelor's degrees in engineering or other technical fields, as well as MBAs—into their fast-track program. These people were told that they were in a risk situation: They had two years to shine, or they were out. They were assigned to a technical position for the first year, and then they would be promoted to a supervisory position the second. Both their technical skills and their managerial skills were being evaluated, and if after two years they were successful, they would be promoted again. However, the company had to reorganize and flatten, and there simply were not enough supervisory positions available. The reality was changing to the new paradigm, but the recruiting and apprentice practices were firmly stuck in the old one.

A career development program was implemented to educate both these high-potential employees and their managers about the new realities. Quick learners, the employees got the message clearly and set about creating their own development plans with their managers' help. But the recruiting process took longer to change, so new recruits kept being hired with the old expectations. And there were no systems in place for the individuals to explore opportunities on their own, to be supported in moves to other departments, or to get information about the new direction of the company in order to plan their development accordingly. Those who felt betrayed or stuck were quick to take their high-potential talent elsewhere.

Selection policies in organizations—recruiting, internal staffing, and succession planning—must be aligned with the development message to build a development culture. If individuals are to be more proactive in managing their own careers, they must have the information and the freedom that will allow them to do so. A starting point is to take a serious look at existing policies and procedures. Some may be supporting the development direction, while others may be fundamentally sound but require some tweaking. Still others may need to be changed substantially in order not to reinforce the old behaviors and undermine the change of culture. New systems may need to be designed and implemented to meet new needs. In many cases, individuals need to be educated about the systems and how to use them to their best advantage.

For example, many organizations have a job posting system. This may appear to be a valid way for individuals to find out about openings and for managers to have access to candidates; however, the expectations of the system and the way people use it may need to change. If job posting is the only way employees learn of opportunities, and if not all openings are posted, people will feel that the system is flawed. If job posting is the only visible tool for employees to manage their career, they will expect too much from the system and probably use it incorrectly. Employees may not recognize that using the job posting process to apply for a position is almost the last step of a career management process, not the first. If the first time employees think about a position is when they see it posted, it is far too late. They can be assured that by this time others have been targeting the job, exploring requirements, building a relationship with the hiring manager, identifying and developing skills that would transfer, and even preparing for the interview.

In some organizations, individuals gain a reputation as malcontents because they apply for everything that comes along, never being seen as viable candidates. They are written off for any opportunity, but no one ever tells them why or educates them to the essential steps necessary in planning, decision making, and preparing before they present themselves for an opportunity. If it is taken for granted that employees should know how to operate effectively in these systems, then they will need to know when the systems have changed. Adapting existing practices and educating employees on their use are essential to a development environment.

If informal methods are used for internal staffing decisions—networking, who you know or who knows you, managers' cross-department communications—then employees need to know that these approaches are real. The informal staffing and selection processes don't stop in a development culture, but there is open communication about them. If employees do not recognize that building a network is a strategic element in managing their career, they will develop a cynical attitude about office politics. It is important to know people and have them know your work in a rapidly changing, quick-response environment. A vice president in charge of all the regional offices reinforced this message in the kickoff to a career development system by saying, "Don't take a vacation day when I'm visiting your office. Home-office hiring is based on who I recommend that I know in the regions." The organization created a flowchart that showed how the staffing and selection process worked, with networks, job posting, and external recruiting lined up equally as sources of candidates.

Mobility Systems

Another source of conflict between the development message and existing practices is often the issue of employee movement between departments or even business units. When an individual wants to make a move, has identified an appropriate opening, and the hiring manager wants the candidate, is it legitimate for the current manager to prevent the move? An objection managers sometimes express to active participation in career development is, "If I develop my good people, won't they just leave? I have a good team, and we are productive. I don't want to break them up and have to start over again at getting everyone working together. Our results will suffer."

This is a legitimate concern and must be addressed. Otherwise some managers will hold people back, thinking they are justified because they have pressing business needs and the individual is a critical contributor. In some nondevelopmental environments, the people who move freely are the very ones managers are glad to see go. Written development policies can ensure consistent practices and balance the needs of the manager with the needs of the individual and ultimately the needs of the organization. One organization defined a mobility policy so that a manager could prevent an employee's move once because of pressing business needs and deadlines, but could not do so twice. This may not work for some organizations, but it worked for them. If employees and managers are working together to write and implement development plans, managers won't be surprised when an employee decides to move. Together they would recognize the types of opportunities that would be developmental for the employee—some may be in the present job and others may at some point require a move. Both manager and employee must be guided by benefit to the company as well as benefit to the employee.

When the development message says that flexibility is needed to meet changing business demands, and that functional silos need to be eliminated by having people prepared to make lateral moves, management and human resources practices must find a way to support this direction. Mobility systems should be defined or created where none exist today. For example, one information systems department determined as desirable that 25 percent of its workforce change roles annually, with the assumption that few if any would stay in one assignment longer than four years. This policy supports the business need for flexible, multiskilled individuals who are constantly learning and updating their technical skills. In their project-oriented environment, changing roles might not mean changing managers, but taking on totally new projects. It could, however, mean performing the same role in another division, or even changing careers. The policy also supports the individual's need to develop marketable new skills to keep up with the latest technology.

When mobility means geographic moves, there needs to be information provided by the employee and kept in a database about availability for moves or acceptable areas for relocation. Assumptions by managers about who is or is not mobile are often discriminatory and definitely a remnant of the old-culture paternalistic thinking that they as managers know what is best for their people.

Succession Planning

In a hierarchical culture, succession planning was a secret process of identifying candidates for top positions in the organization. The process brings up the image of a smoke-filled room with senior managers discussing heirs apparent who would be ready to move into executive spots.

People were put on "the list" of high potentials without their knowledge. The argument supporting this process was based on the assumption that if the targeted individuals knew they were on the list, others would know they weren't and therefore be demotivated. This practice often led to valuable employees leaving because they didn't know there was any opportunity for them in the company. How can individuals be developing for greater responsibility if they don't even know they are being considered? Secret processes have no place in a development culture.

In a development culture, strategic objectives of the company lead to assessment of talent to determine future staffing needs and bench strength. The assessment may be by a 360-degree instrument with feedback to the participants on which to base development planning. Candidates for key positions are still identified, but the strategic objectives are communicated to everyone, and with the expectation that everyone would have a development plan, so there isn't an "us-versus-them" environment set up. Succession candidates' goals and needs (such as mobility) are incorporated into the succession planning process, and their development plans are based on competencies needing development. A joint planning process requires that senior managers be prepared to have career discussions with candidates about gaps between their present competencies and those needed for the future. Then specific development opportunities are sought to build the skills and knowledge needed to prepare strong candidates. In some organizations, an HR administrator updates a database of skills and candidates annually.

This open process results in a management replacement plan in which individuals are ready for immediate backup of key positions; it also results in a succession planning system that provides a way to identify candidates across functional lines.

Compensation Systems

Reward systems—compensation and recognition—are slowly changing to catch up with the changed paradigm about careers in organizations, but many have far to go. Traditionally, base pay was determined by hierarchical grades with increases driven primarily by seniority, until the top of the range was reached. Even when increases were based on performance, good performers reached the top of the salary grade sooner, but were still "topped out." Employees felt they were entitled to raises, and even marginal performance usually was rewarded with a minimal raise. Many employees saw no relationship between stellar performance and pay, so the focus on promotions was reinforced because that was the only way to get more money once the top of the range was reached. Even merit pay or skill-based pay was still fit into the hierarchical compensation structure.

Traditional compensation systems were based on market comparisons for narrowly defined jobs or levels with limited flexibility or manager discretion. Bonus pay was usually for top managers only, and few employees at any level saw a relationship between their effort and rewards or the company profitability and their paychecks. Pay was linked to the job, not the person. There was no mechanism for rewarding team contributions. Sometimes lateral moves that would benefit both the individual and the organization were punished financially or even not allowed because the pay structure didn't have the flexibility to accommodate them. No wonder lateral moves are seen as a punishment in some organizations today, at a time when that very flexibility is required in many reengineered environments.

Employees recognize as important that which is rewarded. So it is not so much the amount of compensation that contradicts or supports the development culture message as it is the approach to compensation and other rewards and recognition.

Now with the focus on development rather than promotions, there is frequently conflict with the realities of the traditional compensation systems. Instead of motivating employees to add value and contribute to business results, the old systems reward only those who move up. Employees still stuck in the old paradigm, which is reinforced by the reward system, say, "Why should I put in the time and effort to learn new skills or take on more responsibility when the company doesn't show it values them—either by giving me an opportunity to use the skills or by increasing my pay for being more valuable? What's in it for me?"

Organizations with constantly changing technology find that their technical people may not be keeping up, nor are they being paid at the going market value for the skills they contribute. In order to attract the new talent they need, these organizations must offer competitive compensation. This often results in internal inequity of pay among employees.

Jobs are expanding their scope, and responsibility is being pushed down in the hierarchy. The hierarchy itself is flatter or has changed totally to self-directed teams, and development no longer means climbing the corporate ladder. So in a development culture, compensation systems must change to reward the new behaviors and attitudes instead of reinforcing the very behaviors that need to change. Table 10 shows the discrepancy between the new-culture message and the old-culture compensation systems.

Table 10

What We Say and What We Reward

What We Say (New-Culture Message)	What Our Compensation Systems Say (Old-Culture Message)
Your value is directly related to the contribution you provide to the company.	The people who have been around the longest make the most money.
We expect you to complete degrees, and we have tuition assistance to support that goal.	Once you graduate, you are not assured additional money or a promotion.
Teamwork and good interpersonal skills are critical to your success.	Promotions and advancement often are not based on demonstration of competencies or results.
We encourage breadth of skills and want you to add value in many areas.	Your pay is increased by moving up, with specialization encouraged in most salary administration systems.
We encourage managers to develop employees.	Managers are rewarded solely on the basis of achieving the numbers.

From "Career Development and Compensation—A Marriage Made in Heaven or Hell?," by S. Bicos and P. Simonsen. Presentation to the national conference of the American Society for Training and Development, June 1995.

Pritchett and Pound (1996) say that "today's marketplace has changed its reward structure. It doesn't reward companies simply for showing up, or for trying. The real world rewards results." Compensation systems must reward results in the workplace as well, keeping "all rewards out of reach of those people who don't contribute to the new culture."

New compensation systems are based on roles rather than on narrow job descriptions, have greater flexibility to reward contribution, and have variable pay incentives for all employees. Many are seeking ways to reward the person instead of the position. Figure 10 illustrates a person-based pay system. Instead of pay being determined by the level and expected results of the job, in a person-based system compensation is determined by the contribution the individual makes, the level of competence he or she brings, and the extent of learning that allows him or her to add continuing value.

Broad career bands, or at least having fewer salary grades, allows development on the job and increased responsibilities to be compensated without a promotion or even a move to another job grade. Minimums, midpoints, and maximums have given way to market pricing. Individuals' performance and development are evaluated against competencies rather than job tasks. This is not to say that there should be an unlimited pot for

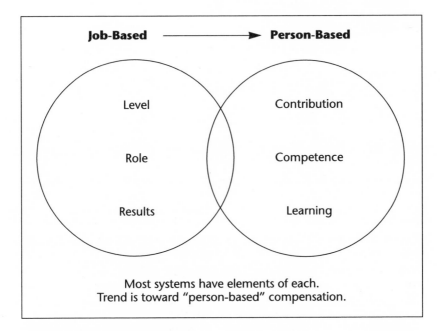

Figure 10   Competency-Based Pay
Adapted by permission, James T. Kochanski, Principal, *Competency-Based Management in Career Development Planning.* Alexandria, VA, September 26, 1996, Sibson & Company

compensation and benefits; it may be the same amount as in a traditional system, but administered differently. In order for this shift to succeed, there needs to be open communication to managers and employees about the business objectives and results, and variable compensation based on individual, team-based, and organizational results. Table 11 illustrates some of the changes occurring in compensation practices that support the development philosophy.

Other nonmonetary rewards that meet individual values and definitions of success are increasingly sought—such as more challenge, autonomy, or time flexibility. "For any such strategy to be seen as a reward, it must not be presently available to the employee, and the employee must view it as personally important" (Leibowitz, Farren, and Kaye, 1986).

Even when desirable to individuals, nonmonetary rewards lack the status and esteem of promotions and titles, and to the extent that employees are motivated by recognition and public acknowledgment of success, additional rewards and recognition must be incorporated into the system.

Table 11

Development Culture and Compensation: The Emerging Needs

Traditional	Needed
Increases based on tenure	Increases based on contribution
Secretive; mutually distrustful	Open; shared expectations
Reluctance to differentiate	Willing to reward people differently
Salary administration system based on moving up	Job worth determined by competencies
Many salary ranges and grades	Large salary bands to discourage emphasis on "moving up" and to reward growth
Job families encourage high degree of specialization	Generalists highly desirable
Compensation driven by market/ salary surveys	Compensation determined by internal worth
More financial opportunities for management jobs	Financial opportunities for superior contribution—professional or managerial
Bonuses reserved for executives	Wider prevalence of stock options, broad-based or team incentives at all levels

From "Career Development and Compensation—A Marriage Made in Heaven or Hell?," by S. Bicos and P. Simonsen. Paper presented at the national conference of the American Society for Training and Development, June 1995.

These changes, while slow to occur, support a development culture and reinforce the message that behaviors and career actions must change. Successful integration of compensation with other development elements requires extensive communication and training. It is important to initiate the changed culture before introducing new compensation systems so employees first learn that change is needed. It is not about compensation. The changed compensation system supports the development message but cannot drive it.

Recognition Practices

In addition to compensation, other recognition practices need to be integrated into the total development process. People value status, although it takes different forms for different people. Those whose anchor (see "Career Anchors" section in Chapter 2) is expertise (technical/functional competence), for example, might be motivated by a "Distinguished Contributor" title and the perks that go with it. There are fewer layers in most organizations today and therefore fewer titles, so even with substantial compensation packages, people need some public way to be recognized for success and achievement. Since our mores don't approve of talking about how much we make, other perks or recognitions are more sought after. For example, assignments with visibility by senior management or other business units may be seen by some as recognition for superior contribution.

Team successes need to be celebrated separately from team compensation. Sometimes friendly competition among teams can be the culmination of a successful project. Organizations with a motivating environment frequently like to celebrate company successes with an event that recognizes the contribution of all.

Those whose anchor is service and dedication want visible thanks, perhaps a gift and a plaque on the wall. And those who are trying to balance all aspects of their lives may find flextime or Friday afternoons off in the summer to be employee-friendly practices that say the company cares about their needs. In recent surveys, it has been found that many employees would choose to make 25 percent less income if they could work 25 percent less time. This may not be possible in our leaner organizations, but it does support the assertion that compensation is not the only outcome people want from their work. When compensation becomes an overriding issue for a group or an individual, it often means, "They don't pay me enough to work in an environment I hate." Jennifer Laabs (1996b) comments: "We must realize that money—while a huge motivator—isn't everything to people. People still want meaningful work and want to feel valued by their organizations, in addition to receiving their paychecks."

In a development culture, managers are in touch with individuals' driving forces and needs and have the flexibility and resources to reward and recognize accordingly. When staff contribute beyond expectations to respond to a crisis or achieve a department goal, they are acknowledged in a tangible, meaningful way, though not necessarily a costly one. A development culture has no place for the manager who says, "Why do I need to thank them? After all, that is what they are paid to do; it's their job!" (The response to this out-of-touch manager is, of course, "But do you want them to keep doing it?")

Benefits

Benefits fall into the category of "satisfiers." They don't motivate behavior, but the lack of them causes dissatisfaction. Adequate benefits in the form of insurance, vacation time, retirement funds, tuition assistance, family-friendly policies, and so forth have become an expectation for most employees. How do benefits programs, then, contribute to a development culture?

Innovative benefits programs that are linked to development programs are contributing to individual development and supporting career goals. One compensation and benefits firm has developed a benefits program for clients (and implemented it with its own associates as well) that individualizes benefits that most support the needs of the individual. Their plan is a "cafeteria plan" that allows employees to choose from a selection of benefits offerings. This is based on an assessment of values and goals, so that individuals choose those benefits that most contribute to their own goals. If a person is new in her career, for example, and advancement is her primary goal, she might choose tuition assistance to get a master's degree. Another, older employee concerned about retirement might have more of his benefits contributed to a retirement fund. Still another, trying to juggle work and young children, might select child care and additional health insurance benefits. The firm has found that this approach actually costs companies less money per employee than standard benefits programs.

The important point to remember is that all of the human resources systems in the company must contribute to rather than contradict the development message.

Communicating the Scope of a Comprehensive Career Management System

All of these policies—selection, development, and rewards—need to be formalized and communicated as part of the development process. Some people instinctively know how to operate in the system—they have their antennae up and can read unspoken messages and expectations. But most cannot, especially in a changing culture in which the old rules have changed. In many environments, the old rules said, "Do a good job, but be passive. Someone will recognize your talents and take you under his or her wing." That was not a functional way for most people to manage their careers; it was detrimental for women and minorities, and it doesn't work for anyone in today's rapidly changing, demanding work environments. Employees must be proactive; passivity can be deadly to one's career.

Everyone typically needs to see and hear how all of the human resources systems in the organization support a development culture. Career development is not an isolated event that happens in a workshop, nor is it something that should be paid attention to only when a crisis occurs or when employees are unhappy with their jobs. It is an ongoing process supported by managers and the organization and reinforced or enhanced by human resources systems. It is critical that people in management and human resources analyze the messages of the organizational systems and set about aligning systems with each other to support the business needs of the organization. Changes are not easy to implement, even when the recognition is there that systems need to change. But most employees will understand and value the efforts being made to update selection, development, and reward systems, even if they need to be told to stay tuned because all the work is not yet completed. A brochure with a model of the ways in which all the components link and interrelate can be a strong message to employees and managers. Consider career development to be the glue that pulls all the other supporting systems together.

Roles and Responsibilities in a Development Culture

A Shared Responsibility

We became convinced that we had a responsibility
to put employees back in control of their lives.
—Marianne F. Jackson, Sun Microsystems

Creating a Development Culture

In a development culture, we say individuals must be responsible for
their own development and not dependent on their manager or the organization for their growth and career opportunities. Even so, individuals
are not the only players—or stakeholders—in a development culture,
and they certainly cannot change the culture by themselves. This process
is a shared responsibility with benefits to all parties. Each group fills a
specific role and has different responsibilities.

One of the most notable characteristics of a development culture is
the involvement of various groups with a commitment to their responsibilities. In today's overloaded work environments, it takes significant
effort to gain and sustain the commitment necessary to make this work.
It requires a significant change in behavior for some, particularly managers who have been rewarded for their technical expertise rather than
their people development skills.

The development culture team includes employees, of course, because
they are the primary beneficiaries of development. But it starts at the top
of the organization, with commitment—both verbal and active—from

senior managers who represent the organization and its philosophy of a development culture. The banner then needs to be carried by managers, who need to understand what's in it for them to make the commitment to developing their people. And there is a role for human resources or training professionals, although they cannot be the primary sponsors of the process if the process is to become part of the culture and system. Some organizations also establish mentoring relationships, career counselors/ advisors, and/or advisory teams to ensure the commitment and skills for an ongoing, successful intervention. Table 12 summarizes the roles and responsibilities of individuals and groups in a development culture.

As you consider all the stakeholders who are critical in creating a development culture in your organization, you need to assess both their readiness and their capability to contribute to your desired future state. Development Culture Survey 2: Readiness and Capability Tool can be used for this purpose. Lack of readiness on the part of the stakeholders indicates that you need to get their attention about why they must be actively involved. Lack of capability requires an educating or skill-building intervention. Both must be considered as you begin to design your development process.

Senior Management's Role

Senior managers have a primary responsibility to establish and communicate a philosophy of development in their organization. If development becomes a pervasive message, and senior managers provide leadership to bear it out, there will be much more likelihood of an impact on the culture. Senior managers need to be champions at every opportunity to reinforce the message, to be role models, and to hold others accountable for their responsibilities. Commitment from senior management is a powerful force for change in organizations.

Gottlieb and Conkling (1995) say that one definition of leadership is "the exercise of interpersonal influence." They observe that "many otherwise excellent initiatives have failed in organizations because no effort was made to bring the opinion leaders on board." While others in an organization may very well be opinion leaders, people *expect* senior managers to perform this role. Senior managers need to lead the development culture process to the same extent that they carry the torch for other organizational initiatives such as quality, market competitiveness, or reengineering. Otherwise, promoting the development culture will be seen as a "program of the month" pushed by human resources.

Table 12

Roles and Responsibilities in a Development Culture

Role	Primary Responsibility	Means	Outcomes
Employees	Take responsibility for managing their own careers and development	Engage in self-assessment, reality checking, goal setting, action planning, and implementation	Achievement of career goals and job satisfaction
Managers/ Supervisors	Provide support and opportunities for growth	Coach and provide feedback about performance on present job; advise and provide opportunities to achieve career goals	Highly motivated workforce that takes personal responsibility for their performance and development
Senior Management	Support the introduction and continued efforts of the development process	Communicate organizational goals, needs, and opportunities	Motivated and capable workforce prepared to meet current and future company needs
Human Resources Staff	Provide information, resources, systems, and assistance to facilitate development	Offer workshops, assessments, career centers, organizational information, HR staffing systems, training, compensation systems	Enhanced information for decisions regarding staffing and development needs; systems that support development
Mentors	Provide encouragement, advice, reality testing, and organizational perspective	Establish rapport with mentoree; communicate expectations and realities of the organization	Passing on of organizational knowledge and culture; contribution to bench strength
Career Advisory Team	Provide guidance, organizational perspective, and continuity to a development process	Give input and feedback on the design and implementation of development resources; serve as communication liaison to the organization	Successes in helping individuals set and and achieve goals and make a greater contribution to the organization

From *Managing Career Development,* by P. Simonsen, 1994. Rolling Meadows, IL: Career Directions, Inc.

2

DEVELOPMENT CULTURE SURVEY

Readiness and Capability Tool

Readiness: Willingness; having motives and aims
Capability: Power, influence, authority to allocate resources, the possession of information and skills required to carry out the necessary tasks

In the left-hand column, list the individuals or groups who are critical to building a development culture as you envision it in the "future state." Then rank each (high, medium, or low) according to their readiness and capability to take part in the change effort.

Individual or Group	Readiness			Capability		
	High	Medium	Low	High	Medium	Low
1.						
2.						
3.						
4.						
5.						
6.						
7.						
8.						
9.						
10.						
11.						
12.						

In research conducted by Gutteridge, Leibowitz, and Shore (1993), comparisons of career development in the United States with other parts of the world showed less commitment by senior management here than elsewhere. Eighty percent of U.S. respondents said they agreed or strongly agreed with the statement: "Senior management believes career development is an important part of employee development." In contrast, the percentages of respondents who agreed or strongly agreed in other countries were as follows: Australia, 92 percent; European countries, 94 percent; and Singapore, 100 percent. Respondents from all four samples interpreted this statement in a similar way: "Senior management feels that career development is an important part of employee development and should be tied in with the organization's strategic plan."

The question occurs, then, that if about 80 percent of senior managers in the United States believe in career development, and most probably know the importance of employee development to remaining competitive, then why do so many organizations lack their involvement in career development initiatives? Could it be that most programs do not emphasize a link between career development and the strategic plan? Do senior managers not see career development as a driving force for a development culture? Or is the major change of behavior they expect from employees not seen as changing the culture?

There are two issues to be addressed: (1) Senior managers must believe in career development and its role in building a development culture, and (2) others in the organization must know they do. The issue brings up this question: How do you find out if your management team believes in a development culture and in career development as a significant influencer to move in that direction? Consider some structured interviews with as many representatives of your senior group as possible. If you are in a division of a large organization, your unit leadership may be who you target, but knowing where the company's executives stand on these topics can be useful as well.

The intent of interviewing management is to determine what they consider key development issues for the future. What are their concerns for achieving the strategic plan? What vision do they have for the workforce? What outcomes do they expect from a career development program in the company? Do they share your definition of a development culture and of career development?

Sometimes senior managers are still operating in the old paradigm: Career development means moving up, and since upward mobility is limited in most organizations today, they may resist the idea. Most leaders, however, recognize how quickly organizations must move today to remain competitive, and they see the need for developing people as a competitive advantage. Others may have a pressing problem to address, such as loss of highly skilled employees or key successors—so they see the need to address these problems although they may not call the intervention career development and they may not expand their thinking beyond solving the problems at hand.

Once you identify the pressing or future needs recognized by senior management, you can be sure to target those in your development philosophy and approach. You may need to interpret their perspective to ensure understanding by others in the organization, but you can be sure you will not get their endorsement or support of a process or program if these concerns are not addressed. The concerns of senior management that might lead to this kind of change effort could range anywhere from a desire for a total change of culture to a desire to "just improve the scores on the employee opinion survey next year on the career development question." The latter, of course, will not change the culture unless all of the interventions happen too, with one result being a rise in positive scores on the survey.

Another approach to involving senior management and getting their support for a development process is an executive briefing. This can be held at the onset of your planning and might include a presentation about intent, purpose, and how the process will contribute to the company direction. Or the presentation might have more impact after you have completed planning and some design so that it could include more detail and answers to questions. This positions you to gain senior management's active support as you move the process forward, while allowing them to give their input before implementation.

Visible senior management commitment can take many forms, such as a letter in an initial communication piece to employees explaining why the process is needed and encouraging their active participation, an introduction by the president at an all-employee meeting, or an orientation conducted by senior management representatives providing attention-getting reasons why the company is launching a development initiative. Senior management's attendance at career development sessions can also go a long way toward convincing managers and employees that they support this process and expect participation. Whether they attend as participants or visit a session to endorse it and provide a big-picture perspective on the company's needs, their role is valuable. And, of course, being a role model throughout implementation is critical. If managers are expected to have career discussions and work on development plans with employees, there should be similar expectations regarding senior managers and their direct reports. If senior managers aren't willing to take the time or emphasize the importance of the process, that message cascades throughout the organization. As organizations envision their future ideal state of a development culture, they need to think about the role senior management will take. How can they be sponsors of the process of building a development culture?

Human resources representatives of Motorola's Land Mobile Products Sector (LMPS) in the Plantation facility initiated a sectorwide task force to consider issues of career development for its professional ranks of employees. They gained the support of top management, who—because of rapidly changing technology and global competition—recognized the need to have a continuously developing workforce that would meet Motorola's business needs. The task force focused on employee responsibility for development to change the mind-set indicated on annual employee surveys: that individuals expected the company to provide career development opportunities. Development Culture in Action: Case 6 illustrates how LMPS recognized the importance of shared responsibility in their career development intervention.

Supervisors' and Managers' Role

Managers have the responsibility to carry the development message to their unit. "Top executives can conceive the vision, but managers are the midwives who must help give it birth" (Pritchett and Pound, 1996a).To build a development culture, each unit must work on it. Many organizations traditionally have had good managers who believe in and act on their responsibility for developing people, but if this effort is spotty the organization cannot build a pervasive development culture. When a few managers stand out by comparison with the rest of the organization in promoting the development culture, major effort will be needed to make those behaviors valued throughout the organization. People will lose faith in the vision if managers "sit on the fence, second guess top management, or only give lukewarm support" (Pritchett and Pound).

case 6   DEVELOPMENT CULTURE IN ACTION
Motorola Land Mobile Products Sector

Shared Responsibility

The first response to the career development effort in the Plantation facility was the opening of a Career Resource Center, staffed by a professional career counselor who served as the manager of career development services. The purpose of the center was to deliver a comprehensive package of career services. The services included in-depth career counseling and a full range of career training classes as well as ongoing career awareness activities and programs that ultimately were delivered by the stakeholders themselves. For example, managers led a "Career Discovery Series" of informal sessions focused on organizational information. Employees and managers were invited to attend to gain more information about other departments and current projects.

Shortly after the opening of the Career Resource Center, an Engineering Career Team was established to consider issues of career development for engineers in the facility. Made up of senior managers, managers, and human resources representatives, the team worked together with the Career Resource Center manager to respond to their customer needs. They identified two unmet needs in the organization: the need for all Motorolans to better understand the changing roles in career development in corporate America, and the need for tools and information to facilitate the career development planning process and to drive and direct individual development.

The Engineering Career Team determined that in order to achieve the first objective, a change in the culture was necessary. To create ownership by all employees of their role in managing their development, organizationwide training was needed for employees and managers. Initiated in 1995, the anticipated outcomes of training were:

▌ Clear understanding of career development roles and responsibilities
▌ Regular career discussions between managers and employees
▌ Completed development plans by all professional employees
▌ More collaborative relationships regarding the organization's needs and the individual's goals
▌ Heightened awareness of career services and other career development supports within the corporation

Today's shared responsibility that has resulted from the career development intervention includes all of the stakeholders:

■ *The individual,* who understands that, ultimately, career planning is his or her own responsibility

■ *The manager,* providing the necessary coaching, tools, and information that contribute to a realistic career plan developed by the employee

■ *The human resources department,* leading the way in career development and providing support to align all parts of the career system

■ *The Engineering Career Team,* who serve as an advisory body for career issues, collaborate with the career development manager, and foster the institutionalization of career development efforts throughout the facility

■ *The manager of career development services,* who leads organizationwide career development, oversees individual career counseling and training, aligns marketing and communication with emerging and expanding services, and leads the efforts to build a development culture by fostering development responsibilities of managers and employees

■ *Top management,* which drives and supports the "human issues" programs that recognize Motorola's workforce as the corporation's most valuable resource

The result of the career development program at LMPS—Plantation was a significant change effort to build a development culture in the business unit that included the integration of many other elements to generate the needed results. In a recent survey, 100 percent of surveyed employees reported that they, or they in conjunction with their manager, are responsible for their own development. They no longer believe that the company will manage their career for them.

Used by permission of Motorola LMPS—Plantation

Communication

A large part of managers' role in employee development is communication. Managers must cascade the business needs and direction to employees, communicate how department goals and plans will contribute to the overall strategic plan, and assist employees in writing appropriate goals. In a development culture, managers are coaches. They build respect not out of fear but out of leadership. In a changing environment, when the past doesn't apply to the present and the present is in flux, people need a leader who "will provide support, a clear purpose, and tasks that are of value to the changing organization" (Gottlieb and Conkling, 1996). The following example illustrates the importance of communication at all levels:

In a rapidly growing software firm, there are strong leaders at the top who communicate their vision to the next level of management. It's an aggressive culture, and the president and CEO epitomize the qualities they expect in their employees. The CEO communicates a broad perspective directly to managers at a monthly one-hour session for those who choose to attend, and then expects them to carry the message to their units. Some do, but there is no translation by the managers from the vision to strategies to individual opportunities and actions. Many actively recruited, highly skilled employees began leaving, and exit interviews indicated that they didn't know where the company was headed and perceived a lack of opportunities.

A process to create a development culture was initiated. In initial data gathering, the most commonly mentioned need was communication. Senior managers said middle managers didn't have the skills needed to lead their people; middle managers said they needed more communication from the top; and employee groups said they needed more communication and feedback from managers. The informal approach to communicating the vision and strategy was being lost in the middle. All three groups were probably right to a certain extent, and in order to build a development culture, a process for communication had to be instituted. Managers at all levels needed to recognize their crucial role in communicating to and coaching their direct reports.

The process of reengineering, downsizing, and restructuring has left the ranks of middle management fairly thin in many organizations. Managers are managing larger numbers of direct reports at a time when more communication, feedback, and development planning is crucial.

Supporting Employee Development

Managers generally need to play four roles in employee development in order to build a base of understanding before assisting with development plans, as shown in Table 13. First, they have the responsibility for coaching employees, which means building sufficient rapport for a trusting relationship, supporting risk taking, discussing employees' desires and needs, and not being evaluative. Good coaching is based on open communication,

Table 13

Four Roles for Supporting Employee Development

Roles	Discussion Topics	Outcomes
Coaching Listen and draw out	*Assessment* Information from employee's self-assessment: work values, interests, skills, and accomplishments	Clarification of employee's desired work characteristics
Reality Testing Provide positive and corrective feedback	*Feedback* How employee is seen; how present performance relates to future opportunities	Realistic view of employee in organization
Advising Offer organizational information and advice	*Information and Advice* Organizational information: opportunities, development support systems, and resources	Organization awareness
Development Planning Offer guidance in setting goals and in development planning	*Development* Realities and limitations of development goals; developmental assignments and activities	Development plan

Acknowledgment is given to Caela Farren and Beverly Kaye for the influence of their career discussion model, and to Career Directions, Inc., *Career Discussion Guide for Managers*.

trust that employees need and will act on company information, and enough time—even in a busy, deadline-oriented culture—to pay attention to individual needs. In a developmental environment, managers encourage and listen to employees' concerns and interests about how their own needs are being met in the organization. By discussing the results of an employee's assessment, both manager and employee clarify elements of work that support development and satisfaction. Coaching is as much about the individual as it is about performance.

The second responsibility of supervisors and managers is reality testing. In taking responsibility for their own development, employees often say they need and want honest feedback in order to know how to focus their efforts. To be sure, some employees need help in accepting feedback, but how managers give it can make a difference in changing performance and behavior. One concern managers have about employee career development is that it may raise unrealistic expectations. If it does, it is because of a lack of honest feedback in the process. Supervisors and managers have a primary role in reality testing.

Feedback can be on several aspects of the development process:

- Present performance—both positive and corrective
- How present performance relates to future opportunities
- Employee's reputation in the organization
- Viability of goals
- Development opportunities and activities

In a development culture, feedback has a future perspective as well as an evaluative one, and it is ongoing rather than an annual event in a performance review. The result of a good feedback process is the employees' realistic view of themselves in the organization.

Supervisors and managers also have the responsibility of providing information and advice, but perhaps not in the way sometimes expected. A human resources manager who resisted having supervisors involved in the development process expressed concern: "Our supervisors are operations people, one step above the people they supervise. They are not career counselors, and I don't want them giving employees advice about the rest of the organization or even telling them what they should do next in their career."

Of course, supervisors and managers should not be career counselors. Rather, they should be trained to have development discussions with their direct reports. Their role in giving advice starts with translating the department needs and directions into appropriate action for goals and growth on the present job. If supervisors don't have any more information about the department direction than employees do, this is a symptom of a need for communication from the top down. Career discussions should be driven by the individual, with the supervisor or manager in a coaching role. This means that the conversation agenda should be the employee's, with perspective provided by the supervisor or manager.

If the individual has interest in exploring other areas of the company for future opportunities, the manager is not expected to have all the answers about requirements or possibilities, nor does he or she need to do the homework. Instead, the manager can be a referral agent or a liaison or can make recommendations about resources. Supervisors and managers benefit from having a strong network. Some organizations have formal systems for employees to explore other options, as discussed in Chapter 11, but most still rely on informal network contacts.

Employees can use network contacts for information, planning, and reality testing, or to build relationships or find openings.

Managers can give their opinion, but it is not their role to tell employees they should or should not pursue a particular goal. They can give advice on how difficult they think the goal is, or on the personal and organizational barriers they think the employee will need to overcome. And if they have been honest in feedback up to this point, the employee has the benefit of that perspective. The outcome of this part of the discussion should be broader awareness on the part of the employee of the organization and its realities.

The final role for supervisors and managers in the coaching process is to collaborate with employees on development plans to achieve their goals. There usually needs to be agreement about what can be done on the present job to contribute to future goals, whether short- or long-range. Training courses may be appropriate, but managers also need to seek or invent development options on the job, and employees need to be willing to use self-directed resources. In a development culture, employees own this process. They are not passive or dependent on their manager to create a development plan for them, but jointly agree on a development plan as an outcome of the career discussion. Employees commit to continuous learning, and the company ensures that their skills don't become stagnant or obsolete. Development often means opportunity for expanding their skill sets and therefore their marketability. Building skills and competencies for an employee's goals becomes a criterion for success.

The Collaborative Process

While supervisors and managers are asked to support the development of employees, they have careers too; it is important for managers to be participants in their own development process. Managers need to do their own development planning, especially values-based assessment. If they understand the process, they will be more effective at helping employees. "Today's leaders are required to take a large measure of interpersonal and professional risk. In order to take these risks, the leader must begin with a clear idea of what is important to him or her personally" (Gottlieb and Conkling, 1995). Development discussions must therefore be held at all levels, from senior management on down through the ranks.

There are some important questions to be answered in initiating a development focus. Program designers need to anticipate the types of conflict that will arise when a manager's best interest collides with an employee's need for development. For example, when a good employee who is working on a critical project is offered an opportunity in another department, how do you create a win-win outcome? In a development culture, does individual development always take precedence? If it does not, how do you manage the apparent contradictions that employees will experience?

The answers may lie in the collaborative process necessary in a development culture. Employees will stay longer in a situation they have outgrown, and will be more willing to maintain a high level of performance, if they believe their manager is truly concerned about their development and well-being. They may postpone an opportunity because of present departmental needs if they know they won't be "stuck" as a result.

Joline Godfrey (1996) suggests that female managers may demonstrate collaboration skills and relationship building more than males do, and may be role models in this process:

> What female business owners called normal was now being tagged the "new paradigm" by business gurus worldwide. The new psychology on women revealed that relationships are a source of power that women are comfortable nurturing. Success among these women is less a matter of conquest than of collaboration.

For many managers, however, actively supporting employee development is a new role. These skills need to be developed and reinforced. Technical managers in a fast-paced environment, or long-term managers stretched by new demands, need to be held accountable for developing people, or the responsibility becomes a "nice-to-have but I don't have time" function.

Some organizations circumvent supervisors and managers in the employee development and career development process because these people may not have the motivation or the necessary coaching skills. Mentors and advisors can help fill the gap, as can "development managers" in a matrix structure, but it is difficult to establish and maintain a development culture without managers' significant role in the process. A better approach is to guide employees who don't want to or don't have the skills to manage people to individual contributor paths instead of into manager roles. In the meantime, before today's managers retire, there needs to be a major effort to bring supervisors and managers into the culture change. Many managers say they want to help employees in their development and are willing to have career discussions, but they don't know how. That is a training need. For those not willing to move with the changing needs of the organization, that is a performance improvement need. As we deemphasize the goal of moving up the ladder, we need to allow for and value moves back, so good technical people who are not good people managers can contribute their skills appropriately.

Employees' Role

Even while benefiting from leadership by their immediate supervisor, employees carry substantial responsibility for their own career development. To start with, they must recognize the need to actively manage their career. This awareness is essential to move away from the dependency mentality that leads to blame ("Why don't *they* . . . promote me, tell me what I need to do to get ahead, pay me more, and so on?").

In a development culture, employees buy in to the need for active development. Sometimes this message needs to be interpreted, because in the old culture, individuals who didn't want to be promoted really could ignore their own development and just do their job. In our changing organizations today, that is no longer a long-term option. The basis for successfully changing the culture is a critical mass of employees who recognize their responsibility and are ready and willing to take action. The following is an example of an organization in which employees were not prepared for change:

A data management company was phasing out one of its processing units. Many of those about to lose their jobs had been in the same positions for many years and had only the data entry skills needed for their function. The company had a generous tuition assistance program and also offered opportunities to interview for positions in other units, but few employees took advantage of either. Many continued to believe that it wouldn't be *their* jobs that would be eliminated.

Finally, when a deadline for closing the unit was set, human resources decided they needed to take action to get employees moving. They conducted an orientation session to announce self-directed career planning resources for employees to use, and to introduce the need for active career management. Involvement was not mandated, but a majority of employees did attend the orientations and indicated a willingness to participate. They received workbooks or career planning software and had the option of a career discussion with an external career counselor if they chose.

Managers were not involved, nor was there direction from senior management about the impact of the scheduled changes. Only two employees out of 125 whose jobs were affected took advantage of the career counselor. A few made moves within the company, but no one initiated additional tuition-assisted courses. Most of those who participated completed some self-assessment, but took no action on their own behalf. Why? Inertia is strong, and without someone pushing for action, communicating expectations, encouraging goal setting, or linking development with performance evaluation, it was easier to fall back into the ostrich syndrome and to hide emotionally from the life-affecting changes of job elimination.

Employees heard—but did not internalize—the message of change and the need for active career management. Offering resources was not sufficient to change the culture.

Perhaps the most intransigent group of employees in any organization are those who *like* the status quo. When organizations offer voluntary development programs, these employees are the ones who don't choose to participate. Those who are unhappy with their present situation are the first to enroll—whether motivated by negative feelings about the company, their manager, and their lot in life, or by a desire to be proactive about their own development. In a stable organization, it may be acceptable in the short term for employees to say they don't want to change, but it is not acceptable to still be thinking in the old paradigm that career development means promotions. In dynamic environments, with market forces driving companies to be competitive, yesterday's skills won't be acceptable in tomorrow's organization. So employees need to get the message clearly that the status quo will no longer exist; *everyone* needs to be developing new skills, even if they don't want to make a move.

For those who do have a future focus, career development opportunity starts on the present job, so employees need to mentally link performance feedback—in the form of performance evaluation and reviews— to future opportunities. They need to actively seek to build skills and competence for today as well as tomorrow, even when they may not know just what tomorrow will bring. This is why it is so critical for managers to be involved with employee development, even though employees need to drive the process. Only supervisors and managers, not career advisors or mentors, can link development to present performance.

That is not to say that career development and performance management are the same, or even that they should be discussed at the same time. But if there is a proactive performance management process, including planning and feedback discussions between employees and managers, the basis is there to move forward with career planning and discussions. A rule of thumb is that performance management discussions are driven by the manager, and career discussions should be driven primarily by the individual.

A good career discussion won't happen by completing one question about career goals at the bottom of the performance review form with no attention to discussing career plans. One cynical employee, when asked how he had decided what to include in response to such a question, replied, "I put the opposite of what I want, because it seems they make a point of giving you the opposite of what you write." A development culture requires that a critical mass of individuals be actively engaged in their own development. It becomes an expectation, not an exception.

Self-Insight

A critical responsibility employees have for managing their careers is ongoing self-insight. This may take the form of formal or informal assessment—either individually or in groups. Individuals should revisit their self-assessment each time new skills are learned, new accomplishments are achieved, or new experiences contribute to self-awareness (see Chapter 12).

A critical element of self-awareness for individuals is clarity about their *work values.* In a changing environment, the clearer individuals are about what is important to them about their work, the more they can (a) adapt their environment (assignments, relationships, and so on) to support their values, and (b) recognize that their dissatisfaction is caused by values conflicts and make informed choices about whether to stay in the position or make a move. In today's demanding workplaces, all employees need to be clearly aware of their capabilities and the value of their capabilities—their marketability. With a constantly moving target, this needs to be an ongoing, or at least a regular, process.

Employees need to recognize that to achieve career success, first they need to define—or redefine—success. Then they need to set goals and communicate their goals to those people who can help the employees achieve them. Usually this means career discussions with managers as well as with co-workers, managers of other areas of interest, mentors, and perhaps a spouse or significant other.

Goals are better defined, communicated, turned into action, and measured if they are written down. It is employees' responsibility to create a development plan for themselves, but in some organizations this is also a

Table 14

Development Plans—Personal or Organizational?

Benefits of Sharing

■ Company has a record of employee's interests, mobility, and goals.

■ Information can be available in a database for selection decisions and HR planning, taking individual's input into account.

■ Development needs of the group form a needs assessment for training curricula and development planning options companywide.

■ Development plans can be a measure of active individual involvement in career management.

■ If the business driver is a need for everyone to upgrade skills and keep them current, an annual development plan is a means of accountability.

■ An ongoing emphasis, rather than a one-time program, can be maintained by requiring an updated development plan annually as a basis for career discussions.

Limitations to Sharing

■ If employees are truly responsible for managing their own careers and development, a *required* development plan can be seen as contradicting the message.

■ If there has not been a trusting environment, employees may not be open about career development goals and plans. They may write what they think should be written, rather than what they want.

■ Shared goal information must be administered, whether on paper copies or in a database. If a database is to be kept, who enters the data?

■ The purpose of shared information from employees must be clearly communicated. Will it be used for staffing decisions? To ensure bench strength? For HR planning? For training needs assessment? Without a perceived benefit to employees and managers, it becomes one more administrative requirement.

---

shared document. Whether to use development plans for organizational planning or to have them be only a discussion guide between employee and manager is a design decision to be made as you establish parameters of a development process. There are pros and cons of each approach, as shown in Table 14.

Employees in a development culture are not dependent. They take on a self-employed attitude, recognizing that change is not optional. Cliff Hakim (1994), in *We Are All Self-Employed,* describes a self-employed attitude as one of being interdependent with the organization, being a perpetual learner, doing what you do best, and satisfying your customers. A self-employed mentality generates both independence and interdependence.

Dependence generates an entitlement mentality, blame, subservience (in a time when innovation is needed), passivity or animosity, and a past (rather than a future) focus. In a development culture, independence is encouraged. As leaders in a Fortune 500 retail company changed from a paternalistic to a self-directed environment, they communicated the message to all employees: Act like owners.

The following chapters in Part II provide an overview of other roles that support managers and employees in building a development culture.

CHAPTER

7

Leaders of the Change Process

Great opportunities to help others seldom come,
but small ones surround us every day.
—Sally Koch

The Role of the Human Resources Department

Human resources as a department, along with senior management, represents the organization to individuals. HR may provide leadership for the change effort to address business issues creating the need for change. They can have a significant contribution to make in promoting a development culture.

HR representatives must be careful to build their reputation as facilitators and not as gatekeepers. They must be seen as adding value and as being personally effective before they can be effective change agents.

A primary human resources responsibility is to build—or redesign—HR systems to support a development culture and ensure that employees and managers don't experience contradictions between what is said and "how things really work around here." In other words, is the organization espousing a new culture and expecting changed behaviors, but operating out of and continuing to reward old-culture behaviors? Selection/staffing systems and reward/recognition systems must be aligned with development expectations, or at least be moving in that direction (see Chapter 5). For example, if new employees are recruited who expect and are promised upward mobility (old-paradigm expectations), but the reality is that most growth will occur by expanding responsibilities in place, the development process will suffer, and a new business need will be created by the loss of high-potential talent.

Another responsibility that typically falls to human resources is providing development resources to employees and managers. This may take the form of systems, people resources, training, written or computer resources, a career center that houses written and media resources, or, increasingly, a virtual career center. Systems include elements of a career development process such as means for self-assessment and planning, a process for linking career development and performance management, perhaps a mobility system if that is a business need, and access to organizational information and so on (see Chapters 11 and 12).

A critical responsibility of HR in a development culture is to establish a mechanism or build into the design a means to keep the development emphasis alive and ongoing. If individuals and managers are putting energy and time into creating development plans, is there a way to incorporate them into human resources planning? If not, people will feel that development planning may be a nice thing to do but not something they will continue to place emphasis on. Are managers at all levels accountable for developing people? Is there a process for updating development plans annually or on an as-needed basis? The outcomes that were expected as the process was implemented will need to be measured. If there is a process for communicating business goals and direction annually, is there a process for ensuring that this information is directly tied into individuals' development planning?

Human resources leaders may be driving the whole development initiative, either responding to a charge by senior leadership or facilitating a grass-roots effort because of expressed need. But in either case, the responsibility for implementing a systematic approach typically rests with HR. Human resources departments with a small staff or lack of expertise in the field often seek consulting help to design or implement a comprehensive process when they realize quick-fix approaches will be considered the "program of the month" by employees and managers. As HR specialists move toward an internal consulting model, or as they move out of corporate and into field offices, they increasingly recognize the value of a collaborative model for designing and implementing a process that has the goal of creating a development culture. There may be task forces or teams already in place addressing such needs as diversity, reengineering, or skill improvement. If everyone involved can see how career development can be the glue that holds a change effort together, there is opportunity for a synergy of all the initiatives. A multipronged approach not only has more possibility of changing the culture, but the outcomes will likely be more successful if everyone sees how they all link together.

Facilitating Change

The Change Agent Role

Whether you are a manager, a human resources specialist, or an associate in a function selected to contribute to a task force or advisory group to design a development process, you will need to play the role of change agent. The American Management Association defines this role as follows: "Change management is the developing discipline of planning, organizing, and controlling organizational change to better solve present and future business problems" (cited in Laabs, 1996a). Whether you will act formally as a change agent or informally as a proponent of creating a development culture, you will be facilitating change. Use "Development Culture Survey 3: Change Agent Competencies" to assess your own ability or that of others in the change agent role.

If you are involved in the design and implementation of a career development system in your organization that is intended to change employees' and managers' views and behavior about career development, you will need to facilitate change. If your process is intended to affect their behaviors to result in *strategic career management,* defined as "planning, preparing, implementing, and monitoring career actions in ways consistent with the direction and needs of the organization" (Simonsen, 1993), you will be actively managing change—especially if the needs of the organization are changing rapidly. When you initiate activities that invite adults to develop personally and organizationally, your intervention requires you to be a change agent and facilitator.

Other Roles

In its competency work for the human resources profession, the American Society for Training and Development (ASTD) defined fifteen roles in which HR specialists may need to demonstrate capability (see Table 15). Many of these roles are essential to managing the change process and building a development culture.

DEVELOPMENT CULTURE SURVEY

3

Change Agent Competencies

A change agent role requires the following characteristics and skills. Rate yourself or your collaborators on a scale of 1 to 5. Circle the number that best describes your capability on each item.

1 = Can't do it at all
2 = Below-average ability
3 = Average ability
4 = Above-average ability
5 = Exceptional ability

1. A thorough knowledge and understanding of the change process	1	2	3	4	5
2. Vision	1	2	3	4	5
3. A positive outlook that encourages continual learning and growth	1	2	3	4	5
4. Strong employee focus, grounded in company values	1	2	3	4	5
5. Being innovative, with ideas focused on improving the quality of work life	1	2	3	4	5
6. Flexibility and adaptability	1	2	3	4	5
7. Knowledge of the business	1	2	3	4	5
8. Highly developed human relations skills	1	2	3	4	5

Score

8–16 points	Get help and improve your skills before championing change in your organization.
17–24 points	You have some strengths, but you have much to improve for a smooth roll as a change agent.
25–32 points	You have a moderate chance of success as a change agent. Work on your own capabilities even as you are helping others adapt to change.
33–40 points	Your scores indicate strong capability in the characteristics and skills of a change agent. You may want to test yourself by getting feedback from others and by applying your skills in managing a real change effort.

Assessment based on "Expert Advice on How to Move Forward with Change," by J. J. Laabs, © July 1996. Used with permission of Workforce/ACC Communications, Inc., Costa Mesa, CA. All rights reserved.

Table 15

Roles for Managing the Change Process
and Building A Development Culture

Strategist	Marketer
Group facilitator	Instructor
Individual development counselor	Transfer agent
Evaluator	Program administrator
Needs analyst	Training and development manager
Task analyst	Media specialist
Program designer	Theoretician
Instructional writer	

Adapted from *Models for Excellence*, by P. McLagan. Copyright 1983, The American Society for Training and Development. Reprinted with permission. All rights reserved.

Choosing Your Battles

Facilitating change is a difficult process to step into. With change happening so fast, you can never be an expert on everything—you need to choose your battles. Jonathan Kozol (cited in Pritchett and Pound, 1996) says, "Pick battles big enough to matter, small enough to win." Pritchett and Pound (1996) describe the concept of "zero defects" as alien to managing transitions and change: "If the organization waited until the changes could be made perfectly, they would never be made at all."

To get buy-in for a comprehensive career development effort, Marianne Matheis, career development manager for the Aerospace Corporation, says, "Think systems, sell programs." Although you may be well aware of the scope of the changes needed, you may first need to gain acceptance of elements of the process. While you are convincing stakeholders of the need to move forward with practical steps, you can be inventing the comprehensive system you know will be needed. As Pritchett and Pound say, "The best way to predict the future is to invent it." That's good advice as you start on a major effort to build a development culture in your organization.

Partnering with Management and Teams

Much of your work in initiating a major change effort will involve partnering with management and employee groups to determine their needs and to contract with them to create the kind of help they need. Whether this relationship is built with one department or across the organization will depend on your function and your role in leading the change of culture to support a developmental environment. If you are working on a team, your partnership will also be with team members to determine roles and the best use of everyone's skills.

Building these partnerships will help you understand real needs, the kind of resistance you might expect, and the outcomes the group needs from a successful intervention. It will also build a solid relationship on which to gain trust. Your role may be to help managers and leaders who have influence over organizational change to understand the scope of the effort.

Facilitation Skills

Beckhard and Harris (1987) describe managing change as an art:

> It is obvious that the process of intervention is complex. One of the biggest traps for large-system change efforts is the failure of [those managing the change] to resist the temptation to rush through the planning process to get to the " 'action' stage." Although the pressures for immediate results often arise from a need to eliminate the acute negative consequences of the problem, it has been our experience that a great portion of large-system change efforts fail due to a lack of understanding . . . of what the process of intervention and change involves. . . . Management must gain a basic understanding of the whats, hows, and whys of the change management process, and be able to recognize its developmental . . . nature as a necessary condition for success in planned change efforts.

In the process of building a development culture, leaders will find facilitation skills essential. If these skills are not in their repertoire as the process unfolds, consider hiring a consultant to serve both as facilitator for the partnering and data gathering and as role model for the internal team's learning. In order to build a collaborative development culture, you must have buy-in from many stakeholders. To obtain buy-in, you must consult and facilitate rather than advise and train. The following outputs are identified for group facilitators in the ASTD competency work (McLagan, 1983):

- Group discussions in which issues and needs are constructively assessed
- Group decisions with which all individuals feel committed to action
- Cohesive teams
- Enhanced awareness of group process, self, and others

The role of group facilitator is defined in the ASTD competency model as "managing group discussions and group process so that individuals learn and group members feel the experience is positive" (McLagan).

Career development delivery usually involves both facilitation and training. Work in the area of self-assessment for individuals, in large or small groups or individually, involves using processes that uncover self-insight. While models of career development and concepts may be taught, most of the effort is in facilitating people's own awareness of what these models and concepts mean for them. Whether in workshops or in small group-counseling sessions, the goal is to lead participants to new insight about themselves and their role in the organization as a basis of their own development planning.

Education for managers in their role in managing employee development will also involve both training and facilitation. In introducing new concepts, the leader is most likely to be training, that is, disseminating information and ensuring learning by the participants. But in building managers' coaching and feedback skills, the process requires facilitation because the best outcomes result from drawing out and building on the awareness and skills the manager already has. Managers come to this process with tremendous variations in levels of readiness, skill, and willingness to support the development of others. The facilitator must model the very behavior expected of participants and address their various needs. When dealing with human behavior, there is no one answer, so a facilitator must be skilled at coaching and feedback in the session itself to contribute to learning from real examples and from needs managers bring to the training.

Development Needs

Just as other employees and managers at all levels of the organization need to be building their own development plans, so too do those responsible for coordinating the design and implementation of the career development process. Change agents, like any other employees, need to ensure flexibility by building skills in areas not previously in their job descriptions. Some may find they are strong project managers who can shepherd the process through all sorts of pitfalls, but they are not as skilled in the change management or facilitation process. These people need to identify development actions in those realms for themselves. Others may be strong in the delivery of career development training or counseling, but not as good in the big-picture strategy planning of a comprehensive process that links to broader HR systems. Their growth may require taking on some of the planning processes, perhaps initially under the tutelage of a consultant or colleague who demonstrates these strengths.

Generalists who are managing the development implementation need competencies in the areas of organizational understanding, adult learning, consulting, communication and feedback, organizational behavior, group processes, marketing, presentation, negotiation, and computer skills. The ability to project trends and visualize positive outcomes, sometimes called *futuring*, is another important competency needed. This may be a tall order, but it is no greater a demand than that being asked of managers and employees, who must build new skills, change attitudes, and participate in continuous learning. All are required to successfully create a development culture.

8   Career Advisors

If you don't know where you're going,
you might end up somewhere else.
—Casey Stengel

Career Specialist Versus Manager

There are a variety of roles for career specialists in an organizational career development program. The most successful outcomes will be attained by using career specialists as a supplement rather than a replacement for managers. While managers have day-to-day contact with employees, specialists have particular training or a targeted focus in the field. They may be professional career counselors, career advisors selected and trained for the role, trainers who focus on career development, or even personnel from an information systems department who link with a career specialist to produce virtual resources for employees. Mentors who are trained and supported in the development process can also add strength to an overall development program, as discussed in Chapter 9.

    Career specialists may be internal employees who have the advantage of knowing the company and the issues affecting people's careers, or external consultants or counselors with the advantage of professional training in the field and objectivity and confidentiality in dealing with employees' career issues. Although manager involvement in career discussions is crucial, there will be issues and situations beyond managers' capability or function. For example, an employee who doesn't fit in the manager's unit may not know where else in the organization his or her interests and skills fit. It isn't up to a manager to do the research for the individual, and sometimes, especially in a large or changing organization, it is difficult for an employee to do it alone. A career advisor or career counselor can provide counseling and research assistance for a major career change, perhaps saving a good employee for the company and launching the individual on a more successful track.

Employees typically prefer discussing moves away from their manager's area with an advisor or mentor rather than with the manager, especially if friction with the manager is driving the employee's need for a move. A mentor or advisor can often provide a broader perspective on the organization's needs or developments in another unit of interest as well.

Organizational information is an important part of career planning, but it can be addressed by means other than a formal career specialist role. If having a person in this capacity does not fit in your culture or budget, there are informal ways to involve senior professionals or managers to coach and advise individuals who are not their direct reports. Increasingly, there are formal and informal mentoring programs initiated to supplement managers' roles in supporting employee development, as addressed in Chapter 9.

Particularly in a career development process, employees may need to talk to someone confidentially about career issues. If they have a superb relationship with their manager or a mentor, some may be able to discuss sensitive concerns or needs with that person, but on occasion people need an objective professional view. There will be times, even in the best environments, when an individual clashes with his or her manager, or when the manager is the reason career actions are needed. In these cases, employees are likely to seek help or advice from human resources representatives.

Especially in organizations without other career development support or resources, many HR professionals are put in the role of career advisor. This is like putting a finger in the dike of a flood of needs. In a comprehensive system such as the one proposed in this book, the career advisor has a more defined and supportive role in the career development alliance. The role of career advisors is not to replace managers in developing employees; rather, it is to supplement and offer more in-depth assessment assistance than can reasonably be expected of managers. In addition, they can provide a broader perspective than most managers, whose expertise is largely confined to their own units, and can also provide access to resources about opportunities in the company as a whole.

Managers provide support and opportunities for growth. Their role is to coach and provide feedback about performance on the present job and advise and provide opportunities to achieve goals. Career advisors provide unbiased assistance to individuals for career planning within the organization. Their role is to provide assessment interpretation, counseling, feedback, advising, access to resources, mediation, and decision support.

Contractor Versus Internal Advisor

Career advising can be defined as providing guidance and information and making recommendations regarding a decision or course of conduct that affects an employee's work and career. It needs to be distinguished from career counseling, which is provided by a professional counselor utilizing psychological methods and testing. "The term *counselor* implies—and in many states requires—professional training and certification in the field. [In some environments,] employees may negatively equate counseling with therapy, something they may think they neither need nor want" (Simonsen, 1995).

Some organizations prefer to use outside counselors who have professional credentials and experience in career counseling. A major rationale for this is the issue of confidentiality. A resource who is not an employee has no loyalty to or political connections with the company and is thus potentially less threatening to employees. Employees also tend to believe that a counselor can be more objective. A master's-degreed counselor also can administer and interpret assessments not available to a human resources professional.

The disadvantages of using outsiders are that they do not know the business, nor do they have firsthand knowledge of the type of work done in various departments and established networks for referrals or information. So a contractor needs training and orientation to the business needs and organizational information, while an internal advisor typically needs training in the advising process and counseling skills.

Career Advising Competencies

Function of the Career Advisor

Before you decide on the background appropriate for advisors in your organization, define the functions they will need to perform; some typical ones are identified in Table 16.

Table 16

Career Advisors' Functions

- Providing assistance to individuals for career planning within the organization
- Conducting formal and informal individual assessments and interpretation
- Identifying relevant written resources and making information available to employees
- Identifying and coordinating organizational resources, such as contacts, networks, or executive briefings
- Making referrals to external resources, such as counseling, testing, training, or outplacement services, as appropriate
- Providing support to managers for career discussions or coaching with their employees
- Gathering demographic data regarding the needs of the organization, departments, or individuals
- Consulting management on decisions affected by or affecting employee retention and development

---

From "Basics of Career Advising," by P. Simonsen. *InfoLine,* April 1995, p. 9. Reprinted with permission.

If the function of the career advisor is primarily to conduct assessments because individuals are not in tune with their skills and limitations, and managers are not very good at coaching and providing feedback, it may be wise to hire an external counselor. If, on the other hand, the function is to serve primarily as a resource for individuals who want to make internal moves, find resources for development planning, or deal with limited opportunities, perhaps an internal human resources specialist would be better. In either case, both need training to be able to provide a full range of assistance.

Skills Needed for Career Advising

There are a number of skills that career advisors need to be effective. People with good human relations skills have the basics of many of these, but competencies may need to be focused or expanded to successfully address the range of needs employees bring to the advisor. As described in the sections below (from Simonsen, 1995), skills are needed by advisors in coaching and diagnosing to assist employees with self-assessment, in providing reality testing for viable goals and plans, and in goal setting and motivating to action.

Coaching   Advisors need to coach employees in career development decisions. Good coaching involves the following skills:

- Establishing open communication with employees
- Encouraging employees to share insights or the results of their self-assessments
- Listening rather than talking
- Probing to understand employees' values, interests, skills, and needs
- Identifying additional assessment needs that employees may have
- Focusing on the issues important to the employee

Diagnosing   Advisors may not know the employee who comes to them for help. Yet the advisors need to determine what real issues or problems employees may have. Diagnosing involves the following skills:

- Dealing with emotional issues and providing emotional support before addressing any career issues
- Withholding judgment of the problem until it is clearly diagnosed
- Forming a hypothesis about the problem and using appropriate questioning techniques to identify the real issues
- Remaining objective and not acting on personal biases

Reality Testing   Advisors can be an important source for reality testing, providing feedback in an environment where no one else "tells it like it is." They can also reinforce feedback that an employee may have received from managers or other sources. Reality testing involves the following skills:

- Maintaining a developmental approach as opposed to an evaluative one
- Helping employees understand how present performance affects future opportunities
- Defining strengths, weaknesses, and developmental needs
- Helping employees recognize the importance of their reputation
- Assessing the viability of goals and action plans
- Providing support and "prodding" as needed

Goal Setting   Advisors can play a key role in formalizing employees' career goals. Most people, even when they have completed a thorough assessment process, still need help defining and writing viable goals. But when employees are expected to pursue multiple goals, or goals for development rather than a move, they typically need help. Goal-setting assistance involves the following skills:

- Helping employees define viable career goals based on their preliminary assessment and planning
- Helping employees write specific, measurable, positive goals
- Analyzing employees' goals to determine action steps
- Providing reality testing when goals are unrealistic

Motivating to Action   Depending on how the advising function is designed, advisors may have ongoing contact with advisees, encouraging and supporting their progress. This may include the following skills:

- Determining developmental actions to help employees reach their goals
- Completing a written development plan as a communication tool, a working document, and a record of developmental actions
- Identifying barriers and figuring out ways to overcome them
- Offering encouragement and prodding to keep employees moving ahead
- Celebrating successes

The following case example illustrates how one company recognized the need for skilled career advisors:

With pressure looming for billable time, a consulting organization decided that managers' time needed to be spent with clients rather than in coaching employees on career development issues. In addition, employees were often working on more than one project, off site most of the time, so managers weren't closely in touch with their work. With a traditional partnership structure, the emphasis was on moving either "up or out." The expectation for development had always been up, even though in a flatter organization that was no longer realistic.

When employees had career needs, the only resource available was recruiters. The recruiters knew what positions were open and so were able to provide that information in response to inquiries. However, no other career advising process was in place, so "next job" information was all employees got, even when their issues revolved around other needs, such as how to balance intensive work weeks with personal lives or build skills needed to be more successful on the present job. Many employees' efforts to change positions had been unsuccessful because there had been no self-assessment to determine the right job fit, there was no effort made for career focus to determine how one's skills matched with position requirements, and no goals or development plans were in place. The process reinforced employees' unrealistic expectations that career development meant promotions; it also neglected the need to implement active development plans to meet changing business needs and customer demands.

Because of these dynamics, career development project managers decided to implement a career advising function rather than expect managers to play an active role in employee career development. They selected human resources professionals with generalist, employee relations, and recruiting backgrounds to be trained as advisors. People with generalist or employee relations backgrounds quickly demonstrated the skills necessary for good advising. But the recruiters, firmly stuck in their experience of helping people make moves, took longer to internalize the development message and to prepare to help employees with broader development planning. Once the advisors really understood that employees needed to work through assessment, career focus, and goal setting before thinking about which positions were open, they began to build appropriate skills needed to reeducate employees away from next-job thinking and toward ongoing development planning.

Career Development Concepts

In addition to career advising competencies, advisors require knowledge about career development concepts, including the importance of work values to career development planning and success, how to link goals to the direction and needs of the organization, providing information, and general organizational savvy. As with skills, some areas of knowledge may not need to be tapped if managers are doing a good job of advising and providing information about the organization and if there is a system for ensuring linkage of individual goals with the strategic direction and business objectives. The topics listed below should be part of any career advisor's knowledge base (from Simonsen, 1995).

Importance of Work Values   While there are many assessment instruments available to measure *interests*, the value of understanding *work values* has been underrated. Work values are the core elements that determine work satisfaction or dissatisfaction, motivation and preferences, and alignment with the organization's values. Advisors should know the following:

- How values influence job satisfaction and success
- Which important values are missing in an employee's work and which unwanted circumstances are present

- Ways to help advisees identify and clarify their values
- Differences between exploring values ("What is important to you about your work?") and identifying interests ("What kinds of things do you like to do?")

Advisors can ask employees specific questions such as these to help them clarify their work values:

- What gives you satisfaction from your work?
- Which work values are most important to your satisfaction on the job?
- Of those, which are not being sufficiently met in your present job?
- How can you meet your top work values here?

Linking Goals   A typical objection to career development initiatives in organizations is that career planning will raise unrealistic expectations. However, effective career advising must realistically link individuals' career goals with the direction and needs of the organization. Advisors need to state clearly the importance of this linkage and help advisees plan accordingly. Specifically, advisors should understand the importance of the following:

- Balancing individuals' wants with organizational needs
- Knowing the strategic direction of the company and making sure employees' goals contribute to that end
- Targeting organizational competencies by job families or levels rather than by jobs or positions that can change

Providing Information   Once employees have completed their self-assessment, they often need help finding and evaluating information about the organization. Once they get this information, some employees still need help navigating the organization to use the information. Providing information includes the following:

- Knowing about positions, departments, trends, and requirements, or knowing where to find such information
- Understanding the strategic direction of the organization
- Understanding and communicating the policies and procedures for the company's staffing, training, compensation, and personnel selection
- Having or building networks
- Helping employees understand the dynamics and culture of the organization
- Communicating organizational realities such as limitations and opportunities

Organizational Savvy   With newer employees (and even with some long-timers), advisors need to communicate any informal organizational systems critical to career advancement and opportunities. These include the following:

■ Industry and organizational trends and issues that may affect career development
■ Importance of reputation and sponsors in achieving career goals
■ How to build a network using appropriate protocols
■ Behaviors valued in the informal organizational culture that contribute to success

The Career Advising Process

Regardless of whether you decide to (1) develop advising skills within your organization to supplement an integrated career development process or as a major resource for employees or (2) hire a professional career counselor, you will need to determine the best process. Which approach will best contribute to the development culture you are building? In a development culture, advisors do not replace managers in the role of supporting employee development. Employees may receive some much-needed help from an advisor in managing their careers, but a development culture cannot be built without managers' active involvement.

In designing an advising process, you will need to determine the way the process will work and how and where the services will be provided. Will advising sessions be open to everyone, or will people first need to participate in orientation sessions or workshops? By having people first participate in a group session, general information can be shared about expectations, roles and responsibilities, and available resources. Participants can take part in some interactive assessment exercises and receive general organizational information. This makes the advising process more efficient and individualized. Will users first need to complete some self-directed work that will contribute to a richer discussion with an advisor? It is useful to design a model or process chart so everyone understands the total career development process and where advising fits in. Figure 11 is an example of this type of model or chart.

You may need to make some policy and procedure decisions about the advising services. Will employees be able to use the help on company time, or only during nonwork hours? How will communication and reporting be handled to balance confidentiality for the client with

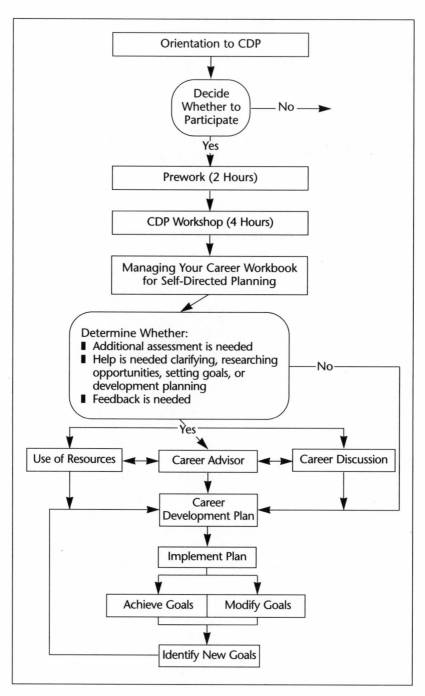

Figure 11   Career Development Planning (CDP) Process

accountability and quality measures for the advising function? What kind of records need to be kept? Usually advisors will keep demographic data (age, department, gender, and so forth) on users, but names are not openly available. This information may be gathered on intake forms and then transferred to a database. Advisors may want to track the type of assistance requested, average number or range of sessions with the advisor, or feedback from clients.

How will services be funded? It is not a good idea to require permission from someone's manager to use career services, because the need for services may in fact be caused by the relationship with the person's manager. What will be the relationship between advisor and manager? What if a manager sends an employee to the advisor to deal with issues beyond the realm of the manager? Should an advisor intervene if there are development issues between employee and manager? Be careful to clarify the difference between an employee relations function and the career advising function.

Another consideration is the communication and marketing of advising services. Working with an advisor should not be seen as an indication of trouble with one's job, or the process will quickly become suspect. If previous individual assistance consisted of outplacement services, a major marketing process will be needed to distinguish and "legitimize" career advising. Employees will not use the service, or will only do so surreptitiously, if there is a public perception that there is something wrong with them if they need counseling. This issue may determine where advisors are housed. A career center with a variety of resources that is in an atmosphere where everyone is expected to write and implement development plans and to have responsibility for supporting a development culture will not have an image problem. If the goal of the total career development process is *strategic career management,* that is, to help people develop in ways that meet their own goals while contributing to the needs of the organization, it is desirable to encourage open use of any resources to assist in reaching the goal.

The Career Discussion

The function of the career discussion itself is critical to the success of the career advising process. As in a career discussion with one's manager, having a framework for the discussion, understood by both advisee and advisor, will reinforce the process and prevent misunderstandings about outcomes or roles (see Table 13, p. 123).

Some action-oriented employees will come to an advisor asking for immediate answers: "What do I have to do to get promoted?" or "How can I get a job in a different department?" In effect, they are starting at step 3 of Table 13, the advising role of offering information and advice. It is difficult for anyone to offer meaningful advice as a starting point, without knowing the employee's issues, concerns, and self-assessment results.

So the career discussion needs to start with coaching in order to clarify or at least communicate the employee's desired work characteristics—what he or she wants and why the employee is seeking help. This step in the process does not need to be lengthy if the employee has done some preparation and clarification on his or her own or in a group session. If the employee has not, then more time needs to be spent in the coaching process before moving on to advice. Without this step, employees are likely to pursue inappropriate options, be unsuccessful in their attempts at development opportunities, or take action that doesn't bring about their desired outcome.

Some other employees may get bogged down in the assessment process, wanting more and more assessment tools or too many counseling sessions. They may need to be pushed to action by moving them through the steps of the career discussion framework. The model for individual career development planning discussed in Chapter 12 might be a useful tool to help clarify things.

In a development culture, individuals could come in to an advisor with a set of goals based on solid planning and a useful career discussion with their manager. They may be asking for organizational information or development planning options to meet their goals. In these cases, the advisor still needs to be brought up to date on the individual's plans, but most of the time will be spent on moving the advisee forward with information or resources he or she has requested.

So career discussions will vary, driven by the level of preparation by advisees, the type of needs they have, and the prior involvement of their manager. Whatever the readiness level, the framework for career discussions provides a useful model for both advisees and advisors to structure the career discussion for the most efficient and effective outcomes.

Handling Diverse Needs

Career advising is likely to uncover more diverse needs than the career discussion between employee and manager. Employees may come to an advisor with emotion-laden issues. Advisors must be able to respond to the emotions before trying to deal with the underlying issues. For example, when frustrated, employees tend to want to move away from their present situation rather than proactively moving toward a selected goal. Their frustration will make them impatient, perhaps ornery, and probably blaming of their manager, the company, their co-workers, or all of the above. Before any rational planning can occur, the advisor and the employee must deal with the frustration and its cause. This requires coaching and counseling skills as well as time. If the advising session is less than forty-five minutes, any help will likely be disjointed, with unfinished discussions carried from one session to another.

Advisors cannot be all business and information, but must be prepared to handle diverse needs. If all they do is provide organizational information, they will be seen more as administrators or librarians than as advisors. Even when employees come in asking for answers, advisors must deflect the question until they understand the real needs driving the employee. For example, an employee's presenting problem might be, "I'm tired of my job—what else is there?" The wrong answer would be a response like the traditional one of recruiters such as those in the consulting firm case example on page 148: "Well, let's see what's available." Instead, advisors need to employ good coaching skills to question, listen, draw out, and explore the issues underlying "tired of my job."

We recommend the advisor form and test a hypothesis before coming to conclusions. Quick answers to presenting questions are seldom right, and may even cause the employee to distrust or argue with the suggestion. This leads to "yes, but . . ." responses: The advisor makes a suggestion, and the employee sees something wrong with it and says, "Yes, but. . . ." Instead, the advisor needs to listen and probe to determine the issues underlying the employee's surface statements. If the advisor is forming an unspoken hypothesis, he or she can direct questions to confirm or change the assumption. When it is appropriate, the advisor shares the hypothesis with the employee, along with reasons for forming it, and discusses the individual's perspective (Career Directions, 1993).

It is critical that advisors not infuse their own values into the advising process. In our manager training, we caution managers about that as well, but they are in a position to expect or reward certain kinds of behaviors. Advisors are not and should not be evaluating employees. An advisor needs to be an objective sounding board, a coach, sometimes a mentor, perhaps a referral agent—but never an evaluator of individual performance or values. The closest advisors come to evaluating is in reality testing and giving feedback. This is a useful role advisors play, because often they are filling a void created by lack of feedback from managers. When naysayers object to career development because it might raise unrealistic expectations, it is a red flag that there is not enough or honest feedback in that environment. One responsibility of the advisor is to ensure that the employee gets useful feedback, either by coaching the employee to seek feedback on performance and reputation from his or her manager or by providing feedback on topics relevant to the career discussions between employee and advisor. But such feedback should always be developmental—provided to help employees overcome personal or organizational barriers in order to achieve their goals.

Advisors may also need to be alert to cultural or ethnic differences. The whole issue of "promoting oneself" by self-assessment or communicating accomplishments is contrary to the privacy or modesty mores of some ethnic groups. Equal opportunity or discrimination perceptions will occasionally be a concern in career planning. When lifestyle issues surface for individuals, these may be brought to an advisor rather than discussed with a manager. Employees often ask, "Won't I be negatively influencing my manager's opinion of me if I tell him or her that my outside responsibilities or interests are more important to me than my job is?" They might prefer to discuss these issues in confidence with an advisor and be ready to communicate them to their manager only after goals are determined.

There is the potential for dependency by the employee on the advisor. Some needy individuals will show up often "just to talk," and perhaps never take action. Some individuals will expect magic—they want the advisor to solve their career dilemmas for them without any effort on their part. Others may share noncareer issues such as family problems that are beyond the scope of the advising function. So the parameters of the advising function must be clearly communicated, and advisors must be clear about their role, the limits of their services to individuals, and approaches to take when people overextend the process. If a counseling referral is appropriate, advisors need to be informed about employee assistance or external resources and when to use them. It is wise to communicate with other services during the planning of resources so employees are clear about the advising role and understand the differences.

The career advising function, in addition to the other components and resources already discussed, contributes to the development culture. When confidentiality is an issue or a company is too small to support regular time from an external counselor, some organizations refer their employees to local career counselors whose services are targeted to the needs of the individual and the outcomes expected by the company. For example, a good employee may be in the wrong job, as determined by herself, her manager, or emerging performance problems. Rather than fire her, the company may choose to refer her to external career counseling to assess the needs and determine a plan of action. Another person, either newly promoted or being groomed for greater opportunity, might be referred to an external counselor for coaching and to create a development plan. These services are less likely to be needed if the organization has a comprehensive development process with managers actively involved, but in many instances, a selection of resources is the chosen approach.

As you contribute to the design of a comprehensive career development process for your organization, consider carefully the role of career advisors. By themselves, they cannot build a development culture, but they can be a resource to help in the transition until every employee is taking responsibility for his or her own career management and every supervisor and manager is truly supporting employee development.

9 Mentors

Wherever there are beginners and experts, old and young, there is some kind of learning going on, and some sort of teaching. We are all pupils and we are all teachers.
—Gilbert Highet, *The Art of Teaching*

Institutionalizing the Development Mind-Set

Mentoring relationships are typically a contributing element in a development culture. Whether a formalized process or spontaneous, mentoring provides an ongoing approach to development for individuals. When an organization provides a facilitated mentoring process, the message is communicated that it values the insight and organizational knowledge of the mentors and encourages open communication and learning by mentorees.

Mentors are not external consultants or counselors, not a separate functional unit like human resources, but respected managers or senior professionals in business units. The mentoring relationship is not part of an annual process required of managers and employees as performance management typically is. As a voluntary process, mentoring requires initiative on the part of both mentor and mentoree. (The term *mentoree* instead of the traditional *protégé* is used because the latter implies a dependent, subordinate relationship—not the message needed in a development culture, where emphasis is on independence and initiative and away from the sense that someone else will take care of good employees.)

Mentoring is a mutually beneficial relationship that gives the mentoree access to the expertise and experience of the mentor for self-development and career management. It provides the mentor with an opportunity to contribute to the development of others.

Mentors are valued for the following:

- Showing employees the ropes
- Communicating the organizational culture and protocol
- Recommending developmental actions that may be broader than those needed for the present job
- Referring mentorees to their network for broader visibility
- Being employee advocates

Facilitated mentoring is defined by Margo Murray (1991) as "a structure and series of processes designed to create effective mentoring relationships, guide the desired behavior change of those involved, [and] evaluate the results for the protégés, the mentors, and the organization." Facilitated mentoring benefits the organization and contributes to a development culture in the following ways:

Improved performance. Mentorees' performance can be increased by greater motivation, performance planning and improvement, increased teamwork, and greater accomplishments. Mentoring relationships can be very results oriented, with motivation and accountability by the mentoree.

Cost effectiveness. Additional staff isn't necessary, and time spent in development discussions by mentors and mentorees typically pays off in greater dividends than the time and cost of classroom training. Developmental activities recommended or supported by the mentor are likely to be very relevant to the developmental needs of the individual and can add more value to his or her role in the organization.

Increased organizational communication and understanding. In times when organizations are trying to lower the walls of divisional or functional silos, a mentor in another business unit or department opens lines of communication. Mentorees gain access to information about development opportunities and needs in other areas and also build a broader base of understanding to make a greater, or more flexible, contribution to the organization.

Becoming a development opportunity. Respected individuals who have stores of organizational knowledge to relate often find the role of mentor an opportunity to make a greater difference than their regular job provides. Especially in flatter organizations in which the opportunity to move higher to positions with broader impact is limited, being a mentor can be developmental. Besides, long-time employees may benefit from a new perspective brought by younger mentorees.

Sponsoring development for succession planning. As layers of management have been eliminated in many organizations, decision makers are finding that they have no systematic way to prepare future leaders. Mentoring can ensure development to meet future business needs as well as to improve performance on the present job, which is likely to be the focus of an individual's manager.

Facilitated mentoring expands the opportunities for mentorees who might not be sought out by a mentor if left to informal relationships. With the overall focus on individual development, the process communicates that the organization is serious about expecting and providing support for individual development efforts.

Mentoring Responsibilities

The mentoring relationship is one of "trust and respect between two individuals who are interacting for their mutual benefit to reach some agreed-upon goals that focus on development and learning. The relationship requires an investment of time and effort for both participants, the mentor and mentoree" (Career Directions, Inc., 1996a).

Mentors—typically managers or experienced individual contributors—are role models who are themselves high performers, believe in a development culture, and want to make a contribution. Career Directions, Inc., (1996a), in a mentoring training program, defined ideal mentors as people who

- Care about and respect others
- Feel secure about themselves and are not threatened by the success of others
- Are trustworthy and trust others
- Know and believe in the organization's mission, goals, values, and policies and also value their own work
- Possess personal power and prestige
- Are open and innovative, patient and tolerant
- Can tolerate ambiguities and are willing to take risks

Table 17

Mentor's Responsibilities

- Making time available to the mentoree and establishing a climate of open interaction
- Setting realistic expectations and working with the mentoree to set realistic goals and appropriate action plans
- Listening to and being openminded about the mentoree's ideas and opinions
- Working to foster the relationship
- Offering challenging ideas and providing growth experiences
- Encouraging professional behavior and confronting negative intentions, behaviors, or attitudes
- Helping to identify obstacles and exploring ways to overcome them
- Offering encouragement and standing by the mentoree in critical situations
- Offering wise counsel and identifying appropriate resources
- Triggering self-awareness and providing genuine confidence-building insights and experiences
- Sharing critical knowledge and insights into organizational realities
- Encouraging mentoree to explore options

From *Mentoring: Focus on Career Development,* 1996. Rolling Meadows, IL: Career Directions, Inc.

- Have an extensive network of resources, both within the organization and outside of it
- Are committed to staff development
- Are willing and able to demonstrate leadership

The mentoring relationship is one of responsibilities shared by the mentor, the mentoree, the mentoree's manager, and the organization. These responsibilities include those listed in Table 17.

In a development culture, mentorees play an active role in managing their own development, and share responsibilities with their mentor. The mentoree's responsibilities are listed in Table 18.

It is essential when introducing a mentoring process not to imply that managers are being replaced, or to allow managers and supervisors to abdicate their responsibilities in developing their employees, even when the individuals are also benefiting from a mentor's guidance. Managers may be mentors to individuals who don't report to them, but still must

Table 18

Mentoree's Responsibilities

- Assuming responsibility for his or her own growth and development
- Being willing to write goals and to stay goal oriented
- Actively seeking challenging assignments, greater responsibility, new experiences, and learning opportunities
- Working to foster the mentoring relationship
- Clearly communicating problems as well as possible solutions
- Being open and sincere about needs and feelings
- Remaining receptive to feedback and coaching
- Learning to adapt to change
- Understanding the protocol of the mentoring relationship and maintaining appropriate behavior
- Knowing how to maintain confidentiality

From *Mentoring: Focus on Career Development,* 1996. Rolling Meadows, IL: Career Directions, Inc.

be involved in coaching and developing employees about performance on the job. The manager's responsibilities in the mentoring process are listed in Table 19.

The organizational environment for a development culture also contributes to successful mentoring. The organization is responsible for establishing the mentoring program and setting guidelines for it, including those listed in Table 20.

Mentoring Competencies

Mentors typically need to be volunteers who are trained in the expectations of the role as well as in the skills needed for coaching. The framework for the discussion recommended for advisors in Table 13 (see p. 123) is useful for mentors as well. There are a number of skills that mentors need to be effective in the process. Good communication and human relations skills form the foundation of mentoring competencies. While contributing to the development of others, mentors can focus on their own development as well. Career Directions (1996b) provides a list of the skills needed by mentors, which is included in the following sections.

Table 19

Manager's Responsibilities

- Understanding the benefits for all involved in the program as well as for the organization
- Knowing the purpose and goals of the mentoring program
- Participating in orientation and training sessions for the mentoring program in order to better understand and support it
- Clarifying what is acceptable time away from the job
- Being flexible and keeping an open mind
- Continuing to fulfill the role of supervisor/manager in providing feedback, coaching, on-the-job training, and so forth
- Appreciating the mentoree's developmental attitude and offering help when appropriate
- Keeping the lines of communication open between manager and mentoree and manager and mentor

From *Mentoring: Focus on Career Development*, 1996. Rolling Meadows, IL: Career Directions, Inc.

Interpersonal Skills

Mentors need interpersonal skills to build and maintain the relationship, perhaps with individuals who have backgrounds quite different from their own. Interpersonal skills include the following:

- *Establishing rapport*—building a comfort level in working with mentorees
- *Collaborating*—contributing as part of a team, accepting and supporting others' ideas
- *Resolving conflict*—managing differences of opinion effectively to facilitate win-win solutions

Communication Skills

Much of the mentor–mentoree relationship is based on clarity of understanding and straight talk. This involves the following skills:

- *Active listening*—paying full attention to the meaning and feelings behind another's words

Table 20

Organization's Responsibilities

- Communicating the program goals and the guidelines to all
- Gaining commitment from those proposing to be mentors
- Establishing a selection process to the mentoring program that provides and allows choices
- Providing orientation and training for those involved in the program
- Actively supporting the program and individual mentoring relationships
- Providing resources for those in the program
- Monitoring and evaluating the program
- Responding quickly to any problems that arise
- Permitting withdrawal from the program

From *Mentoring: Focus on Career Development,* 1996. Rolling Meadows, IL: Career Directions, Inc.

- *Giving feedback*—communicating one's perceptions in a way that maintains self-esteem
- *Speaking clearly and effectively*—articulating thoughts and getting the point across in oral communication

Leadership Skills

Mentors are role models, and as such they demonstrate the leadership that is desired as a result of development or opportunity to contribute. Leadership skills include the following:

- *Providing direction*—making appropriate recommendations for decisions or actions
- *Motivating others*—providing encouragement and reinforcement in line with an individual's own motivators
- *Championing change*—seeking out, initiating, supporting, and managing change or new organizational strategies
- *Valuing diversity*—avoiding prejudging those who are different in some way, and actively involving them in organizational activities
- *Leveraging networks*—building informal networks across functions or externally

Business Skills

One expectation mentorees often have of mentors is help in learning the organization, understanding the culture, and gaining savvy not easily learned except through experience. The business skills needed include the following:

- *Knowing the business*—keeping up-to-date on work requirements and new developments and how they affect the organization
- *Organizational savvy*—keeping up-to-date on organizational goals, trends, culture, and needs

Problem-Solving Skills

Positive results occur when mentorees can bring work or relationship problems to a mentor and both can use good problem-solving skills to determine an appropriate course of action. Skills needed for problem solving include the following:

- *Diagnosing the problem*—defining the issues at hand and identifying the cause, symptoms, and possible solutions
- *Identifying and analyzing alternatives*—developing multiple alternatives to increase the quality of the solution
- *Making sound decisions*—maximizing the positive outcome or minimizing negative outcomes
- *Taking action*—implementing agreed-upon solutions, measuring results, and making adjustments if necessary

In addition to the characteristics of ideal mentors listed above and the skills needed for mentoring, Shea (1994) identifies behaviors to avoid:

- *Giving advice.* A "You should . . ." approach can encourage dependency. Rather than telling mentorees what to do, skilled mentors listen and encourage them in their problem solving and decision making. Educating on why things are done can help the mentoree learn and apply the knowledge in the future.
- *Criticizing.* Mentors do have the role of giving feedback, but factual information about a situation followed by discussion of the desired outcome will yield better results than criticism.
- *Rescuing.* Mentors can help mentorees learn from their mistakes, see patterns of behavior that contribute to problems, and define behaviors

to change. But rescuing—taking responsibility for solving a problem the mentoree has caused—leads to dependency.

■ *Sponsoring*. In the old mentor-protégé relationship, it was common for the mentor to negotiate special treatment for the protégé, as a confirmation of the mentor's power. In a development culture, the mentor should help the mentoree to be ready for opportunities, and build networks to open doors for themselves.

The Mentoring Process

A selection process is typically used to determine who will be mentors and, in some organizations, who will be mentored. The simpler the process and the less structure imposed by the organization, the more likely mentoring will become an ongoing means of development. The process should not require extensive administration. Having fewer qualifying criteria eliminates the need for lengthy sessions to determine which volunteers should be allowed to participate.

In some organizations with a historical lack of trust between individuals and management or anyone in authority, there is a need to avoid the perception that the process is unfair or favors a chosen few. If criteria and responsibilities for mentorees and mentors are developed and communicated, individuals who are interested and feel they meet these characteristics can volunteer to participate. Success factors critical to the facilitated mentoring process include the following:

■ Ease of administration
■ Perception that the process is fair
■ Support of supervisors/managers
■ Ongoing rather than short-term participation
■ Realistic expectations of the process on the part of mentorees

One approach to establishing a mentoring process includes selection and training of mentors, orientation for mentorees, and a list of mentors for mentorees to choose from. The key to a successful mentoring relationship is establishment of a comfort level by both parties; arbitrary pairing, or even planned pairing by a third party, can often cause difficulty.

In this process, since individuals seek their own choice of a mentor, there is no perception of unfairness in selection or pairing. Once mentors are selected and trained, there is little administration required. However, because it is possible that some mentors may be chosen by more mentorees than they have time for, some individuals may have to be turned down. There is also the possibility that some mentors are not selected, causing them to lose interest. A modified approach is for the administrator to match the mentoree with one of three mentors they select, so there is better distribution of mentorees with mentors. In some organizations, pairing is done by an administrator based on employees' goals and mentors' areas of expertise. This process runs the risk of a partnering without rapport, which prevents building an ongoing relationship, and also requires more administration and therefore less individual choice.

In any process, it is wise to create a mentoring agreement with no-fault exits by either party. Facilitated mentoring does not generate spontaneous relationships, so participants need to understand that the roles may be short-term or may last longer.

Training for mentors and mentorees is valuable. You can conduct an orientation for all who are interested in the process before they decide to participate. This provides awareness of the process—what it is and what it is not—and clarification of responsibilities and qualifications. (Usually the only qualification for mentorees in an open program is acceptable performance on the present job. Mentoring is not intended to be a remedial process or to take the place of performance management.) An orientation can also provide information about how the process will work and how much time it will take. Once volunteer mentors are selected, they can benefit from training in the following areas:

- Establishing the relationship
- Valuing diversity
- Coaching, feedback, and other mentoring skills
- Discussion about potential pitfalls
- Possibilities for defining and creating developmental suggestions for mentorees

A successful mentoring process contributes to a development culture by expanding the ways employees manage their growth and development. Employees recognize that their mentor does not have a magic wand to make things happen for them, but that together they can continue to add value to the organization, which values their contribution. Mentorees appreciate the direction and perspective of a good mentor, and mentors have the opportunity to contribute their knowledge and wisdom for the development and success of another individual.

As you consider all the roles that contribute to a development culture, consider the value that a facilitated mentoring process adds to the organization. Mentors by themselves cannot create a development culture; however, along with managers, employees, and other resources, they can infuse energy and direction into the ongoing efforts to change behaviors that result in a development culture.

The Development Advisory Team

Friendly counsel cuts off many foes.
—Shakespeare

Contributions of the Advisory Team

Building a development culture obviously cannot be accomplished by one individual, no matter how skilled or enthusiastic. A supportive team can make a major contribution to the planning, design, implementation, and evaluation of an ongoing change process. It is essential to have as broad a base of support for the change effort as can be garnered; a diverse advisory group representing various stakeholders can help build that support. Advisory teams have varying levels of decision-making authority, depending on the organizational level of their members and the control needed by the persons who chartered the group.

Advisory teams can be used for many purposes in the planning, design, and implementation stages of the change process:

▌ Envisioning the desired future state of a development culture (as described in Chapter 3)
▌ Defining a mission and philosophy of development for the organization (discussed in Chapter 11)
▌ Keeping a finger on the pulse of organizational needs
▌ Representing various areas, levels, and the diversity of the organization

▌ Identifying stakeholders' expectations of a development culture and objections to change
▌ Gathering data as a basis of a development process
▌ Giving feedback and critiquing elements of the design process
▌ Serving as a liaison between internal or external consultants and the rest of the organization
▌ Linking with other change agents and intervention teams in operation concurrently
▌ Determining success indicators and measurements
▌ Developing action plans to move the process forward
▌ Contributing to implementation
▌ Promoting the process
▌ Building support coalitions

Task Force Versus Advisory Team

There are differences between an advisory team and a task force. The task force may be self-directed, and its members may need to become subject matter experts and skilled implementers. They are likely to commit extensive time to do all the work, sometimes in unfamiliar territory, and much of their effort becomes trial and error while they learn. The advisory group, however, works with subject matter experts or a project manager or consultant so as to not have to start from scratch in their learning. The advisory group provides organizational perspective on plans and makes group decisions on key issues. Instead of implementing, they advise and support. The differences are illustrated in the following case example:

A division of a manufacturing company established a career development task force to respond to concerns expressed on an employee opinion survey about lack of development opportunities. The task force was made up of employee representatives of various constituent groups—manufacturing, support staff, engineering, information systems, and human resources. Although the task force reported to the human resources director, they operated very autonomously. The group met regularly for a year to define career development, identify what that meant in their culture, define the changes in employee attitudes necessary in a changing environment, and generally learn about organizational career development. Their efforts resulted in a career development booklet that outlined employees' responsibilities for managing their careers and identified existing resources. The content was good—it represented the research that the task force had conducted about the new paradigm needed for career development in today's organizations.

The task force distributed the booklet to all employees but were disappointed and frustrated when they got very little response to the booklet and there appeared to be little change in employee attitudes about career development in the organization. At this point, the human resources manager called in consultants to work with the group. The consultants worked with the task force to become an advisory team. Although their work became the basis of a more comprehensive system, the former task force had spent an undue amount of time achieving limited outcomes. With help from the experts, the new advisory team made decisions about a career development process that included a communication strategy, orientation for all employees and managers, a workshop and career advisor for self-assessment and career planning, demographic data about company human resources needs, and beginning plans to train managers in effective career discussions. The advisory group was able to affect behavior in the organization. Employees began to participate in the career development process and implement development plans—the very changes in behavior the group had anticipated in their initial efforts as a task force.

Benefits for Team Members

In addition to the contribution that an advisory team makes to building a development culture, there are benefits that its members receive from their involvement. These benefits include providing opportunities for the following:

- Developing and/or demonstrating leadership skills
- Building their own knowledge and skills as change agents
- Expanding their network of contacts
- Increasing their visibility
- Influencing the direction of the organization
- Receiving recognition for achievement of a successful change effort

Selecting and Defining Tasks of the Advisory Team

The advisory team will serve as a resource for the design and implementation of the career development project. The ideal size of the team is eight to twelve members. The team should be a diverse group of people representing a variety of levels and departments within the organization.

Table 21

Advisory Team Tasks

▪ Provide input and feedback on each phase of the project (This feedback will be used for project recommendations.)

▪ Act as a resource for information about employee attitudes, organizational culture, internal systems, and so forth

▪ Contribute to the communications strategy for project implementation

▪ Help obtain employee and manager support and buy-in to the development process

▪ Meet approximately two to three hours per month during the design and implementation phases of the project

The selection of advisory team members can be guided by answers to these questions:

▪ Who will best represent stakeholders?
▪ Who are the people most respected in the organization?
▪ Who can work collaboratively?
▪ Who are willing to speak openly and give honest feedback?
▪ Who have time to contribute?
▪ Who have experience to speak for the groups they represent?
▪ Who will be supportive of a development philosophy?
▪ Who are the thoughtful, creative problem solvers as well as results-oriented achievers?
▪ What representation of various departments, levels, and demographic groups will make a strong team?

The tasks of the advisory team need to be clarified at a basic level for individuals to decide if they want to and have time to participate. These tasks are defined in Table 21.

Once the team forms, it may expand these tasks. It may choose to define itself in a short-term role, while defining the ongoing roles that managers, employees, and perhaps career advisors or mentors will play in the development culture. The advisory team can define its relationship with internal or external consultants for the design and implementation phases.

Table 22

Responsibilities of the Advisory Team Leader

A team leader guides and manages the day-to-day activities of the team. This involves:

■ Educating team members about the team's purpose, limits, and so forth

■ Tracking the team's goals and achievements

■ Anticipating and responding to changes in timing, schedules, workloads, and problems

■ Helping team members develop their skills

■ Communicating with management about the team's progress and needs (This includes renegotiating limits and discussing priorities, workloads, and resources.)

■ Communicating with the rest of the organization about the team's actions and achievements

■ Removing barriers to team progress

■ Helping to resolve conflict

■ Taking care of logistics (arranging for meeting rooms, getting supplies, and so on)

From *The Team Memory Jogger,* © 1995 GOAL/QPC and Joiner Associates, Inc. Reprinted with permission.

Team Leader

After the advisory group is selected and its tasks are defined, it needs to establish itself as a team. This can be facilitated by the convener, or it can be a team-directed process. The internal or external consultant may serve as the team leader, or the team may choose to select a team member to act as leader. What are the expectations of the leader? Is he or she an idea leader or an administrator of the team process? Who will serve in which roles? Table 22 identifies the responsibilities of a team leader.

Establishing the Advisory Team Process

Ground rules or guidelines for how the team will function need to be established for participation. What kind of interaction is desired from each member? How will brainstorming be positioned and facilitated? What process will be used for decisions—voting, consensus, or "minority rule" (i.e., acknowledgment of the role of the leader or subject matter expert)? How will disagreements be resolved? How will the group move forward when it seems stuck or is wandering from the task at hand? How will you assign follow-up action to accomplish results between meetings? How will you determine replacement members when current members aren't able to participate?

A team facilitator or coach is someone who focuses on how the team functions together. This team member's role is to improve the team's efficiency and effectiveness. He or she may provide feedback on the group process observed in team meetings; be a timekeeper to keep the group on track, observe disagreements, and help the group see its own behavior; and lead meetings when the *process* is critical to achieve the outcomes needed.

The advisory team needs to review and understand its charter: Why was it formed? Does everyone have the same understanding of its purpose? What outcomes are expected of it in what time frame? Who needs to sign off on the team's decisions? Who will implement the action steps determined by the team? How will team members represent themselves to managers and employees? What communication should take place to report work in process?

The advisory team also needs to define its expectations of the internal and/or external consultant: Will he or she lead, facilitate, advise, be an extra pair of hands, administer the team, and/or manage the design process? The consultant is likely to be a subject matter expert with experience advising on the design and implementation of a development process elsewhere. However, a process or program that worked in another department or organization is not likely to fit here, so the team needs to be able to balance using expertise with their knowledge of what will work in their own environment. A caution is needed, though: If the attempt is to change the culture, trying to create change by the old-culture rules is doomed to failure. Sometimes an outside viewpoint or objective opinion is needed to help the team reframe its thinking from the old paradigm. A subject matter expert can be used to educate the team members and provide models and a philosophy of a development culture to achieve the desired outcomes. He or she can also predict the pitfalls and land mines to expect along the way and shortcut some trial-and-error attempts.

The essential elements in an integrated career development system (see Chapter 11) and the eight steps in the career development design process (see Chapter 13) can serve as templates for the advisory team and

---

DEVELOPMENT CULTURE SURVEY

4 *Team Startup Checklist*

Check "yes" or "no" in answer to the following statements.

	Yes	No
We have agreed on a **purpose** and written a purpose statement.	___	___
We have identified the people inside and outside the company who can influence or who will be affected by our work (the **stakeholders**).	___	___
We have identified the **limits** and **expectations** for the team's work.	___	___
We have agreed on the **team roles** (who will have which responsibilities).	___	___
We have agreed on **ground rules**.	___	___
We have decided on **logistics** for when and where we will meet.	___	___

From the *The Team Memory Jogger,* © 1995 GOAL/QPC and Joiner Associates, Inc. Reprinted with permission.

---

consultants to determine who will be responsible for which actions in the total intervention. This "contracting phase" of the intervention—determining the expectations of the advisory team and the internal or external consultant and determining how to get started—is important in establishing a working relationship that will generate positive outcomes.

The group will need to determine logistics of its meetings—how often it can meet, what environment is conducive to getting work done, how to work efficiently to take best advantage of members' time, communicating meeting times and places, having the necessary supplies, and so forth.

You can check your advisory team's readiness by using Development Culture Survey 4: Team Startup Checklist. If you answer "no" to any item, attend to these before moving the group forward to make the process and the experience a more positive and productive one for everyone.

The advisory team has an important role to play in building a development culture. The role can contribute to planning and design, program development and pilots, the communication strategy, initial and ongoing implementation, and monitoring and evaluation. It is important, as the team gets started and at checkpoints along the way, to identify the scope and responsibilities of the team in building a development culture. A time and action chart, as shown in Figure 12, is a useful tool to create and update in order to keep the focus on action, especially because most team members have pressing responsibilities on their jobs. It is essential for team members to keep a balance of primary responsibility with the advisory team role.

Elements of a career development system, resources for employees and managers, the design process, and system evaluation are covered in Part III. The development advisory team can contribute to any or all of these steps in designing a career development system that contributes to a development culture. All the people who will be responsible for the design, implementation, and evaluation of a development intervention need to be clear about how much of the process is their responsibility. There is enough work to go around in a major effort to build a development culture so that work does not need to be duplicated; however, critical elements cannot be left out. A coordinated process is needed even if not all elements can be initiated at once.

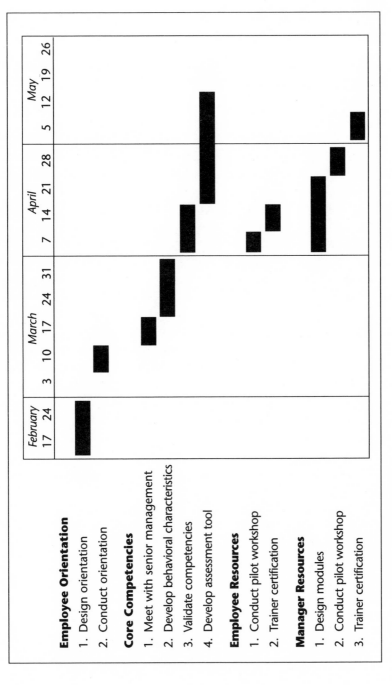

Figure 12 Sample Time and Action Chart

Designing a Career Development System That Builds a Development Culture

Essential Elements in an Integrated Career Development System

Success is relative. It is what we can make of the mess
we have made of things.
—T. S. Eliot

Seven Essential Elements

Career development systems take different forms in different organizations and succeed based on their fit with the culture or contribution to the new culture. However, experience shows that there are essential elements that are part of every comprehensive, integrated career development system. These elements may have different labels, but in some way they are incorporated into successful, lasting processes. Without these elements working together, career development runs the risk of being seen as the "program of the month" or a human resources program, and not integral to the needs of the business. A short-term effort will not build a development culture. Table 23 summarizes these essential elements.

Driven by Business Needs

Career development can be a means to help organizations achieve a competitive advantage. To do this, any program or system needs to relate to specific business objectives. In the life of any long-lived career development system, the business needs may change. For example, a program

Table 23

Summary of Essential Elements in an
Integrated Career Development System

1. Driven by business needs
2. A vision and philosophy of career development
3. Senior management support
4. Communication and education
5. Management involvement
6. Employees' ownership of and responsibility for their own growth
7. Career development resources

started to reduce turnover in a volatile job market may change to closing the gap between strategic competencies needed and employees' present skill base when a downturn occurs in the industry and people hold on to their jobs longer.

The philosophy of a career development program should incorporate the business case for its existence. It can have a dual emphasis on benefits to the company and benefits to the individual, but if it is seen only as a "nice to have" for individuals, it won't survive internal or external changes. As soon as the budget needs to be cut or staff reductions occur or the key sponsor of the program moves on to another role, the program will likely die. If the career development process is seen as contributing to problem solving for the organization, it is less vulnerable. If it is recognized as a contributor to a more broadly based culture change, it will be supported.

The reality of business needs changing and objectives being rewritten annually also contributes to the longevity of a career development process. If a structure exists for individuals to update their performance and career goals annually based on the year's strategic objectives, the process becomes self-perpetuating. Performance planning and career discussions are expected of employees and managers at all levels. Career development planning is no longer dependent on a cheerleader to espouse the benefits to individuals and the organization, but is an expected part of the work cycle.

Virtually any business need can and needs to be translated into people terms that can be justification for a career development process. For example, if the business need is for global expansion, employees may need to be prepared for international assignments, or foreign nationals may need to be trained in the company's values and procedures. The Global Relocation Trends Survey Report published by the National Foreign Trade Council and Windham International in January 1995 reported that only 33 percent of the surveyed companies (which employ collectively more than 24,000 expatriates) pay attention to the career development of those assigned or returning. Even employees not assigned overseas will have development needs to expand their awareness and perhaps add second-language skills. Belief in a development culture will erode if business needs are not targeted as a reason for development.

If the business need is to evolve to a virtual corporation in order to reduce facilities costs and increase speed of response to customers, employees need to have the technical skills and knowledge to operate independently from a virtual office. Roles need to be redesigned and changes in career opportunities communicated to individuals. Then employees need to establish their own career development plans accordingly.

Contribution to business needs should also be the measure of success of a career development intervention. If the business need is to increase productivity, various measures of productivity or of speed of response can be taken as the development planning process is introduced. After people have participated in the process and new systems have been implemented to improve work flow, managers can be questioned about employee initiative and the same measures of productivity can be used to compare. In metric-driven organizations, the development process must show contribution to business needs in a measurable way.

If the business need is to have more people ready with the critical skills needed for changing technologies, then a preintervention evaluation of skills can be made and compared to an evaluation one and two years after the launch of the process. This is a use of competencies that is just emerging. Do people score better in key skills and knowledge now than they did before? Do we have organizational strength in the competencies needed to lead the organization forward?

The information systems department of Motorola's Land Mobile Products Sector (LMPS) planned to develop a comprehensive career development process with the purpose of ensuring that all employees' skills were growing fast enough to keep up with market demands. Development Culture in Action: Case 7 illustrates how they devised a professional development program to meet their business needs.

One company's purpose for the career development process was to light a fire under stagnant employees in an attempt to change their attitude from entitlement to taking more responsibility for their own

DEVELOPMENT CULTURE IN ACTION

Motorola Land Mobile Products Sector, Information Systems Department

Professional Development Program

The Information Systems (IS) department of Motorola's Land Mobile Products Sector (LMPS), a producer of two-way radio products, developed a comprehensive career development process to ensure that all employees' skills were growing rapidly enough to keep up with market demands. Many IS employees, while highly educated and skilled, did not understand how critical it was to develop new skills as technologies changed. Work requiring state-of-the-art skills was already being outsourced, and new people were being hired for the specific technical skills they were able to bring. Many IS employees had been in the same jobs for several years and were not seen as having the flexibility or transferable skills to move laterally.

The career development process was comprehensive. It included the following:

- Career development workshops for all IS managers and employees
- Identification of key IS competencies needed to accomplish business results
- Skill assessment and development tools on an Intranet
- Individual development planning process that links into the performance management system, a quarterly dialog process, and the individual's career plan
- Technical education and certification programs to provide resources for current skills and continuous learning
- Career mobility system to encourage lateral movement into related IS areas
- Review of role definitions and compensation to support a flatter organizational structure
- Intranet technology to communicate and provide access to all the career development resources

The Information Systems Professional Development Program (ISPDP) was announced at a town hall meeting of all local IS employees in the sector. The kickoff was followed by training for managers and employees that emphasized the need for ongoing development and

continued

provided assessment and development planning. Once designed and in place, the total program was announced with all the resources available at an event called The Great ISPDP Adventure, emphasizing the theme of continuous learning and professional growth.

There was still much to learn and internalize about the purpose and need for proactive career management as well as the expectations and resources for the program. Most employees received the program positively, but some were still skeptical. Additional training sessions and management follow-up were provided to answer questions, reinforce the culture change, and help employees apply the new resources to their own situations.

Used by permission of Motorola Land Mobile Products Sector, IS Department

development. How do people demonstrate that they are taking responsibility for their own development? Measures of the actions employees took were one way to evaluate this: How much had use of the tuition assistance program increased? Had use of the skills center increased? What was the change in the number of training hours per employee annually? Another way to evaluate whether employees were taking responsibility for their development was a survey that asked, "Who is responsible for your career and development?" After participating in the development planning program, 100 percent responded that they were responsible or that they and their manager shared the responsibility. No one said it was the company's or their manager's responsibility solely.

With most business needs, any evaluation is not likely to be a pure measure of the specific outcomes of the development process because other factors may be occurring simultaneously. Workplaces are not controlled environments. However, it becomes apparent that designers of the process need to ensure that business needs are defined in actions and behaviors that can be measured. In spite of the difficulty of measuring behavior change, some measure of change is important to be able to take credit for any improvement in the factor being addressed, as discussed in Chapter 14.

A Vision and Philosophy of Career Development

Career development, like any other process that will affect the organization's culture, needs a vision and philosophy. Vision is *what we want to do*. While all involved in designing and launching a development process will have their own ideas of what and why, the group's vision of the process and outcomes needs to be clarified.

A clear vision will be the catalyst and driver of the effort necessary by everyone. It answers "What's in it for me?" and "Why are we doing this?" For example, a vision may be of the company with market dominance achieved by innovative, risk-taking employees whose skills are state-of-the-art and who continue to add value and are ready for changing business needs.

The philosophy is *how we do it*. What actions by managers and employees are necessary to achieve this vision? What systems will support the process, and what resources have been committed to getting there? For example, a philosophy may state that every employee will manage his or her own development by actively participating in assessment, planning, and implementing a development plan. A philosophy might emphasize managers' role in supporting employee development by communicating department goals, coaching and feedback, and creating development opportunities. A philosophy statement might be incorporated in literature launching a career development system, or in a kick-off by a senior manager or sponsor. Some examples of visions and philosophies of career development are provided in the following cases.

TRW's vision and philosophy for development, stated in Development Culture in Action: Case 8, are written in a brochure that every employee receives.

CCC Information Services states its development philosophy, described in Development Culture in Action: Case 9, in a brochure that employees and managers received as their development process was launched.

A philosophy of career development can also communicate concepts or models that define the process and clarify expectations. One division of a manufacturer defined its concepts for defining the process and clarifying expectations in a brochure that all employees received as part of the communication about their career development process. This new model is related in Development Culture in Action: Case 10.

Senior Management Support

Visible support from senior management is essential to a comprehensive, sustained development process. Career development systems that are introduced in a traditional environment will be suspect without the endorsement of senior managers. A total culture change must have leadership and buy-in at all levels, most critically from the top. As was discussed

case 8	DEVELOPMENT CULTURE IN ACTION
	TRW

Vision and Philosophy for Professional Development

TRW is committed to supporting a corporate culture that encourages and assists its employees in developing themselves professionally and in achieving and maintaining high performance levels in the workplace.

In an increasingly competitive global market, world-class customer satisfaction requires employees who are continually expanding the depth and breadth of their skills and talents. Professional development is a necessary cornerstone to TRW's business strategy that will make sure TRW is meeting and exceeding customer demands. Development of employees is as important to TRW's future success as research and development or new capital acquisitions. This commitment to professional development is consistent with the corporate mission and values statement, which says, "The men and women of TRW make our success possible." People are responsible for "serving the needs of our customers in innovative ways" and helping us be the best company possible.

Given today's highly complex business environment, TRW cannot unilaterally provide predictable employment and career paths. Instead, the company, in partnership with its employees, must enhance professional development opportunities to ensure consistently high performance levels in the workplace and to enhance employees' prospects for future employability.

Used by permission of TRW, Inc.

in Chapter 3, attempts to change the culture will constantly be sabotaged by anyone who has a stake in maintaining the old ways of doing things or who does not like the new behaviors that are expected.

Managers will not sustain the effort to get their people to change if they don't see role models at the top and are not held accountable for new outcomes. In most organizations today, leadership skills—and often technical skills—of senior managers are as much in need of development as are the skills of other employees. Managers are not exempt as participants in the process of development planning and implementation.

case 9	DEVELOPMENT CULTURE IN ACTION
	CCC Information Services

Vision and Philosophy for a Personal Development Program

As a leader in information processing and provider of business solutions to the automotive claims industry, CCC is positioned to maintain a competitive advantage and achieve market dominance by selecting, developing, and rewarding individuals who

- Are capable and talented
- Continue to add measurable value to the company
- Take responsibility for their own development
- Are results-oriented individuals with a sense of urgency
- Are future-focused and can facilitate change to achieve corporate strategic objectives

Individual development will be accomplished in a culture with a shared vision, open communication, managers who facilitate and support employee development, and an entrepreneurial mind-set in which everyone takes ownership of quality outcomes.

CCC's Personal Development Program requires shared responsibilities. Critical to its continued growth and success are people who are actively involved in their personal development and managers who facilitate and enable employee development. CCC is committed to providing the resources, to supporting ongoing individual and team development, and to measuring and rewarding positive outcomes.

Used by permission of CCC Information Services

Some organizations in the midst of a culture change start from the top. In order to reach agreement on a philosophy statement, senior managers must acknowledge the impact of the process. The process can start with executives by defining the new leadership competencies needed in the changed culture and then using a 360-degree feedback process to measure these competencies. Senior managers can pilot the cascaded development process, participate in training to discuss differences on the assessment as part of a career discussion, and set their own development goals. They

DEVELOPMENT CULTURE IN ACTION

Sales Division of a Manufacturing Firm

New Model for Career Development

In the old model, people expected the organization to take care of them. Successful people managed their careers, of course, but career growth often meant promotion along a predictable career path. Some new ways of thinking are more appropriate in the realities of today's organization.

Career development is a shared responsibility between individuals and their supervisor or manager. Individuals are responsible for managing their own careers. Today successful individuals recognize that they must proactively plan development and act on those plans to achieve their goals. The supervisor's responsibility is to support individual efforts through coaching; provide feedback, information, and advice; and help with development plans. Supervisors and managers have a joint responsibility to work together in helping individuals manage their careers.

Career growth doesn't just mean moving up. The concept of following a set career path doesn't work today because the organization is flatter and jobs change so rapidly. You can't count on a targeted position being there when you want it. Instead, people need to build a portfolio of skills and to continually add value. This provides more flexibility—so individuals are better prepared to respond to opportunities as they occur. But it also means that individuals need to be clear about their own values and goals.

Individual goals must be consistent with the goals and direction of the organization. Individual satisfaction is a primary force in career planning; however, success within the organization requires that individuals align their goals with business needs. As new competencies and market forces become important to the organization's continued success, individuals must respond by modifying their career planning. *Strategic career management* is the process of planning, implementing, and monitoring career progress in ways consistent with the direction and needs of the organization.

demonstrate, by their involvement, their commitment to the process for everyone in the organization. When they communicate the urgency for everyone to be involved in the development process, they are showing their support of and belief in the process.

In addition to being a participant in the development process, at least one senior manager needs to be a champion of a comprehensive approach. In the early stage of initial data gathering to determine attitudes and vision of executives for a career development process, someone will usually stand out as a supporter. This person is in philosophical alignment with the intent of the process, pushing to have this potential process affect business needs. He or she may be a driver of the change in culture. It is important to enlist someone like this as an ally in the career development process if you are defining career development to be broader than just a resource for employees, as is espoused in this book.

Communication is an important element for senior managers if they wish to contribute to the success of the career development process. Regular communication from the top espousing the program purposes and the need for the changes and expressing high-level expectations as well as continued encouragement for participation by managers and employees is important for the career development program's success. Endorsement by the business unit leader at kickoff is valuable, but so is ongoing communication to show visible support. Environments in which career development is implemented as a business initiative leave no question about priorities.

In order for this initiative to build a development culture, accountability needs to be built into the system. If career development is linked with performance management or is an integral part of a comprehensive selection, development, and reward system, people (managers and employees alike) will take it seriously. Managers not held accountable for employee development will revert to prioritizing that for which they are rewarded —making their numbers. Organizations that reward short-term performance (driven by quarterly financial outcomes) will not reap the long-term benefits of skilled, flexible employees who are ready to meet new challenges. That is not to say that business results will not drive effort in a development culture—quite the contrary. Alignment of individual effort to the business objectives is what organizational career development is all about. But there needs to be attention to development to meet the demands of the future as well as handling the crises of today. Senior managers' leadership is essential to help everyone understand and contribute to priorities.

Communication and Education

It is not possible to overcommunicate in an organizational change effort. Communication begins even as the planning and design stages are initiated, and it never stops. Even after everyone has heard the message and perhaps participated in some events, ongoing communication is essential to ensure continuity.

Some resistance to change of behavior is due to lack of understanding of new expectations or misunderstanding of purpose and goals of a new direction. Some people are still firmly stuck in the old paradigm and don't know there is such a thing as a new contract for the employee–employer relationship. Employees and managers—particularly those with long tenure in the organization—may still be operating by the old rules and may not even know there are new ones. They blame all the changes they don't like on poor management, the economy, technology, and so on.

For these reasons, education is necessary for communicating the new message. Merely stating the message is not sufficient to change behavior, and stating it only once certainly will not change resistance or get everyone to jump on the bandwagon. People need to continually hear the message being reinforced by top management, their own manager, human resources, and perhaps a career development advisory team. They need information about what this is about, why the changes are important, and how the new approach or system works, as noted by Pritchett (1996):

> Change just naturally creates an information vacuum, an atmosphere where there are more questions than answers. If you fail to satisfy your people's craving, the rumor mill will fill the void. That leads to worst-case thinking, a lot of warped messages, and an overheated worry factor that gets in the way of work.

There are different viewpoints about what and when to communicate about a career development process. I usually recommend communicating soon and often. For example, a senior manager or senior human resources representative may communicate the intention of designing a career development system and announce that some individuals might be asked to participate in surveys, interviews, or focus groups. A brief definition of the process of and need for career development might also be communicated at that time, with no intent yet to educate the population. Following the data gathering and design, the advisory team or internal or external consultants who are designing the process may prepare a report and perhaps make a management presentation about findings and resulting recommended design. A report may also go out to those who participated in the needs assessment, with results of their input.

As vision and philosophy are articulated, draft versions can be presented to stakeholders. Executive briefings serve the purpose of educating as well as communicating status of the process. It may be at this point that a go-ahead is needed if decision makers have sufficient information to support the process. As components are planned and various responsibilities defined, this information needs to be communicated to all. Brochures or videotapes ensure that all employees get the same message, but a live interaction such as a "town hall" meeting or an orientation session provides opportunity for more education and for questions to be answered. Employees learn that resources are coming and that changes will be expected, and they have time to internalize the message. Some organizations choose to provide a managers' briefing first, with resources for managers to take back to their units and cascade the information. A kickoff by a senior manager at this point ensures that people hear the business need for this effort as well as its priority and importance. Details of program delivery do not need to be designed at this point. Sometimes a pilot program is used for both planning and communication, prior to the launch of a broader system.

Often the design of project components takes longer than anticipated because of changing priorities or staff time, expanded scope of the project, or other unanticipated variables. For this reason, some people responsible for new programs are hesitant to communicate about them until they are ready to deliver. But a more powerful argument can be made that acceptance of new expectations and ways of doing things takes time, and therefore communication about a work in progress can be building readiness on the part of the recipients.

Most comprehensive systems take time to create. Planning, data gathering, and design are sequential elements of the process. Major undertakings like competency identification take time to ensure validity. In the meantime, everyone must pay attention to business and other responsibilities. It is wise to communicate steps along the way and introduce elements as they become ready. Educational sessions for managers and employees can initiate the behaviors required even before all the components are in place.

One organization's belief that its change effort could not be overcommunicated is illustrated in the following example:

An advertising company thought they were doing a lot to communicate a new career development program. Their communication strategy started with monthly senior management briefings on the purpose and status of the project. They had a consultant conduct pilot programs for managers and employees to ensure that the messages were on target and understood and to receive feedback for the design. The training manager held focus groups to ensure that manager and employee needs were addressed and to obtain buy-in. They had kickoff meetings with all employees to launch the total development program and all its elements, some of which were required of everyone. They created a booklet that introduced the total project and showed how career development linked to other human resources systems and resources. They created a videotape about the total development program that was shown throughout the facility, communicated highlights in their company newsletter, and made the training schedule available by e-mail.

After the program was successfully launched, the training manager was asked what he would do differently. His response was, "I would communicate more." Even though he had made a seemingly great effort to communicate the program to employees, he could see that he still did not have everyone on board.

Remember that communication is not just one-way. Input from all the stakeholders is important. Project managers typically communicate at the beginning of a major intervention. But communication is important all along the way to ensure involvement, ongoing course correction, and attention to the changing needs of individuals and the organization.

Table 24 lists some strategies that can be used to market career development in an organization.

Management Involvement

Successful comprehensive career development systems have significant management involvement. Middle managers, who can constitute the biggest barrier in some organizations, actually have the most to gain from active contribution to a development process. As organizations flatten, many managers' jobs are becoming redundant. The changes in today's organizations—technological advances, the need for decisions made on the front line by employees, recognition that the hierarchy is too slow for responsive organizations, self-directed teams, and other structural changes—have changed the role of manager. Many managers are

Table 24

Career Development Marketing Strategies

- Briefings to executive staff and managers
- Career advisory teams whose role is input and communication
- Kickoff meetings
- Cascading orientations (from senior management down through the organization)
- Brochures with vision, philosophy, responsibilities, and program components
- Videotapes, perhaps with endorsement and expectations from senior managers expressed
- Columns in regular company communications
- A regular development newsletter to announce the process, new resources, and "people you should know" and to celebrate successes of individuals along the way
- Career fairs or other events to communicate, educate, and make the program visible
- Electronic messages—e-mail, intranet resources about the program
- An open house if there is a physical space like a career center
- Formal invitations to employees for career development events and to managers to participate in training with their employees
- Celebrations of career development successes (not just promotions) during company events or meetings

working managers, that is, they are individual contributors as well as leaders. Many are project managers, with a short-term relationship with individuals who report to them for the duration of the project.

These macro changes in the way work is organized and performed mean that managers' roles must change, so their own development should be a major concern. For their own sake as well as the sake of those who report to them, managers must understand the development process, be alert to development opportunities, and embrace the changes needed to keep the company competitive.

When managers are excused from the development process because they are too busy or don't have the coaching skills they need, development takes on a very different meaning. Rather than a process linking development to business needs that everyone must be engaged in, development is seen only as a resource for employees who are unhappy in their jobs or otherwise need to make a change. If the purpose of career development interventions or services in your organization is to build or contribute to a development culture, managers at all levels must be actively involved, as was discussed in Chapter 6.

That is not to say that other resources—such as a career center or career advisors—aren't useful, but they cannot take the place of managers and still have the comprehensive effect that is needed. Only managers can be a resource for employees to link performance and development on the present job. Outside resources, skilled though they are, will not have the perspective of seeing employee skills demonstrated in daily activities, or the opportunities for feedback on work and reputation, or the authority to create development opportunities on the job. Even in environments where managers are not held accountable for developing employees, individuals who are taking responsibility for their own development will seek input from their manager or seek a move to an area where the manager will contribute to their growth.

Supervisors' and managers' involvement starts with their understanding and taking ownership of their role in developing employees. In some organizations, this is about development only on the present job, and managers are not asked to help with employees' longer-range career planning. In either case, to succeed in a supportive role for their direct reports, managers almost always need training. The skills and level of understanding of the development process that managers need cannot be read about or learned in a kickoff orientation session. Those can be starting points, but conceptual and verbal skill-building need interaction and practice.

Managers' training also must go beyond coaching. They need to be introduced to new models of career development, just as employees do. If they must help individuals grow in new ways—because the ladder has fewer rungs or perhaps because there is no ladder—managers need new concepts and models on which to base their coaching and feedback. They need to be energized so they can enthusiastically embrace the new possibilities rather than bemoan the fact that the old paths are gone. Finally, the manager's role is made easier if some creative work has been done on development options so that there are established resources for them to use in dealing with development needs. These resources support managers' coaching and development responsibilities.

A critical responsibility of managers in employee development is reality testing. Whether about differences in perception regarding competencies, about reputation, or about viability of goals, managers' input is essential before employees build development plans. A concern often expressed by managers entering the career development process is how to deal with unrealistic goals. Managers may need skills and job aids to handle these potential problem situations, but it is essential that they address the issue with employees rather than have individuals trying to implement plans without any feedback.

If other people, such as mentors, advisors, or career counselors, are available for development discussions with employees, roles should be clarified so managers cannot abdicate their responsibility on the assumption that someone else is responsible for employee development. A development culture has room for many resources for development, and managers are the cornerstone of the process.

Employee Ownership of and Responsibility for Their Own Growth

Development cultures cannot be imposed on individuals. Betsy Collard of the Career Action Center wrote, "Unless employees are convinced that a career-resilience program truly is there to serve them, they won't participate in it" (Waterman, Waterman, and Collard, 1994). For everyone to recognize the need for lifelong learning and actively set about creating and implementing a development plan, there needs to be employee ownership. Management can state the expectations, provide resources and opportunities, and hold people accountable, but development happens inside the individual. It is the composite of experiences, learning, and application of skills that helps people grow, so the organization cannot mandate growth. A development culture requires employees to take ownership of and responsibility for their own growth.

It is essential that employees understand the changing employment contract, hear a clear message about the requirements for success in the future, know clearly the business needs and competencies expected for contribution on the present job, and have the resources necessary for development in order to take ownership of their own careers and development. In organizations in which the process is completely manager driven, employees can be passive recipients of directives who are motivated by threats of punishment for noncompliance rather than evolving a mind-set in which they develop career self-reliance. When employees abdicate their responsibility for managing their own careers, they tend to blame others for their lack of success or bury themselves in their work and hope the changes spinning around them won't affect them.

If you are trying to convince employees to take ownership, make sure their managers are not holding on to the old paradigm of command and control—making paternalistic decisions about what is best for employees and withholding information that employees need to make informed decisions about their work and direction. In one organization that was beginning to communicate the need for individual responsibility for career development, an employee was transferred to a job he didn't want, without any input by him. The contradiction between the new-culture message and the old-culture action was poignantly phrased by the understandably bitter employee: "You said I'm supposed to manage my own career, so why can a manager transfer me without even discussing the move with me?"

For a successful change to employee responsibility, individuals must be able to answer the question, "What's in it for me?" If the emphasis is only on outcomes needed in the present job, some employees will feel that this is a way to "get more work out of us." When it becomes acceptable to plan for longer-range career goals, and in fact employees are encouraged to do so, and when the career planning model is not just about how to get the next job, people will begin to see the mutual benefit of employee responsibility.

A group process can be helpful to gaining true ownership by employees. If they are provided self-directed resources without fully accepting their responsibility, they probably won't take action unless there is enough dissatisfaction with their present situation. However, in a group interactive workshop, employees can help each other recognize the need for change. I personally have seen many skeptics change their tune and leave a workshop saying, "Okay, I get it. It really does matter what I do to manage my career. It is up to me."

Career Development Resources

When some organizations begin thinking of career development for employees, they start by identifying career planning resources rather than designing a system first. In fact, I have known of many who purchased a variety of resources without knowing how they would use them or even who would use them. (The result is often resources sitting on a shelf.) While this element may be the most tangible, it certainly should not occur until some of the planning and design has taken place. Once the design is progressing, a variety of career planning and development resources can be made available.

Other organizations (usually at least somewhat paternalistic) don't even consider that employees may need some guidance or resources to take meaningful action. They prepare communication packages that introduce the concept of career self-reliance and perhaps give instructions on using a career development planning form, but provide little more. When this occurs, employees see the process as another HR form to fill out, have no ownership, and fail to understand the value for their own development. Chapter 12 goes into detail about the career development process for individuals, but an overview of appropriate types of resources is presented here as an important element of the whole system.

When individuals are told that they need to manage their own career in the organization, most don't know what that means or how to do it. Even those individuals who are successfully managing their own careers may not be able to articulate what they do or how they do it. Resources need to be available to educate and guide individuals in the process.

Resources may be provided in a career center or other physical space that becomes identified with the career planning and development process, or they may be provided online for individual access in a virtual center. Workshops, drop-in sessions, career counseling, and mentoring can all be considered resources for employees and managers, as well as assessment tools, information about organizational procedures, and development options.

It is useful to separate resources into *career planning* versus *career development implementation*. Career planning resources include workshops, tools, or counseling to explore self-insight questions such as, "What gives me satisfaction from my work?" and "What are my motivated skills?" Career planning resources also clarify the career focus questions, such as, "What background is needed for positions in the marketing department?" and "What are some development options available in my present role and related ones?" Usually the culmination of the career planning phase is the identification of viable career goals and development of an action plan.

Implementation resources may include in-house or external training available to build skills or competencies identified for development in the planning phase. This may incorporate classroom training plus self-directed or computer-based instruction. Resources may also include assignment to task forces for new learning or application of one's skills, networks, mentors, and other people or tools to help achieve goals once they are identified in the planning phase. Alternatives to promotion must be visible or people will continue to equate career development to promotions. Development in place—without a move—needs to be rewarded if the organization needs future skills.

Often, when asked what type of resources would be useful, employees respond that they want to know the new career paths—if only they knew what jobs to target and exactly what they need to do to get promoted, they feel that they would be managing their careers. This response is clearly out of the old paradigm. Employees obviously need to learn first how the nature of careers has changed. The old paths are no longer there, and no one can predict new career paths in today's organizations. So, while employees may be asking for a recipe to follow, the designers of a career development system need to be ready to offer a *process*. Just as you can't get people to change behavior just by telling them to change, neither can individuals manage their career development just by knowing a progression of jobs—even in the unlikely event that a path defined today will still be viable tomorrow.

So once again, employees and managers need to be educated about the changed employer–employee contract before any number of resources will be usable and seen as valuable. Those who are the most dissatisfied in their present situation will access any resources available, but those who are comfortable in their present situation or who are ignoring the inevitable will not value development resources. And if career assistance in the past has been strictly for outplacement, a major effort will need to be launched to overcome the sense that career planning means you are losing your job. Career resources are an essential element of a comprehensive approach to career development and building a development culture, but they cannot stand alone.

The Career Development Process for Individuals

There are no limits on our future if we don't
put limits on our people.
—Jack Kemp

Introducing Career Management

The first step for individual participation in the career development process is introducing career management. Some organizations make this step mandatory, reasoning that for individuals to make an informed choice about whether to participate further, they need accurate information about what is expected of them, why the program is being offered, and the benefits of participating. The introduction may take the form of an orientation session or kickoff meeting, or it may be cascaded through the company by successive levels of managers. It can be an opportunity to showcase senior management support, communicate the philosophy of the career development program and shared responsibility, or reinforce the career development ideas that have already been presented in a written brochure. This is also a good time to make the business case for the need for individual development.

Presented as an interactive session with an opportunity to learn some concepts or participate in activities and to get questions answered, this introduction begins to build participants' understanding and involvement before they actually start participating in a career development program. Using an exercise that starts everyone thinking about shared responsibility and providing some key concepts of the development process can be a good way to build enthusiasm for participation in the development process. Sharing the components and outcomes expected for all players—employees, managers, and the organization—helps people see which parts of the program are voluntary and which are mandatory. For example, when career development is part of the performance management process, creating development goals is not optional, but writing career goals may be. And having current development plans may be expected of everyone, but participating in a self-assessment process may not be required. These are design issues that need to be determined in an introduction to the career management process.

A Model for Career Development Planning

Once participants are introduced to the concept of career management, they need a model for career development. Without the big picture, people tend to jump in to meet their immediate needs and may not realize that the answer they are seeking may be to the wrong question. For example, when employees are unhappy with their present situation, the question they are likely to ask whoever represents the organization is, "What else is there?" when the question they should start with is, "Why am I unhappy?" As depicted in Figure 13, the first step involves *looking inward* to assess and identify those factors critical to the individual's success and satisfaction from work.

The second step, then, is *looking outward* to understand the organization's needs and opportunities and develop a career focus. If people start their planning with this step, the information may be useless because there is no personal measure to relate it to, or they may make decisions based on images or suppositions rather than a meaningful plan. When individuals are clear about who they are and what they have to offer, they can sort through the organizational information to determine the right course for themselves. Often at this stage participants recognize that "fixing" their present situation rather than making a move would meet their development needs and those of the organization.

The third component of the development planning process is *looking forward*. This involves setting goals and action plans to achieve appropriate

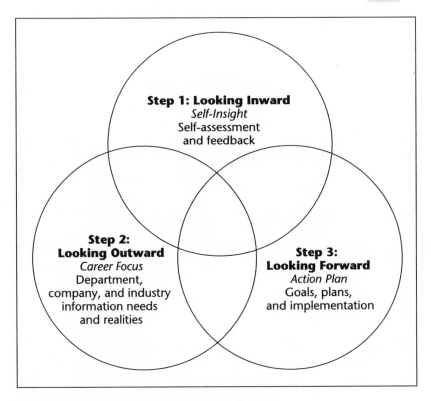

Figure 13   Model for Individual Career Development
From *Managing Your Career Within Your Organization,* by P. Simonsen, 1993.
Rolling Meadows, IL: Career Directions, Inc.

outcomes for the individual and the organization. Based on their self-insight and organizational focus, working through this process then becomes *strategic career planning,* that is, linking individuals' goals with the direction and needs of the organization and building action plans accordingly.

Every successful career development planning process incorporates these three components, although not necessarily in a formal way. People bring varying degrees of self-insight and organizational knowledge to the process, so not everyone needs to go through a formal process to achieve a positive outcome. For some people, summarizing their own self-knowledge may be sufficient. For others, a thorough process may be essential.

Looking Inward

The Self-Assessment Process

The starting point for most individuals in the career development process is looking inward, or self-insight, and usually includes a self-assessment process. This process may be formal and include assessment instruments. But for many people, informal approaches suffice, especially when partnered with a facilitated workshop or discussion with a counselor or advisor. The process may be primarily self-directed, as with use of career planning software or a workbook, or it may be primarily instructor-led, as in a workshop or series of workshops. It may be in a virtual environment, where resources are online to be used at the participant's discretion, or it may require a front-end commitment to participate in a complete program.

Assessment Tools   A career resources person needs to determine and select tools that are appropriate for the targeted populations. Many resources exist that were originally designed for a high school or student population and that are not appropriate for experienced adults. Others are targeted primarily to outplacement, with a job search component that sends the wrong message for career development planning within the organization. There are also many materials available that may be useful for specific populations, such as adults with a low reading level or employees with very basic skills.

Areas for assessment may include work values, motivators, interests, skills and abilities, accomplishments, work style and preferences, needs, personality and/or attitudes, and reputation. Some of these topics are best assessed formally with a validated instrument, but others benefit from an informal exercise and discussion. Most validated instruments require some level of qualification or certification to be administered and interpreted, and therefore can be used only by a qualified professional counselor or trained advisor. The following case example demonstrates the incorrect use of such an instrument:

When employees in a consumer products company with no career development program asked the human resources department for help with career issues, employees were given a formal interest instrument and a computer printout of their responses. No one interpreted the scores or even provided an overview of what the instrument measured. An accountant who had career issues got assessment results that, he said, "told me I should be a fireman!" By the time some career planning workshops were offered, he still had career needs and was angry. No one had helped him find value in the patterns of interests on the assessment, the instrument was wrong for the need and the recipient, and interests were not even what needed to be assessed. The accountant was not ready to leave the consumer products company and be retrained as a fireman; he needed help identifying what was causing his dissatisfaction on the job and how to manage his career within the company. He needed to understand the whole process of career planning, and he needed an intelligent conversation about possible actions he could take to remedy his situation.

The concept of matching individuals and jobs is quickly becoming obsolete in today's world of work. John Krumboltz, a professor at Stanford University with an international reputation for his theories of career choice and development, suggested in a 1994 presentation to the California Career Conference that "instead of taking people and matching them to a job, we need to help them determine career direction, overcome real and perceived obstacles, learn job search skills, avoid job burnout, and prepare for new opportunities."

Identifying Work Values, Work Styles, and Personality Preferences   Identifying work values, work styles, and personality preferences helps employees to answer the question, "What do I want?" Most adults know their values but may need some structure to clarify, name, or prioritize them. Even an employee who can state, "What is important to me from my work is creativity, autonomy, challenge, and helping others" needs to build these concepts into development plans and may need help identifying opportunities to do so. More often, individuals have not put labels on their values; when values are in conflict with some aspect of their work, they may have a general dissatisfaction or malaise without knowing why. Often clarification of values is the element of the self-assessment process that has the most impact on participants. Seeking ways to get their values met can become the focus of their development planning process.

Another area of self-awareness that has impact for adults in organizations is identifying work styles and personality preferences. There are many validated instruments on the market that are useful for this, but all require that employees receive general information about the instrument itself as well as an individual interpretation of results. General information would answer such questions as these: "What is it measuring? How do your answers get sorted into these categories? How accurate (reliable) is the data?" This information can be provided in writing with the results of the assessment, or it can be discussed in a group session.

Understanding one's own results and the application of these to the workplace and to development planning is essential. A group session may be helpful for understanding how one's own preferences differ from those of others, but individual interpretation and development planning can make the assessment information particularly valuable and ensure no misinterpretation. Many organizations are using these kinds of tools for reasons other than career planning, such as team building, management development, conflict resolution, and customer responsiveness. So data from one administration can be incorporated into many organizational activities.

Skills and Competencies Assessment   Employee self-assessment of skills and competencies helps them to answer the question, "What do I have to offer?" Skills assessment tools are most valuable to adults in the work environment when they are related to the needs of the organization. For example, if the organization is moving toward a team-based restructuring, employees need a way to assess their strengths in team skills. Organizations are increasingly using 360-degree feedback assessments to measure competencies or other behaviors needed in today's environment. Again, if this kind of assessment is being used for other purposes in the organization, the results definitely should be incorporated into career development planning. Assessment with feedback from others provides reality testing as well as personal assessment, and it is useful for individuals with low self-esteem who think they have no skills as well as for the overconfident person who thinks his or her capabilities are stronger than others perceive them to be.

However, a broader understanding of skills and abilities can help people understand how skills transfer from one specific application to others. Skills can be classified into three categories: adaptive skills or work habits, functional or transferable skills, and technical or job-specific skills.

- ▮ *Adaptive skills* may also be called *work habits,* but since they are learned and improve with practice, they can be considered skills. Examples include time management, flexibility, and assertiveness.
- ▮ *Functional skills* are also considered *transferable skills* because they represent abilities that can be transferred to many types of jobs. Examples include language usage, instructing, and administrative skills.
- ▮ *Technical skills* are *job-specific skills* and define the knowledge and skills needed for a particular occupation or job. Examples include

programming in a particular language, ad copywriting, and forklift operation.

If skills are defined as *strengths that have been learned and that improve with practice,* people can think in broader terms than specific competencies or skills they are using on the present job or have just learned from work. For people who feel underutilized in their job, assessing all the skills they possess and not just those used on the present job helps them start to define possibilities for growth or new application of their skills. For some employees, career development planning means improving their skills on the present job or to meet changing demands. For others, it means finding opportunities to apply their skills in new ways.

Most career planning programs in companies are not concerned with measuring *aptitudes.* Young people with no work experience may need this kind of data on which to base planning, but most adults can identify and analyze accomplishments for areas of consistent strength. For example, employees usually know whether they have strength in math skills and using numbers, are detail oriented, or have good language aptitude. Tests of these aptitudes are more valuable and more likely to be used prior to enrolling in a skills training program. Adults with low reading levels may be tested to determine the type of remedial work necessary. Technicians about to be trained in a computer-aided manufacturing process might be tested for their knowledge of algebra.

It is important to avoid using the word *tests* when referring to self-assessment or informal instruments or inventories. Workers who have a negative history with tests in school will be turned off to anything defined as a test in the career development process. It is possible that for their development they may need to take additional training, some of which will involve testing, but they need a positive experience first. Participation in a voluntary program requires that employees feel confident rather than fearful of repeating negative school experiences. Development Culture in Action: Case 11 describes how facilitators of the United Auto Workers–General Motors Work-Life Planning Program helped employees gain the confidence to participate in a program to upgrade their skills.

Feedback

Individuals need and want some means of reality testing as they create development plans. Most employees want regular feedback from their manager, although many are not good at receiving feedback, even when it is constructive.

case
11

DEVELOPMENT CULTURE IN ACTION

United Auto Workers and General Motors

Upgrading Skills in the Life-Work Planning Program

In 1993, the United Auto Workers (UAW) and General Motors (GM) negotiated a Career Development Pilot Program as part of their national collective bargaining agreement. The program is administered by the UAW-GM Center for Human Resources (CHR).

The CHR has developed a number of educational programs and resources that have been implemented at every UAW-represented GM plant. These include workplace-based skill centers, tuition assistance for active and laid-off workers, and Educational Development Counselors, who help UAW-represented GM employees choose and prepare for educational opportunities.

The UAW and GM have long recognized that education, skill development, and training must be ongoing if they are to help employees keep pace with changing skill and knowledge demands in the workplace. With a mature, high-seniority workforce, this lifelong learning approach needs to help employees prepare for options that address their work, personal skill development, and lives after retirement.

The UAW and GM representatives assigned to the program from the CHR, together with career development consultants, designed a Life-Work Planning Program titled *Driving Your Future.* A pilot location was selected for a test rollout of the program. The orientation for all UAW-represented GM employees included a "State of the Business" presentation by the plant manager and a union perspective from the UAW shop chairperson. A surprising 65 percent of UAW-represented employees in the plant chose to participate in the pilot. They attended a workshop, created a development plan, and met with a career advisor. Depending on an individual's goals, a plan could include going back to school, among other options. A manufacturing skills curriculum was created jointly with a local community college, and courses were offered on-site at the plant. Participation in the life-work planning process at the pilot site exceeded the numbers of those who typically enrolled in the local skill center (primarily for basic skills improvement in reading, math, and other areas) and those who utilized the UAW-GM Tuition Assistance Program. The participants included production

continued

workers and skilled trades workers. For some participants, high school was their last formal education. Others had taken some college courses or technical training, and some had completed two- or four-year degrees. Skilled trades workers are required to successfully complete an apprenticeship.

Some participants had not previously considered upgrading their skills, assuming that they could "wait it out" until retirement. The manufacturing workplace has changed significantly, however, since they were hired. Jobs typically require more employee knowledge and responsibility on the plant floor. Workers are required to use more skills than they perhaps did in the past. Today, both the UAW and GM know that skill development and training play an increasingly important role in maintaining competitiveness and strengthening employment security for all UAW-represented GM employees. The workshop at the pilot plant offered some enjoyable and enlightening assessment exercises. Participants learned a model for life-work planning that they could apply to present job skill improvement, future opportunities in the plant, preretirement planning or longer-range life planning. People who had been in production or skilled trades all of their working lives were able to identify a variety of their own transferable skills, which increased their self-esteem and their willingness to pursue new learning. Individuals created their own goals and determined action steps. For many, this meant additional education, a step they could now approach with new motivation and focus. Some participants committed to improving their reading and math skills as a basis for additional skill training. One participant shared with the facilitator that the process had already changed her life. She had always felt like a victim of her circumstances. The pilot life-work planning process helped her see how she could take some action. Participants also received individual assistance from a career advisor for additional assessment, exploration, identification of community resources, goal setting, or implementation of their plans.

Change is never easy. It takes a supportive, group process in which people can share their concerns, receive information, and develop a proactive approach to planning and achieving goals that can benefit them in the long run at work and in their lives.

From *Driving Your Future*. Used by permission of the UAW-GM Center for Human Resources and Career Directions, Inc.

Multirater (360-degree feedback) instruments are popular because they are a means of giving and receiving feedback without being dependent on the skills of others to do so. People feel they can be more direct because the assessment they provide is somewhat anonymous, or at least not given face to face. The feedback may be about identified organizational competencies, more generic skills such as leadership skills, or interpersonal skills. Validated assessments provide useful data for individuals to use as a basis for development planning.

Career discussions between managers and employees are another important means of reality testing. Whether analyzing gaps between their scores on a manager–employee assessment, discussing level of achievement on performance goals, or evaluating a just-completed project, regular, honest feedback is an essential ingredient in a development culture. Feedback should not just be given as evaluation during an annual performance review; it is needed for course correction along the way and to reinforce valuable behaviors that the employee has demonstrated. Invariably, managers and employees alike need training in the constructive giving and receiving of feedback. Open communication and developmental feedback are essential elements of a development culture.

Employees need feedback on four topics for career development planning:

- Present performance as it relates to future opportunities
- Reputation
- Viability of goals
- Reality of development plans and options

Present Performance as It Relates to Future Opportunities   The first area needing reality testing, and one essential to performance management, is feedback about performance on the present job. This feedback differs a bit for career development in that it includes a focus on how this performance will affect future opportunities. This is where the performance review and a career discussion are most likely to overlap. While performance must be discussed in a career discussion, career plans should not necessarily be discussed in a performance review.

Reputation   Another important type of reality testing is information on one's reputation. A topic avoided in many organizations, reputation—or how one is perceived by others—has derailed many careers. Lack of feedback about reputation also allows many employees to have unrealistic goals—that is, goals that everyone in the organization except the employee knows are unrealistic. When these goals are continually thwarted, employees become cynical, and any needs for realistic develop-ment go unmet. The following case example illustrates the importance of clear discussions about reputation:

John participated in his company's new career development program because he saw it as a way to get promoted. He had applied for sev-eral promotions over the last three years, but was never successful. The last four attempts did not even result in an interview. John was angry, believing that it was his manager who was blocking his oppor-tunity. When he asked the human resources department why he wasn't considered, the answer was always that others were more qualified. So John came to a career planning workshop with the goal of identifying exactly what he needed to do to get promoted. Others in the class could see that his cynical, critical behavior was not what was needed in a manager.

Discussions about reputation in general managed to shed some light on his own, but he still didn't recognize that the way others perceived him was a critical factor in career success. The human resources manager and John's current manager both said privately that John would never become a manager in that company; his atti-tude, behavior, and interpersonal skills simply would keep him from being promoted. But no one ever confronted John with this informa-tion to enable him either to work on his reputation or to set more realistic goals. John and many others like him in organizations across the country need honest, direct feedback about their reputations to get them on track with establishing realistic goals.

Viability of Goals   Individuals also need reality testing on the viability of their goals. Discussing tentative goals is essential before individuals put much energy into attaining them. This discussion may be with one's man-ager, but it also might be with a mentor, a manager in the targeted area, a career counselor, or an advisor. If the goals require the support of one's manager, then his or her advice and counsel are critical. If the manager doesn't agree with the goal, or believes the goal or the time frame for reaching it is unrealistic, what are the chances that he or she will support the employee's efforts to attain it?

When introduced to their role in managing career development, man-agers sometimes express concern about dealing with unrealistic goals that employees may have. They don't want to be in a position to tell an employee that he or she shouldn't have a certain goal, and they often need help addressing the issue and providing reality testing about goals. Even when others agree that an employee's goal is viable, there needs to

Table 25

Forces That May Support or Restrain Achievement of a Goal

Supporting Forces	Restraining Forces
Organizational need to fill a position or assignment	Limited availability of positions
Organizational need to build bench strength	Organizational changes
Lack of competition	Competition
Appropriate credentials	Lack of credentials
Appropriate experience	Lack of or insufficient experience
Solid skills that relate to the goal	Lack of required or valued skills
Positive reputation and/or visibility	Poor reputation and/or lack of visibility with decision makers
Enthusiasm for the goal	Lack of clarity about the goal
Excellent performance on present job	Present performance problems or weaknesses
Management support	Lack of management support
Right timing	Wrong timing

From *Managing Career Development,* by P. Simonsen, 1994. Rolling Meadows, IL: Career Directions, Inc.

be awareness about the barriers that must be overcome to achieve the goal, and this is best addressed in a frank discussion. A conversation about the existing factors that will contribute to or prevent achieving the goal is a strong means of reality testing. After this discussion, employees will occasionally see the difficulty of achieving their goal and may either identify shorter-term goals that will contribute to a longer-range goal, or they may change the goal altogether.

In this process, everyone involved needs to recognize that not achieving a career goal doesn't mean failure because the efforts to overcome barriers along the way are developmental steps that contribute to growth. Even if they don't result in this particular goal, achievements are valuable in their own right.

An effective way to assist employees in analyzing the viability of their goals is by identifying the forces restraining or contributing to the goal, as presented in Table 25.

By recognizing all the forces working against the goal and identifying all the forces supporting a goal, a clear picture is created of the viability of the goal for the individual.

Reality of Development Plans and Options   Once it is agreed that a goal is worth working on, the fourth type of reality testing employees need in their career development planning is about development options to achieve their goals. They will identify some activities that are obvious, but other options may need their manager's support to achieve. Some individuals get so enthusiastic about their goals and plans that they are overly ambitious and need grounding in how much time is available to work on the goal or the likelihood of having the type of development opportunities they want in the time frame they are counting on. Others are the opposite—they have ambitious goals but lack sufficient commitment to the effort and actions needed to achieve them. In both situations, individuals often need and value input from others to make sure they are on target before committing efforts to development actions.

As you create a career development process for employees, attend to some means of providing feedback or other reality testing. Reality testing needs to be peppered throughout the process for employees. It is not a one-time measure or conversation, but a process that employees need to recognize and value and seek out as appropriate. Employees need to have their antennae up to receive feedback whenever it is available. Regular feedback is essential in a development culture.

Looking Outward

The second step in the career planning model involves looking outward to identify the needs and opportunities in the organization and industry. Some of these needs and opportunities are listed in Table 26. Especially in a changing environment, where the old paths and expectations are no longer viable, participants in a career planning process must have as much information as possible on which to base realistic career goals. Without good information, they are planning in a vacuum or basing their plans on out-of-date information and models, hoping that the goals they set are realistic and can be achieved in the organization. For example, with the old mind-set of career development meaning promotions, people will set unrealistic goals to move up if they don't know the skills needed for the future or the areas of growth necessary for viable lateral moves.

Table 26

Essential Organizational Information Needed for Career Focus

- Organization's strategic objectives and business needs
- Organization and department structure
- Climate/culture
- Human resources policies and systems for selection, development, and rewards
  Staffing systems
  Job posting
  Mobility systems
  Tuition assistance
  Training programs
  Mentoring programs
  Development opportunities
  Compensation system
- Competencies
- Information about departments, positions or roles, job descriptions, and so on
- Information about trends, growth areas, emerging technologies, and so on
- Other resources that support career development, such as contacts in various departments, career fairs, or informal sessions to learn about other areas of the company

There are varying reasons why information for career planning is often hard to come by. Sometimes it doesn't—and can't—exist because things are changing so fast. For example, employees will ask for information about career paths, expecting a road map for their planning. While career paths cannot be defined for most people in most organizations today, some information about positions or roles can and should be available. Even when organizational strategic plans may change because of market forces, employees need a vision and as much information as is available on which to base their short- and long-range plans.

Sometimes the information needed is seen as secret—only a few decision makers should know. For example, in some technical organizations where product time-to-market is shrinking to incredibly short months, not years, it is feared that advance notice to employees will also provide advance notice to competitors. However, if management wants employees who are ready with the skills needed for the future, employees need to know what those skills are and where they might apply those skills. This is where identified competencies can be used for career planning so employees can be developing in ways the company needs, even without a specific job in mind. In a product- or project-driven environment, when career planning means targeting new projects, not jobs, people need to know the trends and new applications in addition to the competencies needed for the future. In a development culture, development needs must be apparent.

There is often an assumption by senior management that employees know the direction and needs of the organization but are not acting on them. Even when such information is published or otherwise communicated to everyone, employees, and often managers, need help "translating" from the big picture to actions they should take. If the career development system starts with and is driven by business needs, these needs will be communicated as an integral part of individuals' planning. But even when people know the business or industry trends and issues, these must be translated first to career implications and then to individual actions. Development Culture Survey 5: Career Implications provides some examples. Implications may be positive or negative for career development, but in either case they are important to recognize for viable goal setting. This process of translating business needs into development plans is difficult to do alone. Most employees will need help from their manager, but a career advisor or a mentor can also be helpful.

Another category of information people need is about resources and systems that support their career planning efforts. How do they get information about other departments or divisions? If the company needs people with a broader base, is trying to eliminate functional silos, and is encouraging lateral moves rather than promotions, how do individuals get information about how their skills will transfer or what experience is important in other areas? How do they know which areas are growing and which are retrenching, in order to plan in advance? Job posting systems are useful to learn of openings, but employees need information and resources to help them prepare in advance for openings. Table 26 lists some important information about resources and systems that employees need to know.

It is essential for informed career development planning that individuals have awareness of the formal and informal culture of the organization as a whole and how culture varies in different business units. The formal culture is that which is published in the annual report or communicated in recruitment brochures. The informal culture is more likely to be learned and picked up over time. There are two pitfalls in trying to read culture today: The culture of many organizations is changing to the point where behaviors and even credentials that were rewarded in the past may no longer be needed or valued; long-time employees may in fact

DEVELOPMENT CULTURE SURVEY

5 *Career Implications*

Fill in trends, career implications, and appropriate actions for your organization. Some examples are provided.

Business or Industry Trends and Issues	Career Implications	Individual Actions
Flatter organizations	Fewer management positions	Create various goals other than promotions
Self-managed teams	Opportunities for team leadership	Improve group facilitation

From *Managing Career Development,* by P. Simonsen, 1994. Rolling Meadows, IL: Career Directions, Inc.

send incorrect messages about the culture to newcomers. If you are using career development to contribute to a development culture, an overt focus on the emerging culture should be a part of the career focus component of development planning. It is valuable in a career planning workshop or in individual career counseling sessions to address the issue of the organization's culture and what that means for informed career development planning. Especially in a transition period, individuals' plans may be off-base if they are not cognizant of the influence of cultural factors on their career plans.

Some of the components of a comprehensive career development system described in Chapter 5, if communicated to employees, can become a source of information for their planning. In addition, career development specialists can organize and schedule information sessions about trends and needs in various areas of the company. These sessions are often led by senior managers and open to anyone interested in learning about the work there. Individuals attend not only for potential moves but also to broaden their understanding of how their work interrelates with that of other departments or to have a bigger picture of the issues in the organization as a whole. This kind of information is essential for anyone targeting a promotion or leadership position. Even in very large organizations, senior managers are saying they want employees to understand the business or "act like an owner."

Another approach to making information available for informed development planning is a network of representatives across the organization who are willing to talk to people about their work and potential opportunities in their field. Not expected to be career advisors, these people may be enlisted from the ranks of those who have participated in the career development process, so they understand what kind of information would be helpful to others and why they are exploring. Some organizations structure this process, with inquiries being channeled through the HR department to manage the contact process. Others simply make the list of resource persons available with other career resources (in a workshop or through a career center).

The difficulty with information today is that it changes as fast as it is gathered and communicated. This is why organizations are beginning to put career management information on an intranet where it can be widely accessible and updated without reprinting and redistributing volumes. As the move to defining roles instead of job descriptions grows, information will not become out-of-date quite so fast. Roles that contribute to the core competencies of the organization will not change and become obsolete as quickly as jobs and therefore job descriptions. Measured less by tasks and more by outcomes, assignments will need to be defined as they come into existence.

And as work increasingly is defined by the incumbent, individual planning will be driven more by knowing one's strengths and the capabilities they bring to their work. As stated above, career planning today is less about matching individuals and jobs, and more about the flexibility and savvy to make a continuing contribution in a changing variety of roles.

Looking Forward

Once individuals have completed some self-assessment and related their needs to the needs and realities of the organization, they are ready to look forward, defining and writing development goals.

Types of Goals

The terminology used to communicate the career development process, and the business case driving the need for career development, will influence the types of goals individuals set. For example, if the organization is flatter and positions carry more responsibility than in the past, there needs to be emphasis on developing in place and expanding or updating skills, rather than on promotions. If the business needs are for individuals who are flexible and can adapt to new assignments quickly, and for the elimination of narrow functional specialties, then lateral moves need to be encouraged and supported by processes that make them possible. In any case, employees need to recognize several categories of goals as viable alternatives. Beverly Kaye, in *Up Is Not the Only Way* (1982), originally defined a variety of goals to guide employee development. Sometimes individuals will choose not to participate in a career development program because they say they are happy in their present job and don't want to move. What they don't understand is that career development doesn't just involve moves, and in changing organizations and development cultures, most of the development that takes place is on the present job.

A list of types of goals can be communicated or posted in a career center to reinforce this message, or they can be included in an orientation session to ensure that people get this message before they choose whether to participate in the program.

Personal Development   Everyone should have goals that result in personal growth. The basis for this type of goal may have resulted from skills assessment, anchors, or values awareness. For example, if technical/functional competence is one's anchor, a goal is likely to be to increase expertise. Changes in the organization may also require that people change to meet new challenges.

Role Enhancement   Often values can be better met, or skills used more effectively, by modifying the present position. If people aspire to more responsibility, it is essential that they seek opportunities to build and demonstrate capabilities *before* they plan for moves. This may require the assistance of their supervisor. Supervisors are able to help articulate enrichment or broadening opportunities and discuss how they will benefit the present as well as the future.

Promotion   If all of an individual's self-assessment seems to lead to the need, sooner or later, to move up, then a promotion goal needs to be considered. If the individual has conducted solid organizational research, he or she will know how realistic this is in the organization and how much competition can be expected. Promotion goals may need to be a longer-range goal, with mini-goals or developmental steps that will prepare the candidate to be ready when the promotion opportunity occurs.

Lateral Moves   If a person wants to broaden his or her base, wants to attain higher managerial levels in the future, or is simply seeking diversity or new challenges, a lateral move should be considered. This can be a position change within the department for cross-training, or it may be a move to another site. If the person's experience is seen as too specialized, or positions are being eliminated, he or she may be forced to move laterally. Making a lateral move can be an excellent way to grow, even for people who have plateaued.

Changing Fields or Functions   A major change of direction, occupation, or field is not an easy move to make, but it can be done. Sometimes the changes occurring in organizations—such as downsizing, relocations, and changing technology—force a change to a new occupation or function. Employees who know they are in the wrong field may need to plan for a major move. If their interests are in one area but their work is in another, a change of direction may be indicated.

Reduced or Changed Responsibility   Sometimes it is appropriate to plan for a move down the ladder to a position that is more desirable. Lifestyle balance or changed needs, as well as pending retirement, may drive the plan to reduce responsibility. Sometimes people move up only to find that the fit is not as good as it was previously. These are conditions in which to consider a move down. Not often understood because of the pervasive sense that everyone should move up, this goal needs to be clearly articulated.

Exploratory Goals   When individuals do not have a clear sense of career direction, even after participating in a career development program, they may want to create an exploratory goal. Rather than exploring as a step to another goal, an exploratory goal can be created as a goal in itself. This goal allows time and provides a plan to seek sufficient information on which to set goals for the future. An exploratory goal could take the form of an internship, an interdepartmental assignment, cross-training, or simply having conversations with people in other departments.

Writing Goals and Development Plans

Goals and development plans need to be written so that they can be shared and tracked and accomplishments measured. While an individual's assessment and exploration of options should be confidential, the goals that result from this process need to be communicated to those who can influence their achievement. A development plan form can serve the purpose of formalizing goals and development actions, providing a consistent way to record plans, and forming a basis for communication. Communication about goals and development plans can be informal, as in a career discussion, or formal, for example, kept in a database for use in organizational staffing, succession planning, and/or training needs assessment. How the written plan will be used or recorded is a design issue driven by the purpose of the development planning process and whether participation is required.

Most individuals and managers need training in writing measurable goals, unless this has been recently covered in introducing a developmental performance management process. How goals are written influences whether they can be successfully attained. Particularly with personal development and enhancement goals, people tend to write vague hopes rather than specific, measurable goals. For example, an employee might write "Improve my computer skills" as a personal development goal or "Take on more responsibility for supervising others" as an enrichment goal. More rigor should be expected in the way goals are written, particularly if achievement of goals will be one measure of success of the process.

Managers and employees alike need to be encouraged to use creativity in identifying development planning activities. Without this thorough career planning process, traditional discussions about development in the old culture resulted in managers recommending that the employee get a degree or take training programs. Often this was an arbitrary decision, driven more by what was available rather than by a specific development need of the employee. In a development culture, internal and external training options should be driven by need rather than selected from a menu of traditional course options. Just as human resources services are changing to a business support function driven by needs of the business, training functions are evolving to just-in-time training determined by the development needs of individuals or groups in the organization.

Development Options

Beyond training or external education, development options should include on-the-job learning activities, self-directed learning, challenging assignments, and even outside activities such as leadership in professional or community organizations. Development options can be selected to do the following:

- Overcome barriers
- Build on strengths
- Create better fit
- Achieve greater job satisfaction
- Expand existing skills sets
- Encourage accomplishments
- Create new challenges
- Prepare for a desired future level of responsibility
- Prepare for a future move
- Keep career planning *strategic,* that is, in line with the direction of the company

Categories of Developmental Experience

Lombardo and Eichinger (1989) have identified five categories of experiences that were found to be most developmental for people who ultimately reached executive levels in their companies. These include challenging assignments, role models, hardships, coursework, and off-the-job experience.

Challenging Assignments   Challenging assignments provide experience in leadership, coping with pressure, and dealing with problems. They require the ability to learn quickly and apply new learning on the job.

Examples of challenging assignments include the following:

- Starting a new operation or process
- Fixing troubled or problem areas

■ Expanding the scope of an existing operation
■ Dealing with the possibility of failure and with visibility to influence others
■ Working when there are tight deadlines or high stakes
■ Dealing with problem people or incompatible groups
■ Juggling multiple demands
■ Influencing people or factors over which there is no formal authority or direct control
■ Utilizing organizational or strategic perspectives

Role Models   Contact with a role model can be a developmental experience. A role model may be a manager, a mentor, or a project director or other short-term manager. Exceptional people, or those with particular skills or experience to teach, become influential to others' development.

The following are some examples of the types of learning from role models:

■ Interpersonal skills or style
■ Balancing technical and people skills
■ Integrity and ethics
■ Leadership versus management
■ Exemplary technical skills
■ Industry or company knowledge

Hardships   Hardships cause learning by pushing people to their limits. Taking risks, overcoming barriers, or making mistakes can cause people to consider the goal and the means of achieving it. People don't seek hardships, of course, but existing problems can be learning opportunities. (Can employees take lemons and make lemonade?)

Some examples of hardships that can be developmental include the following:

■ Limited resources—either budget or staff
■ Having to terminate individuals or reduce total staff
■ Ambiguity of goals or responsibility
■ Dealing with difficult people
■ Systems or procedures that are contradictory or become an obstacle to achieving the goal
■ Lack of support and/or skills or background

Coursework   Internal or external training is developmental, beyond the content to be learned. It provides a chance to build self-confidence, compare oneself with peers (within or outside the organization), learn from others as well as the instructor, and translate the learning to application on the job.

Some examples of ways that coursework can have developmental impact include the following:

I Identifying in advance what needs to be learned and the best forum in which to learn it

I Attendance at courses with others beyond the immediate work group

I Teaching or sharing the learning with others after the course

I Planning ways to incorporate the new learning into behaviors on the job

I Opportunity to learn skills or knowledge not needed on the present job but that can be demonstrated to show readiness for future opportunities

I Requiring a particularly big stretch—an intellectual challenge or major change of behavior

Off-the-Job Experience   External experiences provide a different dimension and opportunities not necessarily available at work. In the case of volunteer contributions, employees can often seek the type of experience that will round out their on-the-job learning.

Some examples of outside experience that can be developmental include the following:

I Community service

I Leadership in professional groups

I Participating in groups for targeting a skill or building experience (such as Toastmasters)

I Activities that provide opportunities to showcase skills or knowledge (such as speaking engagements or writing)

Development Strategies

A variety of developmental options that contribute to achievement of the goal can also overcome the issue of time to work on the goal. For example, on-the-job experiences may not take additional time, but in fact may accomplish a needed task or project while being a learning experience for the employee. Cross-training, or learning another function in the department, can ensure backup skills or bench strength for the organization. But it can also provide the employee with the freedom to expand his or her own role and a learning experience that contributes to his or her developmental goals. Self-directed learning may include the use of a company skills center, computer-based training, reading, or video- or audiotapes.

When writing development plans, it is important to indicate success measures and time frames. Some development strategies are measured in the doing. If a strategy is to assume responsibility for scheduling projects, doing so (with some measure of quantity and quality) is the measure of completion. Comparative or nonspecific words like *more, better, improve, learn,* and so forth do not indicate how achievement will be measured. Sometimes, instead of trying to write measurements into the strategy itself, especially with behavior changes, it is easier to list the outcomes that will occur as a result of accomplishing this action. For example, if a strategy is to gain visibility with decision makers, success measures identified as outcomes might include the following:

- "Be selected for a cross-department task force"
- "Make at least one successful presentation to senior management"
- "Take on a leadership position in the all-company picnic"

Some organizations develop or purchase resources for managers and individuals to use in development planning so each person does not have to research options independently. Databases that match competencies to development options are gaining in popularity because they assist in the transition from awareness of development needs to action needed.

Manager Involvement

A career center or career advisor can be helpful in the development planning process but cannot take the place of managers' active involvement with a direct report's development. Only supervisors or managers see the employee's work on a daily basis and are in a position to identify on-the-job assignments that will be developmental for the employee while meeting the department's needs. The assumption here is that there is a trusting relationship between the two so that a discussion can truly be developmental.

A significant outcome from career discussions between managers and employees is a comprehensive development plan based on thoughtful planning. Important to hold separate from a performance evaluation session, development planning is forward looking and contributed to by both parties rather than evaluative and focused on the past time period. It is also driven by the employee's needs and goals rather than the department's immediate objectives. To the extent that goals come together and are discussed, everyone wins.

Implementation of Development Plans

Once development plans are created and agreed upon by manager and employee, support needs to be provided for implementation of plans. For example, if it is agreed that a leadership development course is appropriate for future roles within the organization, there need to be policies and acknowledgment that allow participation. The course may not contribute to the specific skills needed to perform successfully in the present job and therefore may not be seen as a priority by the manager who has deadlines to meet. For managers, having to juggle the demands for the present with support for development, policies are helpful to guide implementation of plans for employees. All the effort of planning is negated if individuals are prevented from accomplishing their development actions. If managers are participants in establishing the plans, they are more likely to support their implementation. One organization allows managers the latitude to prohibit attendance at a development event once because of pressing business needs, but not more than once. The second time the employee is scheduled to attend, the manager cannot intervene.

Development plans need to be revisited regularly. If time frames are identified for each strategy, they can be checked off as completed. Some strategies may be long term, such as completing a degree, so milestones along the way should be indicated.

If the organization requires development plans, then some measures of completion are called for to measure individuals' progress as well as to evaluate the impact of the development planning process. The number of people with plans is an indication of involvement; the number of goals accomplished in the given time frame is a measure of success for the individual; and the outcomes affecting the business needs are a measure of success of the total process. Chapter 14 describes the career evaluation process in depth.

Annual updating of goals and development plans ensures linkage with business needs, appropriate goals for the changing environment, more action to work toward goals in a consistent manner, and ongoing contribution to a development culture. Even if individuals do not accomplish their specific goals, if they are growing, and particularly growing in ways needed by the organization, they are contributing to the development culture. A program goal is to get individuals to recognize this, take ownership for it, and be rewarded for making a greater contribution. Organizational policy and managers need to support these efforts, and individuals need to take ownership for their own development planning and actions.

All of these components of the career development model discussed in this chapter—looking inward, looking outward, and looking forward—can be provided by a variety of delivery systems. Self-assessment can be done in career centers with a trained career counselor or through self-directed work and in workshops. Managers are better as coaches and providers of feedback. Organizational information is best delivered by managers or mentors and provided as support systems, but information can be housed in a career center as well. Career centers may offer a less viable way for individuals to ensure that their goals are linked with department business strategies, but they can be a good source of ongoing information about current issues and trends.

Goal setting varies substantially from individual to individual. Some goal-oriented people just need to apply the career planning model to their personal approach, and may not need either a career advisor or their manager to help them do so. Others who have not traditionally set development goals may need someone with whom to talk things over and give them feedback on the viability of their goals or the way the goals are written. Whether they prefer to talk to their manager, a mentor, or a career counselor will depend on their relationship with their manager and whether their career goals might be perceived as disloyal. The structure of the process and resources is a design issue and is discussed in Chapter 13.

The Career Development Design Process

Human nature is not a machine to be built after a model,
and set to do exactly the work prescribed for it, but a tree
which requires to grow and develop itself on all sides,
according to the tendency of the inward forces which
make it a living thing.
—John Stuart Mill

Eight Steps in the Career Development Design Process

Up to this point in Part III, we have covered essential elements in an integrated system and components of a career development process for individuals. The question remains then, Where do you start in order to design this comprehensive system that will contribute to a development culture in your organization?

There are eight steps, not necessarily linear, in the career development design process that will contribute to a successful intervention, as listed in Table 27. An advisory team can provide assistance in all steps of the design process.

Identify the Organization's and the Individual's Needs

As with so many organizational interventions, it is important to start with an assessment of needs, perceived needs, and level of awareness, understanding, or expectations from the process. Often the person or

Table 27

The Eight Steps in Career Development Design

1. Identify the organization's and the individual's needs
2. Envision desirable outcomes
3. Get buy-in from stakeholders
4. Determine design elements and the process
5. Design or purchase components
6. Communicate and educate
7. Implement the process
8. Evaluate and keep the process alive

group responsible for developing a career development program believes he or she already knows the needs. There may have been an employee opinion survey that indicated an unmet need by employees, thereby generating management interest in a career development "solution." There may be a grassroots effort by one department with career issues to persuade the HR department to help them implement career development for their people. There may be a ground swell of requests for help by individuals who are stressed by the changes going on and want to be proactive in managing their careers. Career development needs are likely to emerge after downsizing or major reorganization to help the survivors understand the new rules.

So while the *need* for career development may be obvious, the *expectations* various groups have for it may differ considerably. Even the definition of career development may vary by perspective. A needs assessment process can uncover all these variations and reinforce or change perceptions that the designers have about what is needed by whom and also about what will be accepted.

Focus groups with employee groups or managers, interviews with executives or key stakeholders (such as division HR representatives if this is a corporate initiative), surveys of selected populations or across the board, or some combination of these may be the methodology to uncover needs and expectations. Sometimes the data gathered indicates an unrealistic expectation, such as employees equating career development with promotions. This type of finding contributes to the need for education about what this thing called career development is about. Even though your initial efforts may be limited because of time, resources, or

Table 28

Questions for Identifying Organizational and Individual Needs

- Who are the stakeholders? Which groups have what investment in a successful career development effort?
- Who are the supporters and cheerleaders for career development in your organization?
- What are the business issues identified by executives and other leaders?
- How will a career development process relate to performance management or other systems already in place? Do people see them as related? Contradictory?
- How interested/excited/knowledgeable are the masses out there?
- How well do people understand needs and expected behaviors in a development culture? Where are they on the paradigm shift to strategic career management?
- What kind of objections or concerns do people have about the development process?
- What "baggage" do you need to be aware of? What are the prior attempts at career development?
- What would be the consequences of fixing needs? Of not fixing them?
- Who has a stake in keeping needs a problem?
- What changes are occurring that would support your efforts? Hinder them?
- What are people doing now to manage their careers? (This question can lead to pre- or post-evaluation measures.)
- What will work—in terms of acceptance, commitment, and belief in the outcomes? (How complete an intervention do you need or can you undertake?)
- What kind of resources will people use? Will they use a center? Will they discuss career issues with their manager?

budget, it is wise to identify needs through a representative sample of the total organization. The needs in one group may be different from those of another department, location, or division, and the diversity of needs is important to know up front. A budding development culture in one area can be thwarted by a lack of awareness or by linkage to other areas of the company. Some of the questions you may want to ask in your data gathering are listed in Table 28.

These and many other questions can be answered or perspective gained by a needs assessment process. The results can be summarized in a report to stakeholders that is presented in an executive briefing and used as a basis for designing the program. Define needs in terms that decision makers will relate to and understand. Provide support for your opinion that needs can be met by a career development process.

Envision Desirable Outcomes

As was discussed in Chapter 3, a clearly articulated vision of the desired future state is essential in guiding change and supporting the efforts to get there. You may seek a consensus on a vision for the whole development culture: What will the organization look like in this desired future state? What behaviors will be evident? Or you may focus more narrowly on the career development program: What elements of a career development program are important to contribute to a development culture?

This is where an advisory group, a career development team, or focus groups of key stakeholders are important. An *affinity charting* process can be an excellent way to generate independent thinking while benefiting from group dynamics. This process involves having people identify as many characteristics of the desired future state of a development culture as they can think of, in any order, using self-stick notes. You can then have participants post each idea on the wall and arrange them by their affinity to other ideas. In defining a comprehensive approach to career development, look for topics that are related to *selection processes, development processes and opportunities,* and *reward systems.* The topic of compensation is sure to come up in an affinity process. The employee may discuss selection only from the perspective of promotions. Any topics are worthy of consideration, so all get posted and categorized.

The affinity charting process serves several purposes. It taps the thinking and expectations of each person, so no one's ideas are ignored. The frequency with which a topic occurs gives the topic some strength. A sense of the emotions behind certain issues might become apparent, but the participants focus their energy on positives rather than on complaining about present problems. The categories that emerge provide everyone with a broader view of a desired future state than they may have had to begin with. And the facilitator receives excellent input that may provide a new perspective. Sometimes it becomes obvious that an important piece is missing, and the group together can flesh out any weak links. A rich discussion ensues, so that in a short time you have created a solid basis for planning.

This process can be repeated by several groups, if appropriate. Once it has been completed and consistent elements surface, a vision can be written and validated by other stakeholders who were not contributors. Table 29 lists some questions that may stimulate discussion to help groups begin envisioning desirable outcomes.

The answers to these questions can contribute to a process map that outlines the how, not the *what,* including actions and time frames necessary to

Table 29

Questions for Envisioning Desirable Outcomes

Focusing on the Future

- Does everyone share the same vision? If not, why?
- If this vision is achieved, will we be where we want to be?
- What will still be missing?
- What time frame is realistic?
- Where can we start to move toward this vision? What is realistic?

Analyzing the Present

- Where are you now?
- How big a gap is there between the present and the desired future state?
- What will need to be done to narrow the gap?
- What additional resources/staff will you need?
- What are your budget possibilities and limitations?

---

close the gap between the present and the desired future state—a development culture.

Get Buy-In from Stakeholders

If in your needs assessment you identified champions—people of influence who support your efforts and the goal of building a development culture—be sure you enlist them to contribute to planning and to spread their understanding in the organization. Identify others whose support you need. Recognize also those who have objections.

An advisory team or a career development committee or council can be a valuable resource for contributing to the planning and design and also to spread the ownership beyond one person and/or one department. Even if you represent one area, your influence and success can be broader if the process is not seen as territorial. A group made up of representatives of various areas and levels who are willing to meet occasionally and be seen as a liaison between the project designers and the troops serves the additional purpose of influencing popular opinion to gain more support and build enthusiasm (see Chapter 10).

In your process of seeking widespread buy-in for this project, seek answers to some of the questions in Table 30.

Table 30

Questions for Getting Buy-In from Stakeholders

- Who are the people who have a stake in the outcome but are not yet overt supporters?
- What objections are you hearing?
- Are there objections because some people don't understand the intent of the process? Is there a need for educating and informing?
- Are objectors or skeptics concerned about the scope or the reality of achieving the intended outcome?
- How will you communicate the benefits of a development process to the stakeholders?
- What do you have to do to gain support or acceptance?
- Will you choose to ignore some objectors to concentrate on those whose support you need?

It is important to have the commitment of a critical mass. You may remember the story of the chicken and the pig at a ham-and-eggs breakfast —the chicken is involved, but the pig is committed. Beckhard and Harris (1987) recommend "a systematic analysis of the systems, subsystems, individuals, and groups" to find out who is committed to the process.

Gaining support is not a one-time action but an ongoing process. Some people who believe in the concept will support it, but they may withhold judgment to see what actually gets delivered. Some skeptics will need to be converted, perhaps by education, but more likely by actions. A continuing communication about the vision, goals, and status of development of the project can chip away at the resistance, but it can also cause more questions if too much time elapses from announcement of the initiative to delivery of some tangible outcomes.

Acceptance also depends on the culture, the changes taking place in the culture, and the history of "walking the talk." Some people responsible for introducing the process seek some short-term successes, perhaps with a department or group with more urgent needs, as a demonstration of what the deliverables might be. This approach requires caution, however, so as not to be seen as a quick-fix approach or the program of the month when the problem and need are systemic.

Table 31

Questions for Determining Design Elements and the Process

▌ Who are your customers (target population)?

▌ If your target population is varied, such as both professional and production employees, will one system work for all or will there need to be variations?

▌ Will a pilot program or group be useful? If so, how will group members be chosen?

▌ Will budget constraints, staff availability, or time constraints create a need to roll out in phases, or will you plan for full-scale implementation?

▌ How will you incorporate business needs into resources and services for employees?

▌ How will you link and build on existing resources and systems?

▌ What kind of accountability will there be? What records will be kept? By whom?

▌ How will participants be rewarded or acknowledged for changing their behavior and accepting the challenge of managing their careers strategically?

▌ How will you measure success? What baseline data is needed now for comparison after implementation?

▌ Who will pay for participation?

▌ Will employee participation be on their own time or company time—or some combination of both?

▌ Who will be involved in the further design? Will the advisory team continue? Will you use an external consultant? Who has the expertise you need in-house?

Determine Design Elements and the Process

Design elements are not the components of the program, but rather considerations that need to be decided in the design process. Some of these may be clearly known from the data-gathering process, such as which population will be targeted, whether career development will be seen as voluntary for those who choose to participate, or whether everyone is expected to generate a development plan. Some questions to be answered in this design phase are listed in Table 31.

Circumstances and the driving needs may determine answers to these questions, but some of them may be policy issues that need to be determined before finalizing program design. For example, if participants are hourly workers and participation will be on company time, that may drive decisions about length of workshops, or whether a self-directed process with access to an advisor is a better approach. Answers to some of these questions may be generated by the design itself, such as incorporating

Table 32

Questions for Designing or Purchasing Components

___

- How will you ensure that your career development process addresses organizational realities and needs?
- Who will have what responsibility for career management?
- How will everyone be introduced to the concepts of career management?
- How will senior managers be involved?
- What role will line managers and supervisors play?
- What resources or approaches will be used for employees' assessment of values, interests, needs, and skills?
- How will you assess and communicate the competencies your organization needs?
- What information and resources will be available to participants for realistic career planning?
- Will resources be purchased, customized, or developed in-house?
- How will implementation work?

___

a process for communicating business needs that may result in a goal-cascading process.

Design or Purchase Components

Once structural elements are determined, components of the career development program itself can be designed. Considering the essential elements identified in Chapter 11, the process of designing can be launched. It is important to ensure that the model of the process incorporates managers' roles and organizational systems, as well as resources for employees. If the objective is to create a development culture, career development must be integrated with organizational systems. Even employees who fully embrace the new paradigm and work at managing their careers strategically cannot create a development culture without support and systemic change. To achieve your organization's vision, employee behavior must change, but so must managers' and organizational supports. To initiate the planning of career development system components, ask some of the questions listed in Table 32.

If your needs assessment and vision were solid, if your stakeholders contribute leadership and a perspective on the expected outcomes, and if your policy issues have been resolved, these questions may have already been answered. If not, you may need to design a model and get feedback from your advisory board or other stakeholders before moving forward. If you choose to start with a pilot program, make sure you set it up to obtain representative input from initial participants and are prepared to modify the program to respond to appropriate feedback and recommendations.

Communicate and Educate

When planning the communication and education necessary for a successful career development process, consider three uses for any communication efforts: informing and educating people before or at the time the process is initiated, communicating to the various people who are involved at different times and using different resources in the process, and keeping the process alive beyond initial participation and enthusiasm. All three make up the total communication and marketing strategy that is a part of the design process.

Initial communication includes some of the strategies discussed in Chapter 11, with various stakeholders involved at different times and levels. Once some of the preliminary educating is done, with senior managers and perhaps an advisory team, then a broader focus of communication can be planned. Some questions that need to be answered as you get ready to launch a process are listed in the first section of Table 33.

Once people are participating, how will you keep the momentum going? What communication processes or methods will work to encourage further participation, new participants, or completion of the process by past participants? For example, if you plan a gradual rollout of self-directed resources and training for employees, it is valuable to capture the enthusiasm and successes of the first groups to encourage later groups to become involved. Of course, the informal network will carry messages throughout the organization, so it is wise to capitalize on the positives and minimize any negatives that might get into the rumor mill. Some questions to be considered in the design phase are listed in the second section of Table 33.

One company with a corporate office and many field offices decided to create a quarterly career development newsletter. One of the development needs being addressed was the lack of information about home office positions for people in the field. So in addition to all the information built into the managers' and employees' career development planning training sessions, information was communicated via a newsletter. It included successes by participants, highlighting lateral moves and achievement of goals besides promotions to reinforce new thinking about career development. It included interviews with people in a variety of jobs to highlight what they did, but also to illustrate the fact that there was no one career path to various positions.

Table 33

Questions for Communicating and Educating

Getting Ready to Launch a Process

▍ What career development philosophy and approach will you communicate? Who will be the best person to carry the message? What will be the best way to communicate the message?

▍ How will you inform and educate employees and managers so they understand the purpose and scope of the program?

▍ Which publicity strategies will work in your evolving culture?

▍ How do you get attention without leaving the impression that career development is an *event*?

▍ Would an event such as a showcase or open house be a fun and visible way to launch the process?

Once the Process Is Launched

▍ How can you use the positive experiences of some participants to build broader interest and perceived value by others?

▍ How can you communicate successes of some participants to support the value and benefit of the career development effort?

▍ How will you communicate the effect the process is having on achieving business results? On contributing to a development culture? (Quantitative measures may not yet show results in the short term, but interviews with managers may indicate visible behavior change by employees who are participating in the program.)

▍ How will you communicate with past participants so they continue to implement the goals they set and/or revisit the process so they don't perceive it as a one-time event?

▍ How can you use outcomes from the career development program to contribute to an overall culture change?

Implement the Process

With all the design and planning conducted, implementation becomes a procedural management process. Implementation is the *doing*. Depending on the type of services available to employees and managers and the speed of intended rollout implementation, this may be the most cost- and time-intensive part of the process.

If training in development planning is to be conducted for everyone, an intensive short-term effort is needed. If you are introducing a voluntary process, it can be extended over more time. If your resources for employees are primarily self-directed in a career center or virtual center,

Table 34

Questions for Implementing the Process

- How extensive will your initial rollout be? What time period will it cover?
- What administrative preparation will it take?
- What support is necessary for implementation to succeed?
- Who will be the target group? The implementors? The sponsors?
- How will you ensure that organizational systems and the message of development continue to be aligned?
- How will you ensure that development options are available or invented to meet development needs that contribute to the organization's goals?

an initial orientation or open house with doors open for business can be the starting point.

Some organizations implement major efforts over time, with various components and resources introduced as they are completed or incorporated into the process. While a less showy way to implement, this may be more realistic and valuable for employees and managers. In addition, gradual implementation will allow continuing communication to overcome any sense that career development is a workshop or once-a-year requirement.

As discussed in Chapter 12, development options that are available to employees and managers are also means of continued implementation by participants. Skills development, training, on-the-job experiences, or cross-training are means to work toward goals once they are set in a planning component. Some implementation questions to be determined are listed in Table 34.

Evaluate and Keep the Process Alive

Evaluation needs to be based on the business needs driving the career development process and the expectations of stakeholders for particular outcomes. The expectations of your stakeholders will also drive the rigor of evaluation measures. Some companies today expect tangible metrics from every major intervention, even "soft" HR programs. Others resist evaluation because of the extra effort needed to obtain meaningful measures. In any case, to ensure continued support and justification for the process, some measurable outcomes must be assessed. The feedback received by participants upon completion of a training program is valuable at one

Table 35

Questions for Evaluating and Keeping the Process Alive

Evaluating

- What will success look like? Given the desired future state of your initial planning, how will you know when that has been achieved?
- What main result would you like to be able to show two or three years from now?
- How will you evaluate success? Will it be on level of participation, behavior changes by employees or managers, and/or impact on business needs or results?
- What reaction data will be useful?
- How will you measure learning? Behavior change?
- What data needs to be gathered today to use as a baseline for future comparison?

Keeping the Process Alive

- Who will be recipients of the evaluation reports? When?
- Will the evaluation reports be used as progress reports or to gain support for future elements of the process?
- How will you present your findings? Will you have access to some of the same groups—executives, stakeholders, advisory team—that provided input and planning in the beginning of your process?
- Will you have a way to publicize successes—either individual or project—as positive outcomes?

---

level, but not comprehensive. (Chapter 14 provides a more thorough discussion of the evaluation process.) Some questions that can help form an evaluation plan as you design the process are listed in the first section of Table 35.

Once you determine the type of evaluation that is possible and the data that needs to be captured, what will you do with it? The second part of Table 35 lists some questions answered at this stage. A reporting process, which can be a combination of hard data (usually quantitative) and qualitative or more subjective data, needs to be considered.

Even the most comprehensive, well-designed career development process will not stay alive without sustenance and continuous improvement. Just as total quality management requires ongoing evaluation, revision, and refinement, so does a culture-affecting process such as this. Follow-up implementation activities that are available and visible, such as development opportunities and mentoring, keep the focus on career development. The more career development is overtly linked to performance management, compensation, selection, and succession planning, the more managers and employees alike keep up their responsibilities. If career development is a program, it may be seen as an event. For the change in culture to become institutionalized, career development must be seen as a process, with continuing commitment.

Summary of the Design Process

While these design steps are presented in a linear model, rarely can they be so neatly lined up. Several steps must be taken simultaneously, or if action is blocked on one element energy can be diverted to other aspects of the process. But the eight steps can be a guide as you plan and design, so as not to leave a gap that will undermine the ultimate success of your efforts.

It is possible to design and implement a thorough career development process that still does not result in a development culture, given other influences and changes taking place in the organization. But a comprehensive, integrated career development process as described here will make a significant difference and contribute strongly to a development culture. Employees and managers will be better off for moving themselves into the new paradigm of thinking and the new contract. Strategic career management is a proactive way to manage one's career and development, regardless of the environment one is presently in. A longer-range win-win relationship is established, of course, if all parties are targeting the same goals and outcomes, all value the development process and show it in their behaviors and systems, and all reap the benefits of contributing to a development culture.

14

Evaluating the Career Development Process

The means prepare the end, and the end is what the means have made it.

—John Morley

The Need for Evaluation

There are several important reasons to evaluate a career development system. In a development culture, individuals need to be able to measure their growth, and the composite of individual growth is a measure of change in the organization. If the total system is driven by organizational needs, has the intervention met those needs? Evaluation is a way to measure and communicate outcomes, justify the effort and expense of the process, determine continuing needs, and celebrate successes. Desirable outcomes will be different for different stakeholders. Results employees want in order to consider the process a success will be different from outcomes that senior managers expect. To ensure continuing support and involvement, people at all levels need to see tangible outcomes.

Typically, the person or group who designs the career development process will also be involved in its evaluation. In order to measure change in behavior, attitudes, skills, or organizational impact, it is necessary to capture some baseline data before the intervention gets started. Planning for evaluation must occur as the design process is initiated and be incorporated into various aspects of delivery. Evaluation links back to the initial motivation for the process: Why are we doing this? It should link directly to the business needs that are drivers for the process. According to Leibowitz, Farren, and Kaye (1986), "describing the effectiveness of a career development program in the language of business is essential in order to convince the organization of the program's benefits." If one of the issues motivating the career development process was lack of critical skills for changing market demands, are those skills stronger in current employees now? If a driving force was low employee morale following downsizing, has morale improved? The challenge of answering these types of questions, of course, is in how to measure issues such as changes in morale.

While most organizations do some measurement of outcomes from programs, most do not really define measurable results. If your environment is driven by metrics, you probably have many examples from other efforts to follow in measuring outcomes from a career development process. The rigor with which you determine outcomes will depend on the culture, expectations, and anticipated use of the data you collect.

Evaluator Skills

McLagan (1983) describes the ASTD competency study, in which the role of evaluator is defined as "identifying the extent of a program, service, or product's impact." Outputs produced by the process are identified as follows:

- Instruments to assess individuals' change in knowledge, skills, attitudes, behavior, or results
- Instruments to assess program and instructional quality
- Reports (written and oral) of program impact on individuals
- Reports (written and oral) of program impact on an organization
- Evaluation and validation designs and plans
- Written instruments to collect and interpret data

The evaluator needs skills in data reduction and research as well as in using computers, writing, and giving presentations. The person who has the strongest skills as a change agent and facilitator (see Chapter 7) or career advisor (see Chapter 8) may not be the same individual who has these evaluator skills. These varying skills may prompt the need for a career advisory team, rather than an individual, to plan, design, implement, and evaluate the career development intervention.

Table 36

Kirkpatrick's Four Levels of Evaluation

Level 1: Measuring reaction
Level 2: Measuring learning
Level 3: Measuring behavior changes
Level 4: Measuring results

The Four Levels of Evaluation

Donald Kirkpatrick (1975) has identified four levels in the evaluation process, as shown in Table 36. His model has become the standard for evaluating HR interventions.

Level 1: Measuring Reaction

Reaction data, typically the easiest to collect, measures attitudes, feelings, and impressions. It is usually collected immediately after an intervention such as a workshop or a counseling session. This data can be collected by questionnaires, interviews, or, occasionally, in focus groups. One metrics-driven company decided to evaluate the effectiveness of a career management course they had been offering to employees. The total number of responses was tallied and laid out on a pie chart. With 93 percent of respondents to a questionnaire saying they found the course helpful or extremely helpful in managing their careers, a compelling reason could be given to the career team to continue the courses. Particularly appropriate after a pilot group session and before taking a program forward, reaction data is most useful for correcting the program's course, determining program modification, or continuing marketing approaches. What did participants expect coming in? Were those expectations met? If not, why? Will participants be ambassadors of the program because they are excited about their involvement? If questionnaires have ratings as well as open-ended responses, they can be more easily tallied to create metrics or measurements of participants' reactions. Written evaluations are useful to the presenter in a training program, but results can also be summarized for more impact to shape others' opinions.

Reaction data should also be gathered if you are using a career advisor or career center. It can be used not only to determine opinion on the value of the resource, but also to ask for input and suggestions that contribute to strengthening the services provided. Paired with demographic data, a graphic picture can be drawn. How many people participated? What demographic breakdowns does this represent (departments, gender, age, tenure in the company, level of education, and so on)? What percentage of employees found it useful? Do patterns of usage or response appear?

Opinion surveys are a common way to measure overall attitudes about topics. One of the driving forces for some career development initiatives is low scores on the annual opinion survey regarding career development. Questions such as, "Does the company care about your development?" or "Do you have resources available to help you grow on the job?" are asked annually, so changes in perceptions by respondents are a measure of changes in reaction. It may be hard to determine all the causes of positive improvement in scores, but usually some link can be made to success of the intervention, especially if improved scores were identified as one of the measures of this, as illustrated in the following case example:

An organization had very favorable scores on most areas of a comprehensive opinion survey, with the exception of career development. The division manager and his executive team were charged with doing something to improve scores on the career development questions, so they set about designing a career development plan. Quickly realizing that a plan was an outcome rather than a process, they called in a consultant to design and implement a more comprehensive process. Employees and managers participated in a pilot program and made recommendations for a plantwide rollout. The training manager incorporated Managing Career Development™ courses into a total management training curriculum and offered career development workshops for employees. In the first year, although less than 30 percent of employees participated in the voluntary program, the scores on the opinion survey went up by 9 percent, enough to bring scores on career development questions in line with other topics. Because of extensive communication about the career development program, everyone knew that the resources were available, and employees gained a positive perception that the company cared about their careers.

Level 2: *Measuring Learning*

Measuring learning usually requires that a baseline be established at the beginning to compare with outcomes after an intervention. This means planning in advance to gather precourse information. Learning is expected to take place in a training program, but it can also be measured as an outcome for a total change process. Sometimes the outcome expected is learning a new skill or improving existing ones—such as coaching or giving feedback—following a course in managing career development. Sometimes the outcome is acquiring new knowledge or attitudes, as in the following case example:

One of the purposes of the career development process in a metrics-driven company was to change employees' traditional expectation that the company or its managers would take care of them. In preliminary surveys, a majority of employees not only stated this expectation, but complained that the company was not doing it. Courses were designed to educate employees about the new paradigm and their responsibility for managing their own careers. In a follow-up survey six months after participation, employees were asked who was responsible for managing their careers. One hundred percent responded that they, alone or with their manager's support, were responsible. No one said the company was responsible. This survey did not yet measure behavior change—what employees were doing to manage their careers—but it was one way to measure learning.

Learning can be measured either immediately following a learning experience or after application on the job to determine whether objectives for the intervention are being met. One way to measure learning of new career development concepts and processes is through the use of pre- and post-tests. For example, prior to an intervention with employees and/or managers, a questionnaire might be administered asking about understanding and behaviors relating to managing one's development or supporting employee development. Then, following the intervention, the same questionnaire would again be administered in order to measure the change in learning as a result of participation in the process. One organization asked such questions as "Do you have clearly defined career goals?' It found that prior to the career development program 18 percent said they did, and following the process the number responding favorably increased to 92 percent. (See sample questions for a pre-post survey, p. 247.)

Some of these concepts and processes can be observed in the training environment by assignments to apply what the group has just learned, but usually they are informally observed and not specifically measurable. For example, if a career-stages concept has just been learned, can participants use it to determine appropriate development actions? Managers concerned about the application of learning on the job may also ask a participant employee to present a synopsis to co-workers. This overview can be used to determine others' interest in attending, or to share information when all cannot attend. In sharing, the employee demonstrates understanding of the new information, and in fact reinforces his or her own learning.

Level 3: Measuring Behavior Changes

Measures of behavior indicate changes applied as a result of learning. Administered after a period of time has elapsed (typically six months to a year), evaluation techniques might include pre-post surveys of the individual as well as his or her manager or subordinates. Development Culture Survey 6: Career Development Survey is an example of such a survey. Application on the job can be measured by others' observations, such as managers' perspectives of behavior changes as a result of employee participation in the program. The following case example illustrates the efforts of one company to measure behavior changes:

A financial services company used manager and employee surveys in the initial planning of a comprehensive career development process. The data gathered contributed to the design of the process, and also served as baseline data by which to compare outcomes later. The purpose of the program was to change the culture and employees' mind-set from one of entitlement and dependency to one of proactive career management, to get employees to act like owners, and to expand employees' skills to meet increasing demands. The program included communication about the need to change outdated thinking about career development, as well as organizational information, competency assessment, manager training in career development coaching and development, and employee workshops. Six months to a year after the program was launched in each business unit, a follow-up survey was conducted with managers and employees to determine changed behavior. The survey included questions on such topics as the frequency of career discussions and whether individuals had written career goals and development plans. The post-survey identified substantial changes in career development activity.

DEVELOPMENT CULTURE SURVEY

6

Sample Career Development Survey

Please check one of the three columns for each statement, depending on how closely it describes you.

	Very Definitely	Somewhat	Not at All
Career Goals			
1. I have *specific* career goals.	___	___	___
2. I know how to work on solving the problems that get in the way of my career goals.	___	___	___
3. My supervisor has been helpful to me in my career planning.	___	___	___
Self-Awareness			
4. I know what my strengths are.	___	___	___
5. I know what my weaknesses are.	___	___	___
Present Job			
6. I know what is expected of me on my present job.	___	___	___
Organization Information			
7. I know how to find out about other position requirements within our organization.	___	___	___
8. I am aware of the new directions/trends of this organization and industry.	___	___	___
Career Development Assistance			
9. I feel comfortable talking with my supervisor about my career.	___	___	___

Career Directions, Inc.

Responses showed the following statistics:

■ Eighty percent are now playing a major role in their own career development, compared to 24 percent in the pre-survey
■ Eighty-nine percent are continually developing their skills
■ Seventy-two percent have had at least one career discussion with their manager, of whom 70 percent initiated the discussion, as compared with 11 percent in the pre-survey
■ Eighty percent have effective written plans for achieving their goals, compared to 1 percent prior to the program

Level 4: Measuring Results

Measuring the effect of the career development process on the organization is rarely done in career development and other human resources programs. This type of evaluation is essential, however, for determining the impact of changing the culture. Culture is sometimes such a nebulous thing—"How we do things around here"—that attempts are not often made to measure change. But to ensure that career development processes and interventions are given credit for influencing or leading a culture change, you must plan to measure results or outcomes with organizational impact. Usually driven by the business needs or characteristics of a desired future state, data need to be available before interventions in order to draw legitimate comparisons afterward.

Typically collected one year or longer after the intervention to allow time for change to occur, evaluation of results can establish a relationship between career development and bottom-line measures or other significant factors. However, cost data may be available immediately and used to "sell" the career development process, as in the following case example:

A bank undergoing major restructuring offered a generous six-month lead time to employees who were being displaced. They could use internal recruiting resources to find another position within the bank if they chose to do so. A human resources professional who saw the value of a career development process for employees to help them through the unsettling times studied the process people went through to make a successful change. He determined that it took an average of seven attempts in somewhat arbitrary responses to job postings and other leads for an individual to make a successful move to another area. By figuring the cost of employees' time (including a percentage of benefits), as well as that of human resource representatives and administrators, plus the time of the hiring managers, he determined it cost $800 for each attempt. This came to a total of $5,600 for each employee to make a successful transfer (average seven attempts times $800 per attempt). He presented a case for a career development program that would cost only about $700 per person, including time away from the job. Decision makers were convinced and agreed to a pilot career development program. After participating in the program, employees focused their preparation and job targets and reduced their attempts to three before making a successful move. That meant that each employee who participated saved the bank $2,500! (That's three attempts at $800 plus $700.) Since there were forty people still to be redeployed, career development could save the bank $100,000!

Quantifying the cost of the problem to be solved is a starting point for measuring impact. For example, if turnover of highly skilled new recruits is one of the business needs to be addressed by a career development program, determine the costs of recruiting and replacing each employee. Recruiting costs might include advertisements, trips to college campuses, and hiring search firms. Average cost per new hire can be figured by the number hired as a result of each recruiting strategy. Added to that will be costs such as those for the interviewer's time, administrative processes, and the hiring manager's time. Then determine the length of time the new hire is on the job in an apprentice role before becoming fully competent, and estimate the lost income to the department for that time. Without exception, a career development program that retains these talents is cheaper than replacement. In the past, companies frequently said, "Let them leave. If they don't want to work here, we'll find someone who does." With a growing shortage of highly skilled employees, that attitude quickly creates a competitive disadvantage, as the following case example clearly shows:

A software development firm was hearing in exit interviews that the reason why highly valued software developers were leaving was that they didn't perceive any opportunities in the company. In a competitive marketplace, they certainly had options elsewhere. With the company growing at 25 percent per year, senior managers' concern was that they wouldn't have the talent to meet market demands. A comprehensive career development/performance management program was implemented, with managers actively involved in employee development and career discussions. The goals were to create a structure for development and for communicating options and to ensure that managers identified dissatisfaction early and began mediation before the headhunter called and lured employees away. They determined that the direct cost for each new hire ranged between $5,000 and $20,000, whereas the cost of the career development program was approximately $200 per employee. Even if allocated only to the targeted population, the cost of the career development program was approximately $1,000 per person in the department affected. If attrition were reduced by even a small percentage, the program would be cost effective.

A cost of $5,600 per person × 40 persons = $224,000. By reducing the average cost of a move to $3,100 × 40 persons, the cost was reduced to $124,000. So the cost–benefit ratio was 1.8 to 1, saving .8. Anything greater than 1:00 is a return on investment. In this case that amounted to $100,000, enough to be noticed by those paying attention to the bottom line.

Qualitative Measures

In addition to quantitative measures, some of the most significant impact from a career development process may come in the form of personal successes by participants. One employee who felt like a victim of the organizational changes until her company initiated the "Driving Your Future" workshop said that the program changed her life. Another employee came to a career planning workshop because he saw the success of colleagues who had participated and achieved their career development goals. One woman changed her attitude and behavior with her manager from anger and resentment to cooperation. Another finally enrolled in a tuition assistance program and was excited about getting her degree after thinking about it for years. An employee who didn't have the confidence to pursue another area until the career advisor helped her identify and communicate her skills got hired in the new position. A young man was ready to leave the company until his manager helped identify new challenges he could take on in his present job in preparation for a new role that was evolving. A manager embraced his developmental role and built a reputation for being the one to work for.

These kinds of success stories abound as a result of a successful career development process. In order to use anecdotes for evaluation, a method needs to be created to communicate them. One method some organizations use is an ongoing career development newsletter or a career management report in another company publication. Interviews with participants, celebrations of successes, or even anonymous accomplishments make for good reading and send the message that there are positive outcomes from the career development program. Be careful to reinforce the right message, however. If one of the purposes of the process is to change employee and manager mind-sets and create a new paradigm about development, be careful not to announce only promotions. New assignments, lateral moves, accomplishment of personal goals, and actions taken all communicate the development message rather than the promotion message.

If a status report is being written about the program, case studies or anecdotes can supplement the quantitative data being presented. Even personal testimonials, not just about the outcomes for an individual but about their sense of its value (reaction data) can be incorporated. For example, when surveyed several months after attendance at a career development planning workshop, some employees said they knew exactly what to do to manage their career, but didn't have development plans in place because they were overloaded on the job or in their personal lives. They anticipated working more on development when their time freed up. Outcome data from them would not have been very favorable, but reaction data was positive.

Measuring Changes in Culture

"If nobody is going to the trouble to *measure* results, why expect employees to *produce* results? What gets measured becomes important" (Pritchett and Pound, 1996). When people see that you are serious enough about changing behavior and changing the culture to track progress, they have to take the expectation seriously too. If expectations of managers and/or employees are communicated but not measured, it is easy for the old behaviors to return, whether from force of habit, from resistance, or from being rewarded. "Measure change, reward results, and you'll see the whole organization take a different attitude" (Pritchett and Pound).

Be careful to measure appropriate outcomes. For example, is having a development plan sufficient, or is the quality of the plan what matters? Are activities like career discussions an end in themselves, or is the outcome of discussions (such as realistic goals) what is expected? Sometimes activities are an interim measure contributing to a longer-range result.

If you are expecting employees to take responsibility for their own career management, there should not be conflicting messages about the reporting necessary for measurement. The message should be, "In our changing environment, everyone should have a development plan for continuous learning and opportunities, and your manager can help you identify appropriate goals and ways to achieve them," versus "We will monitor your career discussions as well as the quality of your development plans. They must be turned in to HR."

Some organizations choose to measure outcomes by surveys or other anonymous methods rather than building a watchdog process to ensure compliance. The approach should be driven by the philosophy of the process in your organization, and by the business issues driving the need for career development. Measuring impact on the organization, while sometimes difficult, is likely to be better than keeping tabs on employee and manager activity.

However you choose to evaluate your system, determine the kind of data you will need as you begin to design the program. Create an evaluation plan that includes the methods of measurement as well as the desired outcomes and indicators of success. Consider the kind of data needed by different stakeholders. Success to senior managers might be bench strength or solutions to business problems. Success to employees might be a working development plan or achieving their goals. Success to managers might be employees with the skills and attitude to achieve the department results.

Include also the timing and purpose of evaluation. Some measures, such as workshop feedback, may be used for ongoing program improvement. Others, such as usage numbers, may be used for planning and budgeting. Still others, such as business results or return on investment, may be used to obtain or retain support by key stakeholders.

As organizations are increasingly benchmarking, it is those organizations that measure their success who will get the credit. There is too much potential value from solid evaluation data to ignore this important component of a career development system.

Achieving
Your Desired
Future State

It is not the going out of port but the coming in
that determines the success of a voyage.
—Henry Ward Beecher

The Impact of Culture on Organizational Performance

If you have read this book from cover to cover, you will now need to start
taking action if you intend to implement what you have learned. If you
have read and implemented and used this book as a guide to action, you
probably have arrived here with some successes and perhaps some frus-
trations as well. If you need further data or motivation to gain support
for using career development to change the culture in your organization,
consider the work of Kotter and Heskett (1992) on corporate culture and
performance. They have studied organizational culture and its impact on
organizational performance. Their work involved researching organizations to determine which characteristics of culture influenced organizational performance:

- *Strong* cultures
- *Strategically appropriate* cultures
- *Adaptive* cultures

They identified characteristics of all three that influenced organizational performance, as measured by annual net income growth, average annual return on capital, and average annual growth of stock price. The authors describe a *strong culture* as one in which "almost all managers share a set of relatively consistent values and methods of doing business . . . [and] employees tend to march to the same drummer." Strong cultures with shared values create an unusual level of motivation in employees. There is shared understanding of unwritten rules. Economic events had to threaten the existence of the company before managers would question the culture.

But Kotter and Heskett pose the objection to this theory with the issue of causality. Do strong cultures create strong performance? Or does strong performance help create a strong culture? They found that organizations could have strong cultures and weak performance, weak cultures and strong performance, or strong cultures and strong performance! So strong cultures do not necessarily mean strong performance.

The second theory of culture Kotter and Heskett explored was *strategically appropriate cultures.* "This theory explicitly states the direction that cultures must align and motivate employees if they are to enhance company performance." The key concept is that of fit of the culture to the context—the industry, the market demands or the business strategy. For example, "a culture characterized by rapid decision making and no bureaucratic behavior will enhance performance in the highly competitive deal-making environment of a mergers and acquisitions advisory firm but might hurt performance in a traditional life insurance company."

The researchers found that mismatches between the environment and the culture are pervasive in lower-performing organizations. High-performance firms had corporate cultures that better fit their context than their competition's did. However, when increased competition changed the business environment, these cultures had difficulty adapting to changes, fit deteriorated, and performance declined. "An entrenched culture can make implementing new and different strategies very difficult. A culture can blind people to facts that don't match their assumptions." If you have experienced difficulty in championing change in your organization, you know that an entrenched culture is hard to change even when people know it's needed.

The third theory of culture defined by Kotter and Heskett is one of *adaptive cultures.* "Only cultures that can help organizations anticipate and adapt to environmental change will be associated with superior performance over long periods of time." Nonadaptive cultures are bureaucratic,

Table 37

Adaptive Versus Nonadaptive Corporate Cultures

Adaptive Corporate Cultures	Nonadaptive Corporate Cultures
Most managers care deeply about customers, stockholders, and employees. They also strongly value people and processes that can create useful change (e.g., leadership up and down the management hierarchy).	Most managers care mostly about themselves, their immediate work group, or some product (or technology) associated with that work group. They value the orderly and risk-reducing management process much more than leadership initiatives.

Reproduced with the permission of The Free Press, a Division of Simon & Schuster, from *Corporate Culture and Performance,* by John P. Kotter and James L. Heskett. Copyright © 1992 by Kotter Associates, Inc., and James L. Heskett.

and people are reactive, risk-averse, and uncreative. Top-down control dampens motivation and enthusiasm. Kilmann, Saxton, and Serpa (1986) define an adaptive culture as one that supports individual risk-taking and problem solving. Managers and employees are proactive about development and seek to make a contribution to the organization's success. They are receptive to change and innovation.

Kotter and Heskett's comparison of core values of managers in adaptive versus nonadaptive corporate cultures is shown in Table 37.

Kotter and Heskett rated companies on a scale of 1 to 7 on how they valued employees. Higher-performing firms scored an average of 5.8. Some (such as Wal-Mart) scored as high as 7.0! Lesser-performing firms scored an average of 4.1, with some as low as 2.8. Demonstrating that people are valued may be one of the most positive outcomes of building a development culture, with the resulting payoffs to the organization in sustained higher performance. A growing body of research supports the awareness in alert organizations that people are the differentiating factor among organizations today.

Making It Happen

To achieve your vision of a development culture, you and your champions need to persevere in the face of all the elements of culture that arise to block your vision. As you begin to make headway, refer to Table 38 for some tips to help keep your efforts focused.

Table 38

Keeping Your Efforts Focused

- Keep the business case for a development culture and a career development process in the forefront of your efforts.

- Measure and communicate your results. Use measurements for course correction along the way for continuous improvement to the change efforts.

- Keep constant tabs on what the organization is doing and what it aspires to do or be—your desired future state. You and stakeholders will continue to need clear goals.

- Ensure a base of support so that if players change, the efforts will continue forward. Recognize that the commitment to building a development culture means you are in it for the long haul.

- Communicate, communicate, communicate. Remember that people don't change their behavior by hearing about something once, but repetition, along with supporting resources, can begin to get their attention.

- Celebrate successes! Acknowledge and reward those aspects that are working well—and the people that are making it happen.

Success breeds success. You may not be able to undertake the extent of change in the whole organization that your vision needs, but do attend to groups of stakeholders and their needs and expectations from a development culture. It is usually better to implement a comprehensive process with a smaller group than to provide a surface intervention with everyone.

Be sure to avoid the "culture-destroying trap of saying one thing and then doing another" (Kotter and Heskett, 1992). A development culture, above all else, requires open communication, trust, and commitment. Your challenge is to add value in ways that make your contribution continue to grow and take root in your organization. In a development culture, career development is a way of life, not just a program.

References

Beckhard, R., & Harris, R. T. (1987). *Organizational transitions: Managing complex change*. Reading, MA: Addison-Wesley.

Bicos, S., & Simonsen, P. *Career development and compensation—A marriage made in heaven or hell?* Paper presented at the national conference of the American Society for Training and Development, June 1995.

Blanchard, K. (1996, January–February). Blanchard management report. *Training Today, The Magazine of the Chicago ASTD*, 3.

Bridges, W. (1994). *Job Shift: How to prosper in a workplace without jobs*. Reading, MA: Addison-Wesley.

Career Directions, Inc. (1996a). *Mentoring: Focus on career development*. Rolling Meadows, IL: Author.

Career Directions, Inc. (1996b). *Assessing mentoring skills*. Rolling Meadows, IL: Author.

Davis, K. (1996, August). Downshifters. *Kiplinger's Personal Finance Magazine*, p. 34.

Deal, T. E. (1986). Deeper culture: Mucking, muddling, and metaphors. In J. C. Glidewell (Ed.), *Corporate cultures: Research implications for human resource development* (p. 27). Alexandria, VA: American Society for Training and Development.

Donahue, J. (1993, September). Speech to International Association of Career Management Professionals, Chicago.

Godfrey, J. (1996, March). Been there, doing that: Mind of the manager. *INC Magazine*.

Gottlieb, M. R., & Conkling, L. (1995). *Managing the workplace survivors: Organizational downsizing and the commitment gap*. Westport, CT: Quorum Books.

Gutteridge, T., Leibowitz, Z., & Shore, J. (1993). *Organizational career development: Benchmarks for building a world-class workforce* (p. 1). San Francisco: Jossey-Bass.

Hakim, C. (1994). *We are all self-employed: The new social contract for working in a changed world*. San Francisco: Berrett-Koehler.

Joiner Associates. (1995). *The team memory jogger: A pocket guide for team members*. Madison, WI: GOAL/QPC and Joiner Publications.

Kaye, B. L. (1982). *Up is not the only way: A guide for career development practitioners*. Englewood Cliffs, NJ: Prentice-Hall.

Kilmann, R. H., Saxton, M. J., Serpa, R., & Associates. (1986). *Gaining control of the corporate culture*. San Francisco: Jossey-Bass.

Kirkpatrick, D. L. (1975). "Techniques for evaluating training programs. Part 1: Reaction. Part 2: Learning. Part 3: Behavior. Part 4: Results." In *Evaluating training programs* (pp. 1–7). Alexandria, VA: American Society for Training and Development.

Kochanski, J. T. (1996). *Competency-based management in career development planning*. Alexandria, VA: Sibson & Company.

Kotter, J. P., & Heskett, J. L. (1992). *Corporate culture and performance*. New York: Free Press.

Laabs, J. J. (1996a, July). Expert advice on how to move forward with change. *Personnel Journal*, pp. 54, 56, 58–60, 62.

Laabs, J. J. (1996b, August). Embrace today's new deal. *Personnel Journal*, p. 60.

Leibowitz, Z., Farren, C., & Kaye, B. (1986). *Designing career development systems.* San Francisco: Jossey-Bass.

Lombardo, M. M., & Eichenger, R. W. (1989). *Eighty-eight assignments for development in place: Enhancing the developmental challenge of existing jobs.* Greensboro, NC: Center for Creative Leadership

Maurer, R. (1996). *Beyond the wall of resistance: Unconventional strategies that build support for change.* Austin, TX: Bard Books.

McLagan, P. (1983). *Models for excellence.* Alexandria, VA: American Society for Training and Development.

McLagan, P. (1996). *Competency systems in the new world of work: Using competency-based tools and applications to drive organizational performance.* Lexington, MA: Linkage.

Meyer, K. M. (1989, September). Coming to agreement: How to resolve conflict. *American Society for Training and Development Info-Line*, p. 1.

Mink, O. G., Schultz, J. M., & Mink, B. P. (1986). *Developing and managing an open organization: A model and methods for maximizing organizational potential.* Austin, TX: Organization and Human Resource Development Associates, Inc.

Murray, M. (1991). *Beyond the myths and magic of mentoring: How to facilitate an effective mentoring program.* San Francisco: Jossey-Bass.

Naisbitt, J., & Aburdeen, P. (1990). *Megatrends 2000.* New York: Morrow.

O'Reilly, B. (1994, June 13). The new deal: What companies and employees owe one another. *Fortune.*

Parry, S. B. (1996, July). The quest for competencies. *Training Magazine*, p. 50.

Pritchett, P. (1996). *Resistance—Moving beyond the barriers to change.* Dallas, TX: Pritchett & Associates.

Pritchett, P., & Pound, R. (1993). *High-velocity culture change.* Dallas, TX: Pritchett & Associates.

Pritchett, P., & Pound, R. (1996). *The employee handbook for organizational change.* Dallas, TX: Pritchett & Associates.

Rifkin, J. (1995). *The end of work.* New York: Putnam.

Schein, E. H. (1978). *Career dynamics: Matching individual and organizational needs.* Reading, MA: Addison-Wesley.

Schein, E. H. (1986). Deep culture. In J. C. Glidewell (Ed.), *Corporate cultures: Research implications for human resource development* (pp. 7–20). Alexandria, VA: American Society for Training and Development.

Sears Merchandise Group. (1996). *Sears transformation.* Unpublished report.

Senge, P. (1990a). *A conversation with Peter Senge.* Framingham, MA: Innovation Associates.

Senge, P. (1990b). *The fifth discipline.* New York: Doubleday Currency.

Shea, G. F. (1994). Mentoring: Helping employees reach their full potential. In *AMA Management Briefing 1994.* New York: American Management Association.

Simonsen, P. (1993). *Managing your career within your organization.* Rolling Meadows, IL: Career Directions, Inc.

Simonsen, P. (1994a). *Managing Career Development.* Rolling Meadows, IL: Career Directions, Inc.

Simonsen, P. (1994b, Spring). Organizational career development. *Career Developments Newsletter*, ASTD Career Development Professional Practice Area.

Simonsen, P. (1995, April). Basics of career advising. *American Society for Training and Development Info-Line*, p. 9.

Waterman, R., Waterman, J., & Collard, B. (1994, July–August). Toward a career resilient workforce. *Harvard Business Review*, 88.

Index

About the Author

Peggy Simonsen is president of the career development consulting firm Career Directions, Inc. Founded in 1979, the firm serves individuals and corporations from its offices in Rolling Meadows, Illinois, and international affiliates. Career Directions designs and implements career development and performance management systems for organizations, conducts career development training for managers and employees, and establishes career centers with trained career advisors or professional career counselors on-site. Clients include Motorola, Sears, Caterpillar, Kraft, General Motors, Mobil Oil, Federal Reserve Bank of Chicago, Harris Bank, Lincoln National Reinsurance, Hewitt Associates, Girl Scouts of the USA, American Medical Association, and American Hospital Association.

A recognized leader in the field of career development, Simonsen has served on the National Executive Committee of the Career Development Professional Practice area of the American Society for Training and Development (ASTD) and is a recipient (1996) of the Walter Storey Career Development Leadership Award. In 1992 she received the Excellence in Training and Development Consultation award from the Chicago Chapter of ASTD. She is a columnist and an invited presenter at national conferences.

Involved in training and development for more than twenty-five years, Simonsen holds a bachelor's degree from the University of Minnesota and a master's degree in education and psychology from Northwestern University, and she has done additional graduate work in organizational development. Prior to forming Career Directions, she held consulting and training positions with corporations and nonprofit organizations.

The publishers have generously given permission to use extended quotations from the following copyrighted works:

From "Basics of Career Advising," by Peggy Simonsen. *American Society of Training and Development Info-Line*, April 1995. Copyright 1995, the American Society for Training and Development. All rights reserved.

From *The Blanchard Management Report*, January–February 1996, by Ken Blanchard, Chairman, Blanchard Training and Development, Inc., Escondido, CA, 1-800-728-6000.

From *Career Dynamics*, by Edgar H. Schein (adapted from chapters 10–12). © 1978 Addison-Wesley Publishing Company, Inc. Reprinted by permission of Addison-Wesley Longman, Inc.

From *Competency Systems in the New World of Work: Using Competency-Based Tools and Applications to Drive Organizational Performance*, by Patricia McLagan. Lexington, MA: Linkage, Inc.

From *Corporate Culture and Performance*, by John P. Kotter and James L. Heskett. Copyright © 1992 by Kotter Associates, Inc., and James L. Heskett. Adapted with the permission of The Free Press, a Division of Simon & Schuster.

From "Deep Culture," by Edgar H. Schein. In John C. Glidewell (Ed.), *Corporate Cultures: Research Implications for Human Resource Development*. Copyright 1986, the American Society for Training and Development. All rights reserved.

From *Developing and Managing an Open Organization: A Model and Methods for Maximizing Organization Potential*, by Oscar G. Mink, James M. Schultz, and Barbara P. Mink. © 1986 Organization and Human Resource Development Associates, Inc., Austin, TX.

From *Eighty-eight Assignments for Development in Place: Enhancing the Developmental Challenge of Existing Jobs*, by Michael M. Lombardo and Robert W. Eichinger. Copyright 1989 the Center for Creative Leadership, Greensboro, NC. All rights reserved.

From "Embrace Today's New Deal," by Jennifer J. Laabs, copyright August 1996. Used with permission of Workforce/ACC Communications, Inc., Costa Mesa, CA. All rights reserved.

From *The Employee Handbook for Organizational Change*, by Price Pritchett and Ron Pound, 1996. Used with full permission of Pritchett & Associates. All rights reserved.

From "Expert Advice on How to Move Forward with Change," by Jennifer J. Laabs, copyright July 1996. Used with permission of Workforce/ACC Communications, Inc., Costa Mesa, CA. All rights reserved.

From *The Fifth Discipline*, by Peter Senge. New York: Doubleday, 1990.

From *High-Velocity Culture Change*, by Price Pritchett and Ron Pound, 1993. Used with full permission of Pritchett & Associates. All rights reserved.

From *Managing the Workplace Survivors*, by Marvin R. Gottlieb and Lori Conkling. Copyright © 1995 by Quorum Books. Reproduced with permission of Greenwood Publishing Group, Inc., Westport, CT.

From *Mentoring: Helping Employees Reach Their Full Potential*, by Gordon F. Shea. In *AMA Management Briefing 1994*. © 1994 American Management Association, New York. All rights reserved.

From *Models for Excellence*, by Patricia McLagan. Copyright 1983, the American Society for Training and Development. All rights reserved.

From "The New Deal: What Companies and Employees Owe One Another," by Brian O'Reilly. *Fortune*, © 1994 Time Inc. All rights reserved.

From *Organizational Career Development: Benchmarks for Building a World-Class Workforce*, by Thomas G. Gutteridge, Zandy B. Leibowitz, and Jane E. Shore. San Francisco: Jossey-Bass, 1993.

From *Organizational Transitions*, by Richard Beckhard and Reuben T. Harris. © 1987 Addison-Wesley Publishing Company, Inc. Reprinted by permission of Addison-Wesley Longman, Inc.

From *Resistance—Moving Beyond the Barriers to Change*, by Price Pritchett, 1996. Used with full permission of Pritchett & Associates. All rights reserved.